Politics of Liberation in South Sudan:
An Insider's View

Peter Adwok Nyaba

Fountain Publishers

Fountain Publishers Ltd.
P.O. Box 488
KAMPALA – UGANDA

© Peter A. Nyaba 1997
First published 1997
Second edition 2000

All rights reserved. No part of this publication may be reprinted or reproduced or utilised in any form or by any means electronic, mechanical or other means now known or hereafter invented, including copying and recording, or in any information storage or retrieval system, without permission in writing from the publishers.

ISBN 9970 02 102 8

Cover Pictures:
Above: *Sudan Government Soldiers captured as prisoners of war by SPLA after the Yei ambush.* Below: *Destroyed vehicles of Sudan Government Army.*

Courtesy: *P. A. Nyaba*

Dedication

There is no other way of marking and celebrating my return to the SPLM/A than by writing these pages which I dedicate to the memory of all the fallen heroes of our people who died fighting on both sides of the political divide.
Honour and Glory to their memory !!

Contents

Abbreviations ii

Acknowledgement iv

1. Introduction 1

2. Background to the present war 14

3. Hatching the conspiracy 77

4. Between guilt and shame 116

5. The Political Charter: No act of chivalry 152

6. Lessons from the Nasir Debacle 169

7. Epilogue: What is the SPLM and where is it? 193

Index 216

Abbreviations

ANC	African National Congress
CANS	Civil Authority in the New Sudan
CCI	Compagnie de Construction Internationale
CCM	Commitato Collaborazio Medico
CCI	Compagnie de Construction Internationale
Cdr	Commander
CI	Combat Intelligence
CPSA	Communist Party of South Africa
CUSS	Council for the Unity of South Sudan
DOPS	Declaration of Principles
DUP	Democratic Union Party
ELF	Eritrea Liberation Front
EPLF	Eritrean People's Liberation Front
EPRDF	Ethiopian People's Revolutionary Democratic Front
FRELIMO	Front for the Liberation of Mozambique
GIS	General Intelligence Service
GPLM	Gambetta People's Liberation Movement
H/Qs	Headquarters
IGAD	Inter-Governmental Authority on Development
IGADD	Inter-Governmental Authority on Drought and Development
ILF	Imatong Liberation Front
INEC	Interim National Executive Council
INLC	Interim National Liberation Council
JUSSA	Juba University Sudanese Staff Association
LC	Leadership Council
MPLA	Popular Movement for the Liberation of Angola
NDA	National Democratic Alliance
NEC	National Executive Council
NGOs	Non-Governmental Organisations
NIF	National Islamic Front
NLC	National Liberation Council
NRM	National Resistance Movement (Uganda)
NSB	New Sudan Brigade
NUP	National Unionist Party
OLF	Oromo Liberation Front
OLS	Operation Life Sudan
PDP	People's Democratic Party
PLO	Palestine Liberation Organisation
PRM	Patriotic Resistance Movement

RASS	Relief Association for South Sudan
RENAMO	National Resistance Movement (Mozambique)
RMC	Resource Management Committee
SANU	Sudan African National Union
SHILU	Sudan Humanitarian Initiative Liaison Unit
SPLA	Sudan People's Liberation Army
SPLM	Sudan People's Liberation Movement
SRRA	Sudan Relief and Rehabilitation Association
SRS	Sudan Rural Solidarity
SSFF	Southern Sudan Freedom Front
SSIA	Southern Sudan Independence Army
SSIM	Southern Sudan Independence Movement
SSLF	Southern Sudan Liberation Front
SSLM	South Sudan Liberation Movement
SSO	State Security Organisation
SSU	Sudan Socialist Union
TPLE	Tigre People's Liberation Front
UNDP	United Nations Development Programme
UNESCO	United Nations Educational, Scientific and Cultural Organisation
UNITA	Union for the Total Independence of Angola
UNPMCC	Upper Nile Provisional Military Command Council
USAP	Union of Sudan African Parties
WFP	World Food Programme

Acknowledgement

It has not been an easy experience for me to start writing this small book which I had intended to carry my reflections on the situation in South Sudan following the Nasir Declaration. Like many South Sudanese intellectuals in Nairobi, who have learnt to live off the crumbs from the high table of international humanitarian assistance to South Sudan, the concept of writing these pages came to me only as a 'project proposal' to scratch a living; that is to get money to sustain myself and my family in the comfort of the Kenyan capital. The fact that this could be a useful contribution to the understanding of the struggle of our people came only as an afterthought, and only when my efforts to get the necessary funding failed. I am happy that I was able to overcome that condemnable attitude.

The war is still raging in South Sudan; people are still paying the price for freedom and social justice and at the same time still suffering the effects of the Nasir double infamy, if we count the Riek-NIF political charter, which was actually negotiated in Nasir where the 1991 coup was staged. I am sure time will come when a full account will be made of exactly what happened and each and every one will be judged accordingly. Dr Riek Machar has decided to pursue not the independence of South Sudan, for which many of us supported him, but its very opposite. Dr Lam Akol is still wavering, hesitating to rejoin the SPLM/A – the mainstream national liberation struggle – because he must make sure of his position in the reunified Movement. But, in the words of Jose Marti, the great Cuban hero, 'real men are concerned not with how they can live better but with where their duty lies'. The people of South Sudan deserve better treatment than being held as ransom for some leaders to acquire leadership positions.

This is a modest contribution to the debate and dialogue for rectification of our mistakes and for the evolution of a clear vision of our destiny. It is my cherished hope that most of our intellectuals, many still sitting on the fence unperturbed by the events, will join in the debate so that a clear definition of the aspirations of the people of South Sudan and their compatriots in the Nuba Mountains, Ingessina, Dar Fur and the Beja can be charted.

This work has been my own initiative, but I take this opportunity to thank all those who made it possible for me to complete it. In this respect my sincere thanks go to Bjorg Mide, former Director of the Sudan Programme of Norwegian Church Aid, who assisted us in Larjour Consultancy with a computer that enabled me to write this book. Many friends who had read the first draft encouraged me to undertake this work. I owe them many thanks.

It would not have been possible for me to undertake this work had it not been for the patience, encouragement and understanding I got from the members of my family. I take this opportunity to thank my wife Abuk Payiti Ayik, my children Keni, Pito, Kut, Agyedho, Payiti and Susan, who have tolerated my irresponsible greed not to have given much of my time to attend to their individual and collective needs.

P.A.N.
Nairobi, Kenya

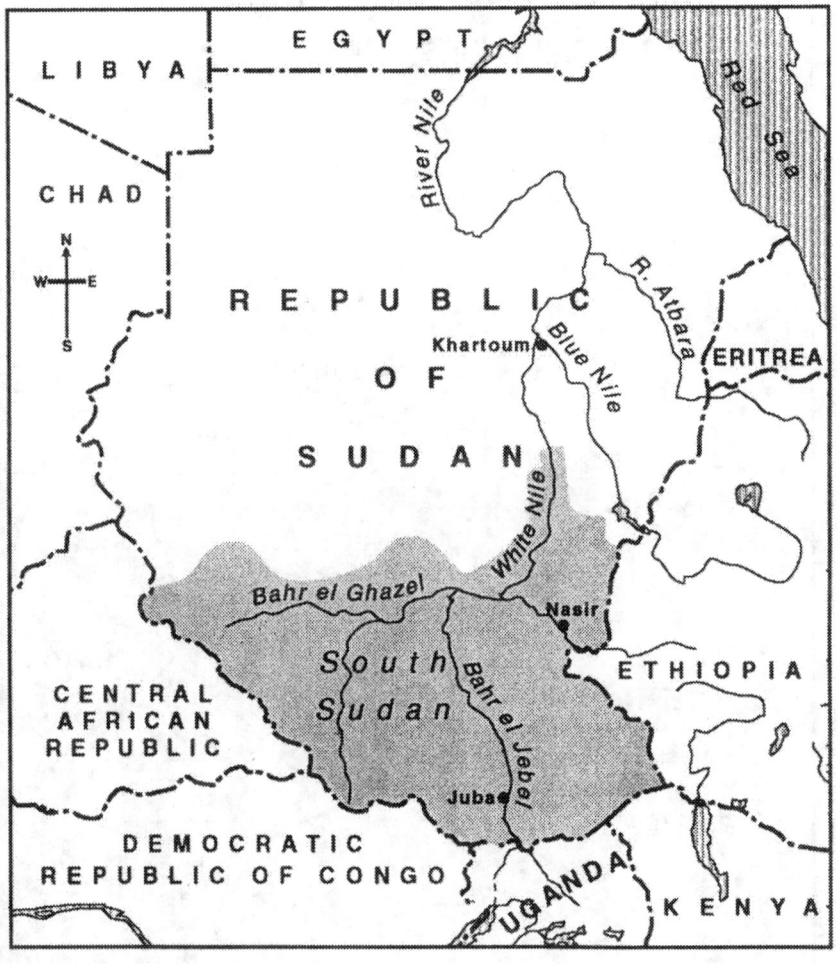

Location of South Sudan

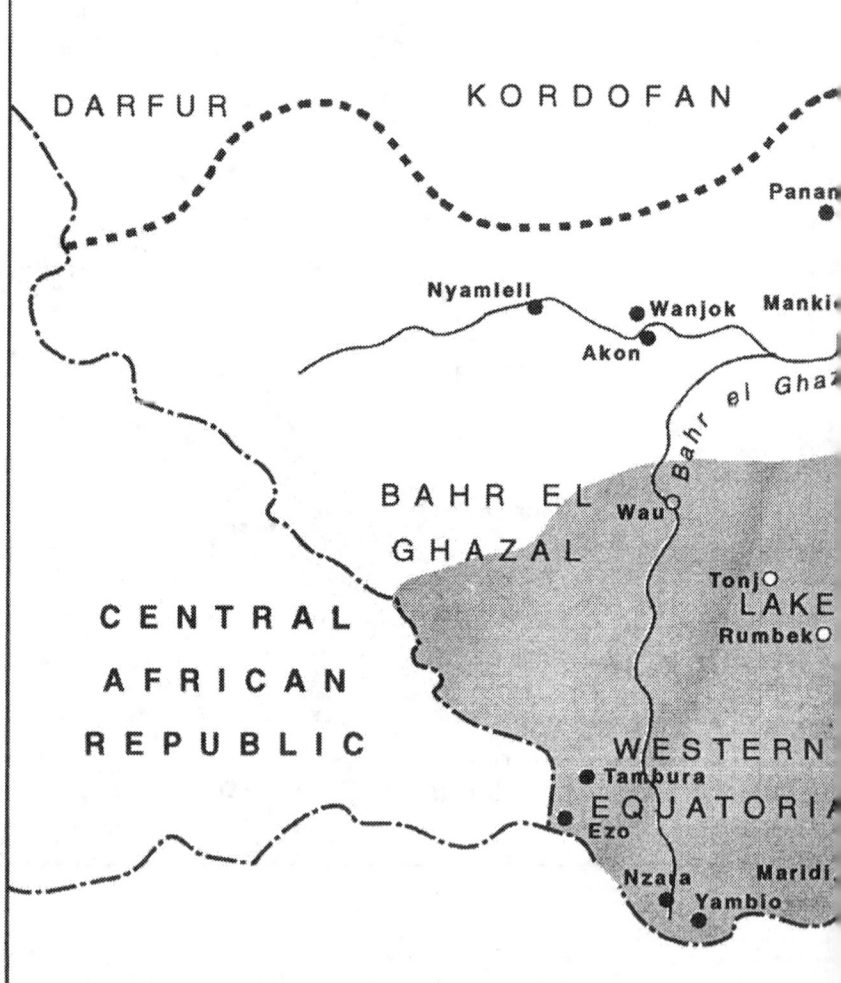

ir coup, August 1991

Towns recaptured by the Government

- ○ Towns captured by Government of Sudan in 1992 and after
- ▪▪▪▪ Location of South Sudan

DARFUR

KORDOFAN

Bahr el Gh

BAHR EL GHAZAL

CENTRAL AFRICAN REPUBLIC

LAK

WESTERN EQUATOR

DEMOCRATIC REPUBLIC OF CONGO

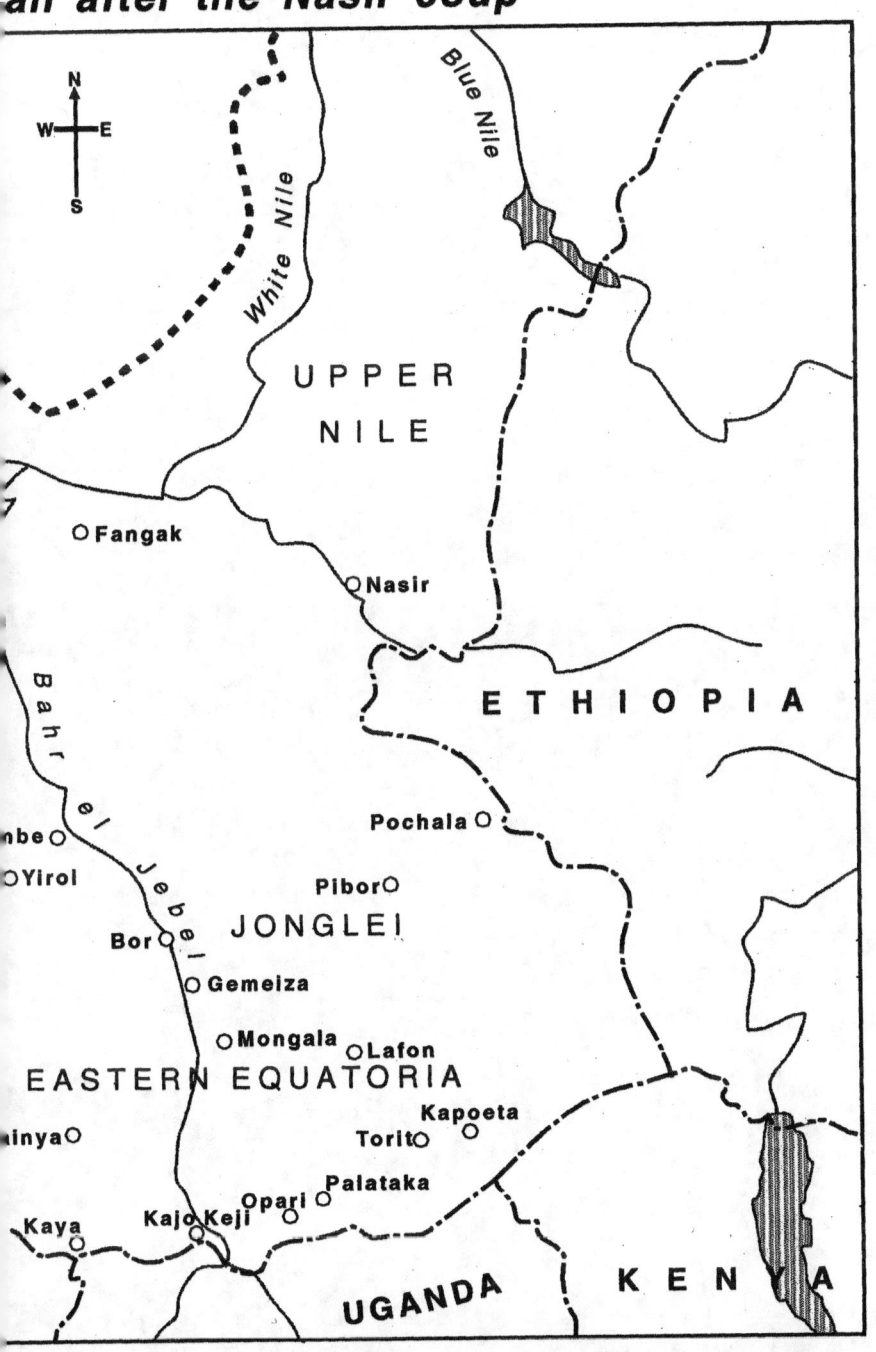

1
Introduction

Those who will read these pages may be tempted to conclude that the author must have been a hireling planted to carry out political sabotage in the Nasir faction. They will be making a mistake. There are times when one has to make a courageous decision to negate a political position one may have earlier taken. This is quite true, especially when the national interest is at stake. It does not boil down to bad faith if adherence to principle demands that one disowns or changes his political views. All that unfolded in the Nasir faction of the SPLM/A, which finally resulted in its disintegration, leading to the eventual surrender of Riek Machar to the NIF enemy, is exactly what has made some of us turn around to condemn it in spite of our initial support.

From its inception in 1983 until the time of the Nasir Declaration in 1991, the SPLM/A policies and practices ran counter to the expectation of many who joined it. However, opposition to and agitation against these policies remained at the level of demand for democratic reforms. The idea of change of the SPLM/A leadership and the concept of its consummation in a military coup was something which Dr Riek Machar and Dr Lam Akol introduced. It was something quite new, given the fact that the two were members of the SPLM/A Military High Command, a position that placed them very close to Dr. John Garang. They, therefore, were not part of the agitation against the situation in the Movement. These men started to identify with the struggle for internal reforms only when they fell out with Dr John Garang in early 1990s.

The idea itself of ousting the leader of a guerrilla army in a coup, as it turned out later, was an ill-conceived adventure. In fact, it marked a complete departure from the political practice in a national liberation movement. Those who opposed some of the tragic policies and practices of the Movement did so in the interest of transforming the SPLM/A into a genuine national liberation movement capable of delivering the people from oppression. The ousting of Dr John Garang from the leadership of the Movement, declared in Nasir on August 28th, 1991, and the failed coup itself proved another way of recreating the conditions of militarism and autocracy in the SPLM/A. It did not take long before the Nasir faction and its latter variations degenerated into the anarchy, autocracy, militarism, excessive human rights violations, etc., against which the coup was purportedly staged.

Democratic reforms, for which people agitated within the SPLM/A, were envisaged to be a slow process of cultivating political awareness and consciousness in the SPLA combatants as well as the people. The process of conscientisation of the people, leading to their eventual empowerment and transformation of their social realities, must of necessity involve their active participation. It cannot be a series of action imposed from above, exemplified in the military coup declared in Nasir.

This approach was disproved by the events in eastern Europe and the former Soviet Union in the early 1990s where strong totalitarian states were brought down not by military coups but by people standing up against them and rejecting them. The totalitarian regimes in eastern Europe were brought down by the same masses of people who had sustained them for four decades. As was the case, it did not matter much, how strong a system buttressed by a machinery of terror and oppression, a determined people are likely to being it down to its knees if they rose against it. The people of Sudan have done that twice in their history. Thus, for instance, when the Nimeri's regime came crumbling down under the pressure of the people's power in March - April 1985, neither his 45,000 men strong State Security Organisation (SSO) nor the Sudan Socialist Union (SSU)- the official political party - watchdogs stood there to defend it. They either melted away like snow without trace or joined ranks with the opposition.

It did not require a military coup to make people conscious of their rights and duties or even their destiny. What was required, especially during those difficult days when the Movement's survival was at stake, was unity in the ranks and file to offset the impact of having lost bases in western Ethiopia. That unity was not going to dissolve the political and ideological contradictions that have sprouted in the Movement. On the contrary, it would have created the necessary conditions for democratic reforms in the Movement that would have made possible the resolution of these contradictions. A big mistake was made in assessing the mood of the people which, unmistakably, was against the internal situation in the SPLM/A and its reflection externally among the civilian population.

It is true the SPLM/A was beset by serious internal contradictions which could have wrecked it into many pieces. Many communities have been completely alienated by the action of some SPLA officers and men and, in fact, some of them decided to cross over and allied with the enemy. For instance, the Murle rebelled against the SPLA in 1989; the Mandari had done so as early as 1984 the Taposa and the Didinga also turned against the SPLA in 1986 and 1990 respectively etc.. In the course of time, and because of the neglect of the objective laws of the people's war and national liberation, the SPLA sometimes posed like anti-people military machine. How else could we explain that the people were running away from or turned against their own liberation movement? It just cannot be explained away that some of these tribes did not want the SPLM/A simply because they perceived it to be a Dinka movement. Definitely, there were excesses, omissions and commissions that needed to be addressed, but to address them did not warrant staging a military coup whose outcome was bound to destroy the whole Movement.

The military action taken in Nasir to oust the leader of the SPLM/A, ostensibly to rectify the situation, became nothing but a bigger disaster, albeit a setback for the Movement and the people of South Sudan. Nevertheless, the Nasir coup received support and was initially acclaimed everywhere in South Sudan. I was one of the first people to lend my approval and support to the coup. In fact, I took an active part in propagating the ideas that precipitated the coup until the hidden agenda of the Nasir leaders and their collaboration with the NIF regime became known. It then became impossible to continue supporting it. It was difficult to believe that the noble slogans raised, which captured the imagination of many South Sudanese, had a treacherous content. But that was it. Eventually, the decision had to be taken to work against it.

However, and in spite of this discovery, some of us remained in the Nasir faction and its latter versions - SPLM/A - United and SSIM/A, which made it a serious contradiction. Why was it we decided to remain in such a treacherous ark? What were the motives for remaining in this den of treason for that long? When was it that we realised that the Nasir leaders had a hidden agenda?

To be honest, the nature of the collaboration with the NIF government was not clear from the beginning. It was conducted in a manner that no information could reach those members of the faction who were likely to oppose it. Moreover, immediately following the Nasir Declaration, the split took a tribal dimension. The passions were so charged in both the SPLM/A mainstream and in the Nasir faction by accusations of murders and summary executions of officers and men who were assumed to be in support. In fact, during those hard days, it was impossible to tell the truth from mere propaganda. Many things just went by.

It was only after the Frankfurt Agreement, the secret meetings in Nairobi between Dr Lam Akol and the NIF representatives that preceded it, and the sending by Dr Lam Akol to Khartoum of a senior member of the Nasir delegation which arrived in Nairobi for the peace talks sponsored by the People of Peace in Africa, that it became clear to some of us that the Nasir leaders had a hidden agenda which ran against their original declaration. This precipitated a crisis and put these leaders on a collision course with some patriotic elements in the faction over the collaboration with the NIF government. It took a long time before any meaningful action could be undertaken. This did not mean that we still doubted and, hence, wanted more evidence and proof of this collaboration. For some of us the central issue was not that 'Garang must go now', as it was articulated by the coup plotters. What mattered to us was the question of a democratic environment and reforms as well as the establishment of institutions and civil structures in the SPLM/A.

The period following the Nasir Declaration was tense with tribal animosities, especially after the invasion of Bor and Kongor counties by the forces of the Nasir faction. This wrought immense destruction and humanitarian disruption on the civilian population. By these ghastly deeds, nationalism was thrown overboard. In fact, it was this that turned things against the Nasir coup, and many who had initially supported the coup defected back to the SPLM/A. Some of us chose to remain in the Nasir faction for long, even though I personally was not welcomed by these leaders because of my outspoken opposition to their policy of collaboration with the enemy. The fratricidal war among the South Sudanese was simply to sanction the existence of the Nasir faction as a counterweight to spur changes in the SPLM/A mainstream. We wanted a situation to evolve within the mainstream SPLM/A in which different political views and opinions were accepted and tolerated. That is why we kept clear of the SPLM/A.

It was clear to me that one cannot struggle for liberation and other ideals in a political vacuum. One needed a forum; breaking away and establishing separate faction(s) could not create that forum. Moreover, the proliferation of factions as a means of solving the contradictions was a sure way of losing sight of the fundamental issues and the objectives of the struggle. It was also one sure way of manoeuvring oneself into the hands of the enemy as it eventually occurred with many of the leaders who broke lose from the SPLM/A in Nairobi and elsewhere outside South Sudan. We persevered in the Nasir faction, suffering psychological and moral trauma of being part of the treason.

But this was because many of us were still apprehensive of the situation in the SPLM/A then and rejected the idea of 'returning to the fold' without sufficient changes having taken place in it. For instance, in mid 1993, following the SPLM/A - United decision to conduct parallel and separate peace talks with the NIF regime in Nairobi, and in the wake of treacherous contacts between the NIF leaders and some SPLM/A - United leaders in Hotel 680 in Nairobi which almost resulted in its complete disintegration, a group of people in the SPLM/A-United decided to call it quits; resigned from the faction and rejoined the mainstream SPLM/A. It was a positive step though it was taken out of emotion and personal considerations. That was why its impact on the internal situation in the fact was not great to change the course of things. On the contrary, it weakened the position of those who remained opposed to the treacherous policies of the faction. By a simple mechanical process of concentration, it strengthened the position of the treacherous elements in the faction. Moreover, it did not immediately create the desired changes in the mainstream SPLM/A.

It was only after the SPLM First National Convention in 1994 and the publication of its resolutions and recommendations that some of us began to take seriously the internal process in the SPLM. We, therefore, immediately started to instigate and nurse political contradictions within the SPLM/A -

United and its leadership, arising out of the policies of collaboration with the NIF government as well as their inability to restore law and order in the areas under its control. This, in effect, was to create conditions conducive for the reconciliation and reunification of the Movement on a much stronger political basis, likely to prevent a relapse into the situation ante the Nasir coup. This was definitely a better political action than that of individual defection back into the fold of the Movement.

Even without that development, and since the Nasir declaration of August 1991, I had never contemplated that the split within the SPLM/A caused by the Nasir coup would last that long. I believed that the point for reforms and other changes in the Movement had been made and that what remained was working for reconciliation and reunification of the ranks and file. Events in the Nasir faction proved me completely wrong or perhaps I was really naïve. Little did I know that vested interests and personal ambitions for power and leadership had overtaken the initial call for democratic reforms in the Movement. The issues of the split had become so personal and highly personal stakes attached to them that reconciliation or compromise became virtually impossible.

In a space of three years, the Nasir faction, the SPLM/A - United and later SSIM/A had split into many ethnically based splinter groups that made the issue of peace and unity among them very difficult. Even much later when the necessary condition was created by the Lafon events, ethnic animosities and hostility prevented any further development of the Lafon Declaration into a meaningful instrument for national reconciliation and reunification of the movement. These leaders showed much reluctance and ambivalence reflective of an earlier commitment to collaboration with the NIF regime. For instance, Dr Riek Machar insisted on separate and parallel existence of the SPLM/A and SSIM/A if he did not become the leader of the reunified Movement. Dr Lam Akol of the SPLM/A-United slighted Cdr William Nyuon instead of praising his patriotic decision as a first step in the process of reconciling and reuniting the national liberation struggle.

The internecine fighting that gripped the South following the Nasir Declaration did not endear many people in South Sudan, least those who themselves were involved alongside these intellectual commanders. In the Akobo conference 1994, one elder asked why the wars instigated by the intellectuals don't seem to end. He was referring to the war unleashed by the Nasir leaders on the SPLA following the failure of the Nasir coup. That was a valid question. Wars are fought for specific objectives and, therefore, must come to an end whether or not the objective has been achieved. The people in South Sudan can understand easily the prolongation of the war with the North because they still can see the 'Arab' or northern army in the South. They still see the 'Jelaba' controlling the market and exploiting them through unequal exchange.

But what the people in Akobo, Waat, Tonga and any other place in the South can not understand is the idea of bringing their children to eastern Equatoria in order to 'fight and defeat Garang'. They could not understand why Riek Machar was insisting of mobilising people to dislodge Garang instead of fighting and chasing the Arab army from South Sudan. That was the reason for which they took up arms in the first place. Therefore, they were right when they ask him, 'where are you going to chase Garang to?' They felt that the fighting to chase Garang away from the South was unreasonable. This explains the desertions and defections within the ranks and file of the Nasir forces that were ordered to go and fight and dislodge Garang from Equatoria. Thus, every time Riek Machar flagged off a contingent of his forces to eastern Equatoria, they easily found their way back home.

This book is a modest appraisal of the events that led to the Nasir Declaration in 1991 and the subsequent developments which made Riek Machar paranoid about the question of the leadership of the Movement and, hence, of the South. Many of the tragic events that occurred between 1991 and 1995 have not been fully documented but the reasons behind them have been highlighted. The internecine and vicious fighting among South Sudanese has reinforced the notion among many foreigners including the North Sudanese that South Sudanese cannot form a viable nation state. But this has been disproved by many of the positive developments in the South Sudan. What could be expected of a people whose perception of and solidarity with themselves as one people have been sufficiently eroded by centuries of oppression, divisions and stereotypes images imposed from outside?

The in fighting that has recently been experienced among the ethnic groups in South Sudan is deeply embedded in the history of our people. In the past, it was reinforced by the colonial 'policy of divide and rule'. The successive northern-dominated governments in Khartoum practiced this since independence in 1956. It has become a straight jacket from which many South Sudanese intellectuals cannot extricate themselves. They have become so conscious of it that they exploit it in the struggle to satisfy their petty needs and ambitions.

Despite many years of common historical development, including fighting together for a common nationhood, many intellectuals now, more than ever before, still identify themselves first as Dinka, Nuer, Moro, Shilluk, Zande etc., and then South Sudanese, even when interacting with each other. This alienation was accentuated by the experience South Sudanese went through in the Southern Regional Government in Juba following the Addis Ababa Agreement in 1972. The political elite who took over the power structure in the South emphasised their tribal attributes and unity with the north at the expense of and against the South Sudanese nationalism which started developing on the eve of the independence of Sudan.

The SPLM/A could have been a way of rejuvenating this nationalist aspiration and many South Sudanese who joined the ranks and file of the liberation movement in 1983 saw this very clearly. Only that they could not realize this dream because of the declared objective of the Movement as spelt out in the SPLM Manifesto 1983. It was at variance with the will and aspirations of many of its members who still believe that South Sudan should secede from the rest of the Sudan to enable a South Sudanese national identity to evolve and develop. Further, the SPLM/A did not transform the rhetoric about a socialist united Sudan into a political and economic programme that put the people in the centre. On the contrary, much time, energy and blood of the people have been wasted simply because of this discrepancy between what the leaders preached on the one hand and the aspiration of the people on the other.

Fears have been expressed, perhaps with justification, given the experience of inter-SPLA fighting and the inability of the leaders to compromise their petty aspirations and ambitions in the interest of the people, that the situation in Rwanda and Burundi might replicate itself in an independent South Sudan. However, and whatever may be said in the context of Rwanda and Burundi, South Sudanese have a big capacity for forgiveness and adhere to traditional mechanisms for resolving such internal conflicts. This was experienced after the Addis Ababa Agreement; the divisions and in fighting among the Anya-nya freedom fighters were forgiven and forgotten in the interest of forging a common unity. It was because of the government's - the Southern Regional Government - failure to reinforce that unity with meaningful development schemes that some of these scars started to resurface.

Moreover, the question of land resources and the struggle over them as in those tiny central African countries is not an issue in South Sudan, at least for the time being. It is our hope that with a good government machinery, democratic dispensation, and economic resources for equitable and sustainable development at its disposal, many people in South Sudan will settle down peacefully to recreate their lives peacefully. In this respect, the splits and in-fighting coming at the present time could have perhaps been a blessing in disguise.

This book is also an attempt to cast light on the bitter struggle that ensued after the Nasir Declaration between leaders of the coup and those who genuinely wanted to reform the SPLM/A and turn it into a dynamic liberation movement which would struggle for the creation of a just and democratic 'New Sudan'. This struggle, unfortunately, did not attain the ideological and political height that would have furthered the aims of the revolution, thus ensuring fundamental impact on the political and military situation in the Movement. It got frozen at the level of personal heckling, bickering and petty squabbles leading to desertions and defections of the combatants to form their own splinter groups with or without military presence on the ground in South Sudan. This played into the hands of the NIF government which exploited the desperate economic and financial situation of many of these leaders to instigate further dissensions and splits, some of them without political or moral basis, through bribery, corruption and blackmail.

This is also an attempt to retrace Dr Riek Machar's political outburst following the Lafon events and the Declaration of 27 April 1995 that generated more divisions and splits within SSIM/A. The acceptance of the Lafon Declaration would have been the surest and cleanest way for Dr Riek Machar and the entire South Sudan Independence Movement - SSIM/A to extricate themselves from the stigma of collaboration with the enemy against the aspirations of the people of South Sudan and their compatriots in the Nuba Mountains and the Ingessina Hills. It would have been a dignified return to the liberation Movement he helped to build and would have also avoided his painful unconditional surrender to the enemy. The Agreement between the SPLM/A and the SSIM/A Forces of Unity was signed on 27 April 1996 by Cdr Salva Kiir Mayardit, the deputy chairman of SPLM and Chief of General Staff of SPLA on the one hand, and Cdr John Luk Jok, Chairman of the Provisional Executive Council of SSIM and Commander in Chief of SSIA, marking the beginning of the process of reconciliation, reunification and reintegration of forces as provided by the Lafon Declaration.

The contradictions that gripped the Nasir faction, the SPLM/A - United and later the SSIM/A proved one salient fact that the Nasir leaders lacked the democratic clout necessary to remedy the contradictions in the SPLM/A which they claimed to rectify by ousting Dr John Garang from the leadership. They, therefore, carried with them into the faction(s) they formed all the distortions they wanted to correct in the SPLM/A. As a result, Riek split with Lam and in turn, Lam split with his deputies; Peter Sule and James Othow in his new faction.

At the height of these contradictions, and since 1991, there has been considerable change of roles and the line of political alliances within the splinter group has shifted so much so that in the course of five years of the existence of the Nasir faction and its political variations; SPLM/A - United and SSIM/A, there has been fundamental realignment of forces suggestive of bitter internal power struggle. For instance, following or soon after the Nasir Declaration, close friends and allies of Dr Lam Akol such as Dr Achol Marial, Telar Deng and others, left the faction in disgust with his methods. Dr Achol Marial became a humanitarian worker, having emotionally reconciled himself with the

SPLM/A in 1992 after performing a traditional Dinka ritual of 'feet washing' to cleanse him of evil spirits which had associated him with Riek Machar and the Nasir faction. People who then very close to the SPLM/A leadership, but later defected to join Riek Machar and the enemy[1] oversaw this ritual. Although Dr Lam Akol had all along been close to John Luk in the Nasir faction and in the SPLM/A - United and in the struggle against Dr Riek Machar, he refused in 1995 to join John Luk in the political and military action against Riek Machar on the grounds that he would accept reunification only if he were made the leader of the new faction.

Contradictions in an organisation are healthy as they become sources of energy for its growth and development if resolved democratically. The solidity and coherence of a political organisation is therefore buttressed by the struggle and unity of the opposite trends inside it. Ideological struggle in a national liberation movement like the SPLM/A is imperative as it is the only vehicle for its development. However, when the organisation is stifled of political and ideological debate, the contradictions are forced to emerge along personal and tribal lines making them complex and very difficult to resolve. This is quite true of the situation that existed in the SPLM/A before the split in 1991, and in the Nasir faction and its political variations after the Nasir coup.

Political and ideological preoccupations on the part of the combatants were proscribed and when issues arose they were personalized, shifted out of their political, ideological and national context. Why on earth would Riek Machar, whose initial intention for the coup was reforms of the Movement, talk of 'over my dead body', in a political contest for leadership as if he were the custodian of the destiny of the people of South Sudan? Is it not simply because he has attached much importance to his becoming the leader of the South Sudan that missing this leadership became comparable to losing his life?

Although a political crisis loomed in the SPLM/A before the Nasir Declaration in 1991, especially at the level of the High Command, its resolution in the form of a military action was uncalled for. The coup did not result from the consideration that a peaceful internal struggle for changes and democratic reforms in the Movement had proved futile. No, the forces for the reforms were weak and still coalescing when the coup was staged in August 1991. It was premature to conclude at that stage that the leadership of Dr John Garang de Mabior had failed and that a military coup to oust him was the necessary alternative. This was the case, given the spontaneous nature of the SPLM/A's birth, and the internal bitter struggles for leadership that marred that birth; it was obvious that more time was needed to correct many of the shortcomings inside the Movement and to allow for the emergence of an acceptable political ideology and structure.

I cherish freedom of opinion, specifically independent opinion, which is not necessarily antagonistic. And being in the opposition politics is a kind of hobby I enjoyed. But, of course, I did not fancy the idea of being thrown in prison for being in opposition. I don't know anybody who enjoys prison tenancy. Thus, when I began to engage in political activity, I had always found myself supporting the view opposed to the establishment in the Sudan. This was due to the fact that there had not been a time when Sudan had a just and democratic regime that satisfied the aspirations of every Sudanese. For instance, the first time I cast vote in an election in the Sudan was only in 1986 following the demise of Nimeri's regime.

When I joined the SPLM/A in 1986, I found myself amongst those who were agitating for democratic reforms and democratisation of the Movement; this was what made me support the Nasir Declaration in 1991 as an extension of that agitation for the establishment of a genuine national liberation movement capable of leading the people's struggle. I supported the coup in the honest belief that it was on the side of the people. However, I did not accept things like the collaboration with the NIF government that unfolded in the Nasir faction at face value. Nor did I condone the lynching of compatriots which took place in Nasir or other places in the wake of the coup. That is why in on time I found myself marginalised to the periphery of the faction and in a state of serious contradiction with the Nasir leadership which branded me a 'trouble shooter', when I exposed their hidden agenda.

However, being against a certain political trend, policy or even a person in a political organisation should not necessarily amount to one quitting and abandoning the struggle. I always preferred to struggle within the precincts of the organisation unless for one reason or the other one is formally dismissed. That explains why I continued to be in the Nasir faction against all these odds. Perhaps something lingered in my mind that it was still possible to effect changes in the faction.

When I came back to Nairobi from the conference in Akobo in October 1994, I had almost made up my mind to leave the struggle, I was so discouraged by the attitude of Dr Riek Machar and his refusal to heed the call of the people at the conference for reconciliation and reunification of the liberation struggle and the SPLM/A that I almost lost hope in the whole liberation struggle. The reconciliation and reunification of the Movement proved difficult if not impossible by that time that the only way was to resign to oneself. But something kept flicking my conscience; it was telling me, ' leave the struggle! in order to do what?' The option of going for resettlement in America, Canada or Australia, like most SPLM/A officers and men, disturbed me so much that I dropped the idea of becoming a retired freedom fighter. I was full of energy; so off I went to Tonga to carry out a survey for a humanitarian agency.

The trip to Tonga would have afforded me an opportunity to assess for myself the level of tribal animosity and what chances remained among the Shilluks for reconciliation and reunification with the rest of the South. To my disappointment, but not surprise, I found the mood in the Shilluk homeland very different and hostile. Nobody was interested in any talk about reconciliation with Nuer or Dinka, especially those who stood to benefit from the status quo. Moreover, the ordinary Shilluks were still bitter about the abuses, atrocities and other inhuman acts they suffered at the hands of Anya-nya 2 and other SPLA groups that roamed the Shilluk homeland between 1985 and 1992[2]. They were specifically very bitter with the Nuers, Anya-nya 2 or SPLA - United of Riek Machar that talks of reconciliation and reunification was a mere waste of time. Moreover, Lam Akol in his quarrel with and dismissal by Riek Machar, and in his bid to gain credibility and acceptability among the Shilluks, had politicised them along tribal lines against the Nuers (SSIM/A) as well as the Dinka (SPLA) to the extent that nobody, at least among those former SPLA officers and men present in Tonga, would listen to my reconciliation and reunification talk. That explains why I had to spend six months, according to Lam Akol, as 'a prisoner of war' in his jail in Tonga.

Arresting somebody for difference of political views was a very radical departure from the principle for which he and Riek Machar staged the coup in Nasir against Dr John Garang de Mabior, the leader of SPLM/A. But, of course, Lam Akol has never been known as a democrat or a humanist, so I was not surprised in the least by his action against me. Dr Riek Machar's action against Commander John Luk and others in Waat in mid 1994 goes to prove that the Nasir Declaration was only an exercise in power struggle over the Movement's leadership rather than a struggle for democratisation and respect for human rights and civil liberties.

Two days upon my arrival back to Nairobi from Lam's jail, I went to meet Dr Riek Machar. This was a few days after the Lafon Declaration had been signed by Dr John Garang de Mabior and Commander William Nyuon Bany on behalf of Dr Riek Machar. After a few moments of courtesy and personal questions about my experience in Tonga, we went into discussion of political issues and the Lafon events engaged us. Without waiting to hear his briefing, I asked him a straight question.

'Dr Riek, why did you miss the opportunity?'

Without allowing me to finish what I had wanted to say, Riek came through in a hurry.

'What opportunity?' he asked. I knew now he was not going to let me continue, nevertheless I continued.

'The Lafon opportunity. I heard your interview with Robin Wright on the BBC; I thought you had missed a golden opportunity to extricate yourself and SSIM/A from the collaboration with the NIF. In my opinion you should have stressed the question of reunification of the Movement and not the position you would occupy in the reunified Movement. It was an opportunity for you to highlight the Washington agreement in which Garang and you agreed on self determination as the basis for resolution of the conflict with Khartoum, and the Nairobi agreement of January 6th 1994 in the wake of the IGAD Peace Initiative.'

'You have been here in Nairobi for only two days and now your small mind is already spoiled, I don't want any more arguments', Riek said,

This left me flabbergasted, asking myself what kind of power Riek Machar so much assured of to warrant that arrogance. I concluded that things were not going to be the same in SSIM/A again. In all honesty, I was not a member of SSIM/A because of the showdown I had with Dr Riek Machar during the Akobo convention in which I declined to take up any political assignment in that faction. However, I believed that my personal relationship with Dr Riek Machar entitled me to go and discuss political and other issues with him. This time things were running against him and, therefore, he saw in any adverse opinion a conspiracy to depose him or deny him the leadership of South Sudan.

Dr Riek Machar's behaviour made me throw my lot with Cdr. John Luk and those in SSIM/A who wanted to further develop the Lafon process and attain the reunification of the Movement. I think that there could not have been a better decision than this. I feel elated and proud to be in the SPLM/A again.

The other point I thought is pertinent here and must be mentioned is my personal reflection. I have realised that at the age of fifty two, one can no longer continue to be an 'opposition activist', at least one must begin to exercise responsible politics of reconciliation and construction. I recall what Lord Churchill, in his poetic way, once said:

> If in your teens you are not a communist, you have no heart.
> But by thirty five you are still a communist, then you have no mind.

Euphemism and flippancy apart, I have both heart and mind. However, But the experience of the last five years has shown me how the best of intentions could be manipulated and misused by some unscrupulous leaders. Dr Riek Machar and Dr Lam Akol were not part of the group that agitated for reforms and democratisation in the SPLM/A. They were obedient lieutenants of Dr John Garang, the SPLM/A leader. Both were favoured and rose to the peak of the SPLM/A in the midst of honourable and diligent military officers who could have been promoted and who would have executed their missions without the qualms of being equal to Dr John Garang on account of their academic credentials.

Both engineers, turned guerrillas, were posted in their own home regions, where they had the opportunity to build individual political power base. They only jumped onto the bandwagon for democratic reforms within the SPLM/A after they fell out with Garang. That I overlooked all these and worked with them is something that still puzzles me. Perhaps, I must have been so overwhelmed by the oppressive situation in the Movement that I opted for the easy way out.

Questions have been put to us, especially by those who have become paranoid about Garang and his leadership of the SPLM/A, who since have remained outside the process of reconciliation and reunification and also by some compatriots within the SPLM/A, who have been timid enough all these years not to put across their views, whether there was change in the SPLM/A or in Garang. Or, to put it in another way, whether things will change in the SPLM/A now that we have rejoined. I say strongly yes! And they will continue to change for the better. Nothing remains the same, especially when there is will for betterment.

But as to whether Garang as a person has changed or will change that is something I don't want to speculate upon. What I can say is that things have changed; that old methods cannot be applicable at the moment, whether it is Garang or somebody else. To this I add that the past thirteen years should be left behind by each and every one of us and we should count them as some of the darkest pages of our history, and most significant, as our collective responsibility, from which no one will be absolved. Nevertheless, these experiences have brought us to a point in time when understanding ourselves is acquiring greater dimensions. We must learn from them that never and never again should they show their ugly face to our people. The people of South Sudan as I have mentioned earlier are kind and forgiving. Even in their weakest moments they are capable of understanding and forgiveness. As such, I say with confidence that our people will overcome the physical and psychological trauma and, therefore, the memories of those dark days, I believe, will light their future.

Notes

[1] Commander Aciek, who was instrumental in Dr Achol's return to the SPLM/A, himself defected to the NIF in late 1996 out of unjustified fear that Dr Garang wanted to kill him.
[2] The memory of the battle with the Nuer forces of SPLM/A-United in 1992 was still fresh in the minds of many of them including civilians, some of who were able to get arms after that battle.

2

Background to the present war

... We are in the midst of a revolutionary war, and revolutionary war is an antitoxin, which not only eliminates the enemy's poison but also purges us of our filth. Every just revolutionary war is endowed with tremendous power which can transform many things or clear the way for their transformation...

Mao Tse Tung

A brief historical synopsis

The history of what is called the Sudan today is long and contains various episodes which still contribute to the present conflict in the country. It is not the subject of this work to trace the historical roots of the problem of the Sudan, but without knowledge of it, understanding of the present complexities will be difficult. It only for quick reference that the following highlights are made.

Until the invasion in 1820 by Mohammed Ali at the head of a Turco-Egyptian expedition, very little was known of the Sudan, except for brief description of Arab travellers who called it 'bilad el sudan' or land of the black people. And this extended well across Africa from east to west following the Sahel belt. The authentic modern historical records of the Sudan begin from that period although sometimes some unscrupulous northern Sudanese historians find it useful to distort for their own narrow purposes.

It is important to note that it was the black, non-Arab, non-Muslim nationalities that really controlled the areas now known as South Sudan, and other parts of west, central and eastern Sudan stretching up to the present Khartoum[1]. Even Khartoum itself derives its name not from the Arabic 'khartoum' meaning the elephant trunk, but from the Nilotic word *karatum* meaning a joint, a meeting place etc., suggestive of the confluence of the Blue and White Niles. These indigenous people controlled the area and the Arab groups, in their migrating across the river Nile from east to west and vice versa, had to seek the permission and guidance of these people.

The Turco-Egyptian invasion, and the establishment of an Islamic Turco-Egyptian regime in the north Sudan from 1821 until the Mahdiyia uprising in 1881, changed the balance of forces in favour of the northern riverian Arabs groups who collaborated with the Turks and Egyptians in the plunder, pillage and enslavement of the areas of South Sudan, the Nuba Mountains and Funj, adding to the worsening relationship between the North and South Sudan.

Slavery and slave trade, still fresh in the memory of many South Sudanese and their compatriots in the west and central Sudan, was factor in shaping the relations between the two parts of the Sudan. Started by the Turks and Egyptians as a means of raising financial resources for their rule, slavery and trafficking in slaves was heightened by the Mahdist's state following its overthrow of the Turco-Egyptian state in the North. The nationalities in the South were ruthlessly plundered by the Khalifa's army who ransacked the South in search of slaves, gold, ivory, ebony, ostrich feathers etc. It is worth mentioning that much of the Khalifa's army latter comprised mainly people from the South and western Sudan who were captured initially as slaves but later converted to Islam.

The re-conquest of the Sudan by Anglo-Egyptian forces brought new factors into play. The inherent contradiction between the national interests of the condominium parties reflected itself in the policies adopted for the colonial administration and the social and economic development of the Sudan. The South took time to pacify and bring under firm control of the colonial authorities. This hostility of the people of South Sudan to foreign rule, coupled with other factors of religious and cultural difference with the North, made the colonial authorities adopt different policies for the administration of the South. This was exacerbated by the rebellion in 1924 of the 'White Flag League' against the British rule under Ali Abdel Latif, and the South, the Nuba Mountains and the Ingessina Hills were sealed off from the rest of Sudan under the 'Closed Districts Ordinance'. The 'policy of the southern provinces' was formulated to consolidate the complete separate socio-economic, administrative and political evolution of the two parts of the Anglo-Egyptian Sudan. From that time until the reversal of that policy in 1947, South and North Sudan were administered as separate entities with formal travel and consular arrangements between them.

The most significant factor of concern in the separate development of the South and North and which continues to affect the relationship of the two people was the colonial concentration of economic, political and administrative development in the North at the expense of the South, thus creating socio-economic and political disparities between the two parts. In this evolution of the uneven development, education was a major vehicle. North Sudan had an advantage over the South because of its proximity to Egypt and the rest of the Arab world to which the northern Sudanese had easy access. Many northern Sudanese found easy access to educational facilities in Egypt. Arab and Islamic heritage, therefore, played an important role in shaping the political awareness of the people in the North which the Egyptians had an interest to further.

Owing to the policy of absolute exclusion, the South had no access to education facilities except from the Christian Missionaries, who were as a matter of policy assigned the complete monopoly of running the school system in addition to their Christian proselytisation. This not only increased the gap between the South and North, it produced apolitical, docile civil servants of the colonial administration. Christian education, which stressed the separation of state from the church, could not be an incentive for engaging in political activity which would challenge the authority of colonial administration. South Sudanese, therefore, were indoctrinated along lines that sought to preserve the status quo. With this missionary education, South Sudanese were discouraged from engagement in politics, political debate and action, and anybody seen practising political dissent was punished and dismissed from either the school or their jobs.

It is common knowledge that politics is both science and arts. As an art it is perfected by practice in political action. A politician is moulded and seasoned in the course of participation in political action. As a rule there must be a political forum on which to act and on which political experience is passed onto the younger generation of leaders. Modern political organisations and parties have devised processes through which their cadres and future leaders must pass and get their political training. In the case of the Sudan, some Northern political parties have had such experiences in their political work and organisation. The proximity of the North Sudanese, geographically, culturally and religiously to Egypt and the Middle East gave them the opportunity to benefit from these experiences; as a result, they acquired political skills in organisation, agitation and action. In contrast, the South Sudanese remained trapped in political backwardness.

The education dispensed to South Sudanese during the colonial rule and after independence retarded the evolution of their national consciousness and awareness. The schools in the South, patterned on the so-called 'Southern Pattern', most of which were former missionary schools nationalised after independence, had certain academic subjects which the authorities perceived would create self awareness among South Sudanese students, intentionally excluded from the curriculum in favour of neutral subjects like biology, chemistry, physics, European history and others that tended to dull their awareness of themselves. Thus, for instance, the history of Sudan taught in primary schools in the North was not included in the syllabus of the Southern schools. A Southern child started learning something about the history of the Sudan, undoubtedly very essential in awareness formation, only in the third year in the secondary school, one year before sitting the Sudan School Certificate (O'level) Examinations.

The gap between South and North Sudan widened in everything conceivable. This was further heightened by the attitude of the northern political elite, in the wake of the struggle for independence, who excluded the South from the political process as a means of marginalising the South to prevent power sharing. The absolute marginalisation of the South from the political, administrative and economic life of the country led to the mutiny in the South in August 1955, just on the eve of independence, and a civil war that lasted for seventeen years.

As a result, South Sudanese political activity commenced and grew within the orbits of northern political parties in the wake of the nationalist movement for independence in Northern Sudan during the forties and early fifties. Since they did not have the capacity to form their own parties, the energies of South Sudanese political activists could only find expression in the programmes of the Umma Party, the National Unionist Party and the Communist Party of the Sudan. The Southern Liberal Party, therefore, was established much later in reaction to and out of frustration with the northern political parties, their Arabo-Islamic eccentricity, chauvinism and arrogance. Although the South Sudanese political activists did at least represent the political interests and aspirations of the people of the South, they lacked the economic muscle to form independent political parties and perseverance in the struggle when conditions became adverse, making them prone to North Sudanese political machinations, blackmail and bribery. They were unable to form solid and coherent political parties due to the instigation of the northern political establishment and their policy of ' divide and rule'.

It is no wonder that South Sudanese, especially among the older generations, displayed a remarkable degree of shyness and indifference to politics, political organisation. The southern 'Liberal Party', the first ever-political party to be formed by South Sudanese came very late, just on the eve of independence. The action of some of its members, vacillating from alliance to alliance with northern political parties, and the name itself is suggestive of lack total of political commitment to the cause, or to stand up boldly, risking one's neck, to defend the interests expressed by these ideas. It is, of course, easy to hide behind the façade of generalities and vague slogans, especially when one is weak and lacks true conviction to the people's cause, or authentic mandate from the people. Most South Sudanese would want to win little favours from their Northern political colleagues by not being seen to be advocating radical ideas like separation, federation etc.

Although there were honourable and strong leaders among this elite, people of strong character, integrity and good will, who really stood up to defy the hegemony of the north, both politically and economically, yet because of their weak economic base, their political action tilted more to where their survival was assured. In fact, South Sudanese elite have a culture of giving their organisations, political or otherwise, names that are so obtuse and so general reflective of lukewarm commitment to their cause, or which should not be identified with their innerselves - i.e. secession of the South which many South Sudanese ascribe to - in order not to offend the northern political establishment.

Since they did not possess the necessary instruments for political organisation, which demands relentlessness in building these structures and instruments, when a regime is overthrown and another is being formed or about to take its place, the South Sudanese politicians hurry to form groups and new alliances to lobby for ministerial and cabinet portfolios. That is usually the time when some form of political action is witnessed; soon after that everybody retires to usual duties. For instance, the over throw of the military regime of Ibrahim Abboud in the October uprising (1964) and the over throw again of the May regime of Nimeri in April 1985 found South Sudanese inside the country unprepared for the political change in the same way the northern political parties were.

Therefore, looking at the Sudanese political landscape in retrospective, we find many of the South Sudanese political groups or parties, that shot up or emerged in the course of a definite political action in a particular era, did not last long after that era had elapsed and new regime had been installed. Because they appeared like political artifacts, out of reaction to certain political situation, and as soon as the condition that brought them into play disappeared or changed, so have they disappeared imperceptibly. To illustrate this point, the Southern Liberal Party was established in response to and under the conditions of the liberal parliamentary democratic regime that existed in the early fifties and which allowed political organisation and action. When that regime was overthrown and replaced by the military regime of General Ibrahim Abboud in 1958, the party politics was outlawed. While the northern parties went into clandestine political activity with the aim of overthrowing the military regime, the Liberal Party dissolved itself voluntarily. Most of its leaders collaborated with the new regime while the patriotic ones went into exile where they formed a completely new and different political grouping to continue the struggle by different methods.[2]

When the military regime of Ibrahim Abboud was overthrown in a popular uprising in October 1964 and political parties activities resumed, the UMMA, the NUP, the PDP[3], the Communist Party, the Islamic Charter Front (as the present National Islamic Front was known then) and others vegetated back to life, maintaining their organisational structures as they were before being proscribed by the junta. Their central committees, political bureaus, branches, and cells etc., which had worked underground[4], issuing statements and printing anti-regime posters, were again out in the open.

The weak economic base of many South Sudanese cannot allow them to remain long in the opposition politics. South Sudanese political elite, who had just woken from the six years of political sleep, came up with something unheard of before. The Southern Front was hurriedly established in Khartoum by government officials[5], intellectuals, students and workers. In exile, the Sudan African National Union - SANU - broke up into two factions. Late

William Deng, leader of the one faction returned to the country in March 1965 to continue his political struggle under the same name. The Sudan Unity Party was a northern party in southern clothing, in the person of Santino Deng Teng[6] and other collaborationists of the military regime. It is worth noting here that, while the Northern Sudanese, who were close associates and who distinguished themselves with the military regime, were scorned, looked upon with disdain and marginalised in the political parties, regimes that succeeded the October government after the elections of 1965, South Sudanese were accommodated by the new ' democratic ' regime.

The reason for what appears like a political discrepancy is simple. The Sudanese state is a Northern institution handed over to them by the British colonial authority on independence in 1956. South Sudan was, therefore, an appendage annexed just on the eve of independence for some political expediency. In essence since 1956 the Sudanese state represented the economic, social and cultural interests of the Muslim and Arab Northern Sudan. Northern politicians like Sadiq el Mahdi, leader of the UMMA party, for instance, talk of the Sudan being a 'family property ' and thinks it is a family/personal duty to protect it by being its permanent rulers.

In 1966, when Sadiq el Mahdi turned thirty years old, as demanded by the constitution, Sadiq el Mahdi had to take over the mantle of power from the veteran and experienced politician Mohammed Ahmed Mahgoub, for no other reason than that Sadiq was the heir to the throne. In 1967, Ahmed el Mahdi, Sadiq's cousin, stroke, with a stick a fellow Umma Party member, a lawyer, during a political rally simply because their views differed. When asked why he beat the lawyer, Ahmed said it was his birth right to discipline dissenters in the party and the whole matter was closed. Such incidences have created serious tensions in the Umma Party, between the political leadership and the elite who did not hail from the immediate Mahdi family. This dichotomy of the Umma Party being a national political institution on one hand and a family institution on the other continues to raise serious political debate to date. Questions are being asked as to whether or not Sadiq el Mahdi should relinquish the leadership of the party in favour of anyone outside his immediate family.

The role Southerners and any other none-Arabs played in this Sudanese state was and still remains that of an apprentice. The South Sudanese, thus, developed the psychology of an outsider in the affairs of their country. As a result, in position of authority in this state, they worked either half-heartedly because of their divided allegiance. For any northern regime coming to power in Khartoum, South Sudanese, whatever their role was in the previous regime, must be accommodated in the new regime. The idea is that while they are still searching for fresh collaborationists from among the Southern politicians, the vacuum must be filled by the old loyalists of the Sudanese state to assist in the implementation of their version of the 'policy of the southern provinces' formulated by the British in the twenties.

The South Sudanese are therefore accommodated on account of the 'Southern Problem' or *mishkalat el Junub el Sudan*, which over the course of time has become a 'sacred cow' for these South Sudanese politicians, orphans of the Sudanese state, to live on. Yes, they are truly orphans of the Sudanese state. This is because their economic interests, social stature and standing in the society is tied up with the position they occupy in this state bureaucracy and its very existence. They are there to be inherited by and ready to serve any regime which takes over the state power, no matter how oppressive it may be.

That is why sometimes they resist the destruction of that state and go to such crazy heights of organising their poor people to defend the regimes serving that state. This behaviour on the part of the Southern elite continued as long as the war continued. What happened during the seventeen years war has been replicated during the Nimeri's regime, and even now, when many of the elite that congregated in Juba between 1972 and 1983 have relocated to Khartoum and other major towns in the north to serve the northern political establishment.

This was a necessary digression to emphasise the lack of commitment among a large section of the political elite in the South. It is comparable to the role the British policy ambivalence towards South Sudan during the last epoch of colonial administration; whether the political development of South Sudan and the future of its people be linked with their kin in East Africa or their lot thrown in with Arab and middle eastern people. It is responsible for the present state of affairs and has contributed to prevent the emergence and crystallisation of a South Sudanese 'national' awareness and consciousness.

The claim to unity by South Sudanese elite all along, especially in their quest for power and dominance over other sections of the society in the South, has not been intrinsic but extrinsic. It has been created by the situation of oppression and reinforced by the continued existence of that oppressive external factor, in the form of North Sudan. This is clearly reflected in the loose attitude; liberalism bordering on indifference and passivity, and lack of commitment to a cause the people of South Sudan are paying dearly in their lives. This explains the ease with which South Sudanese differ among themselves over petty issues, raising them to lethal heights, or their shifting alliances with the oppressive regime to gain immediate and temporary favours and many other unpatriotic moves they undertook which have characterised the behaviour of many leaders who later broke away from the SPLM/A.

The seventeen years war between the South and North was resolved in March 1972 after the Addis Ababa Agreement between the regime of Gaafar Mohammed Nimeri and the Southern Sudan Liberation Movement under the leadership of Joseph Lagu. The Addis Ababa Peace Accord guaranteed the South a regional autonomy within one united Sudan; a Southern Regional

Government (The High Executive Council) exercising executive powers with an independent public service commission; a Southern People's Regional Assembly with legislative powers were established in Juba. It brought relative stability and peace to the South. Although the Addis Ababa Accord did not address the fundamental issues in the South; nevertheless, it was acclaimed through out the South and the rest of the world. An important observation which reflects lack of principle on part of some is that many of the elite who served the Nimeri regime, some of who were very hostile to the SSLM and the Anya-nya fitted themselves, without shame or reservation, in the new regime in the South.

From 1972, the time of the Addis Ababa Agreement, until 1980/81, South Sudan enjoyed a sub-system of the Nimeri regime. The situation amounted then, in some form or measure, to an island of liberal parliamentary democracy in an ocean of one party dictatorship and the personal rule of Nimeri in the whole country. What this sub-system lacked or was denied it was the economic power and resources to sustain it and develop the Southern Region. This was marked by deterioration in the condition of living in the South, economic stagnation and social anarchy.

The South Sudanese elite congregated in Juba, debating their issues, making their own laws and regulations which Nimeri was obliged to endorse except in areas where the authority of the central government was encroached upon. Although the Sudan Socialist Union - SSU, was the legal and only political organisation allowed to function, the elite in the South had their own agenda and organised their political activities along old defunct political parties - Southern Front, and Sudan African National Union - SANU. These clandestine ties created the illusion that the political system in the Southern Region was a multi-party democracy and, in fact, the freedom with which they grilled their leaders and regional government ministers was something that did not exist in the North and was, therefore, a source of envy and sabotage by northern political establishment.

Although the elite in the South presented a façade of unity along their perceived political parties, this did not stand the test of time as ethnic and sectional tendencies overwhelmed many of them to the point of neglecting the southern national concerns and aspirations. The regional government would shuffle and reshuffle the ministers not because they had failed in their task, but because of personal allegiance and how much one memorised and sang the SSU slogans of 'national unity'. The situation in Juba was a reminiscent of people who had attained their lifelong dreams and were, therefore, enjoying its fruits. After attaining what they had been clamouring for over the years, i.e. access to the resources of the state through ministerial portfolios, this elite forgot about what the people of South Sudan had sacrificed their lives in the seventeen years war. The situation was characterised by conspicuous consumption, building personal power bases through dishing out of favours and government contracts to acquaintances or friends.

Instead using this power they had acquired to stimulate the evolution of a southern national awareness, sense of unity and solidarity, social and economic development to alleviate the poverty, backwardness and ignorance, disease etc., in the South, this elite suppressed that national feeling and put the people of South Sudan on a heavy dose of sleeping pill called ' national unity of the Sudan', not because they really believed in that unity, but simply not to offend Nimeri and put their privileged positions in jeopardy. This amounted to a betrayal of not only the people, but also themselves. Because, as a dominant group, it was in their interest to maintain a principled stand vis a vis Nimeri and this could have been possible had they promoted the aspirations of the people and furthered the development of their national awareness as a means of reproducing themselves as a social class.

It is worth mentioning here that between 1972 and 1983 politics in the Southern Region revolved around the personalities of Abel Alier and Joseph Lagu and, in fact, was seen by many South Sudanese in the end as a struggle between the two men, which made it easy for Nimeri to unscrupulously play them against each other. This narrow manner in which the political contradictions were projected did not allow many people in the South to visualise the hands of Nimeri at work behind each of their predicaments. Nimeri took his time playing the southerners against themselves.

Whether or not the southern political elite chose to allow Nimeri to play havoc with them remains to be researched. The truth is that they turned their frustration and anger with Nimeri inwards. For instance, in 1979, perceiving that the issue of oil and change of borders were likely to flare up passions in the Southern Region, Nimeri plotted to have Joseph Lagu, then the president of the High Executive Council, removed and replaced with Abel Alier, whom he knew would treat the matter in a cool manner like the Jonglei Canal crisis in 1974.

When he wanted to abrogate the Addis Ababa Agreement and dismantle the Southern Region in accordance with the Port Sudan Agreement with the National Front 1977 following the resistance to his policies, he dissolved Abel's government (1981), and appointed a caretaker government under General Gasimalla Rasas (until June 1982) to prepare for the election and formation of a new government, ostensibly to oversee the process of administrative decentralisation of Southern Region. He removed Abel as the vice President of the republic and appointed Lagu instead. Thus, to an ordinary mind, it appears Abel Alier and Joseph Lagu were competing for one and the same position.

Nimeri perfected all these machinations and political tricks in preparation for the final dismantling and abrogation of the Addis Ababa Agreement in the Presidential Decree No.1 of June 1983, and the division of the Southern Region into three weak regions - Bahr el Ghazal, Equatoria and Upper Nile - responsible to Khartoum. The unilateral imposition of the Islamic Sharia laws throughout the country and many other tragic policies in September 1983 plunged the Sudan, both North and South, in deep political chaos and anarchy.

In face of all these contradictory political developments, southern politicians did not carry their frustration and anger against Nimeri and his autocratic rule to heights of political agitation or action against the regime. The little resistance that was about to take shape in late 1981, which resulted in the arrest and detention of the members of the Council for the Unity of South Sudan (CUSS) fizzled away for lack of support and solidarity. Worse still, many of them who opposed these policies, turned around to cooperate with and remained obedient servants of the regime. How can the behaviour of all the South Sudanese politicians, who 'agitated for division of the South', be explained? Why did many of those who bitterly opposed and condemned the SPLM/A in its early days come around to pick up senior positions in that organisation when the political tide turned against them with the fall of Nimeri? The only logical answer to these questions seems to be lack of commitment to a particular political ideology and/or principles.

Historically, examples of this behaviour abound among the southern elite. But the case of my colleague, Mr D K Mathews, who instigated and implemented the creation of the so-called 'friendly forces' in order to defend the Nimeri regime against the SPLM/A in Upper Nile where he was governor (1983 - 1985) may suffice for the purpose of this illustration. Interestingly enough, D.K. Mathews himself was not fully convinced that the project he undertook to implement was right. Nevertheless, his shortsighted manoeuvre to remain the Governor of Upper Nile sacrificed the Nuers who made up the bulk of these friendly forces and as such paid the ultimate price defending a state that marginalised and oppressed them just because one of their numbers was a governor. Even the Shilluk Reth Ayang Kur, illiterate and perhaps unaware of the political tricks, was more shrewd than Mr Mathews; he stood up against the designs of Nimeri and refused to raise an army of Shilluk 'friendly forces' and nothing was done against him. He still remained the Shilluk Reth until his death in 1992.

The political crisis that gripped the Sudan in the late seventies and early eighties were bound to have serious repercussions on the delicate and volatile situation in its Southern Region which, at the time, was undergoing its own political despondency. The failure of the regional government in Juba to address the political issues related to the implementation of the Addis Ababa agreement resulted in several armed uprisings between 1972 and 1983. But many of these armed insurrections remained isolated military incidences which did not impact the political situation in Juba. This was partly because they remained expressions of purely military grievances in the barracks. Although they were a reflection of the political contradictions they were not linked to the centres of these contradictions. The only single rebellion that influenced the political situation in Juba and Khartoum was that of the two battalions (104 & 105) in Bor, Ayod and Pibor mid 1983 which heralded the outbreak of the present war and the formation of SPLM/A.

The present war in South Sudan, therefore, came against a background of many contentious issues and contradictions, which fitted South Sudan directly against the regime of Gaafar Nimeri, and the northern political establishment in general. These included, inter alia, the issue of digging of the Jonglei canal which generated a lot of protest from the South (1974), the provincial borders dispute (1980) in which Nimeri attempted to redraw the provincial boundaries curbing off oil rich areas in Bentiu, and the fertile mechanised agricultural lands of northern Upper Nile, with the intention of annexing them to Southern Kordofan and White Nile provinces, respectively; the placement of the oil refinery in Kosti instead of Bentiu (1980) and the unprovoked and continuous interference by Nimeri in the political and democratic process in the Southern Region.

By the close 1981, the political elite running the Southern Region had woken up to the reality of their vulnerability to the political machinations of Nimeri. All along since 1972, they had taken Nimeri and his regime for granted. They put their trust in him more than any other northern politician or leader despite his efforts to play them off against one another. Given their personal allegiances and because of their political and organisational weakness, resulting from their asymmetrical attachment to the regime, coupled with their internal divisions along ethnic lines, the southern political elite was unable to initiate a meaningful opposition to Nimeri's erratic policies. They allowed many opportunities to pass in which they could have taken Nimeri to task, challenged or resisted his policies. On the contrary, they readily succumbed to his 'divide and rule policy' which manifested and expressed itself in their bitter struggle among themselves for balkanisation of the Southern Region, ostensibly to share in the eating of the 'national cake'

Thus, when the first bullets were shot in Bor on 16 May 1983, South Sudan, in general, was already ripe for another military confrontation with the North despite the fact that the political leaders had not prepared the people for it. The insurrection that ensued throughout the South was spontaneous and, apart from the general contradiction and antagonism against the North, every ethnic grouping in the South had its own peculiar agenda for joining the insurrection.

It is imperative to describe at length the different contradictions and ethnic animosity in the South that emerged as a reflection of the deepening of the general crisis of the Nimeri regime in its terminal years. It is necessary also to explain the spontaneous nature and how these contradictions evolved into a political cauldron which led to the formation of the SPLM/A; how they

Background to the present war 25

contributed to the generation of further contradictions linked to the evolution of the Movement's leadership and the concretisation of its political ideology, and the in-fighting which marred the birth of the SPLM/A in 1983. This is because any political action, including insurrection, must have a leadership. A spontaneous action will sooner or latter evolve a leadership that will direct and develop it, giving its form and content.

In fact, from 1980, Nimeri began toying with the idea of redrawing the provincial boundaries in the South in preparation for enacting his policy of ' administrative decentralisation', ostensibly as a means of devolving power to the people. In essence, it was a ploy for diluting the authority of the Southern Region. As a result, the contradictions and rivalries among the ruling elite in the South were automatically shifted to the ethnic arena. Until the formation of SPLM/A in 1983, conflicts along ethnic and sectional lines were not uncommon in the Southern Region as alliances for the control of the regional government shifted up and down. In much of the intervening period, the energy of the people was consumed in the futile struggle for setting up their so-called ' ', sorts of corporate entities of local government formed in the place of old districts. The placement of the boundaries of these councils became a matter of serious concern as it brought a lot of conflict and agony to the poor and innocent tribes who were dragged into conflicts they had nothing to do with their own interests.

Not only was Nimeri's policy of administrative decentralisation implemented to dilute and undermine the authority of the Southern Region which had become restive, but it was also designed to intensify divisions among the people in the South and to turn them against one another. For instance, in Upper Nile, the Shilluk, who have inhabited both banks of the river Nile between Tonga, Kosti and beyond, and both banks of the Sobat river from its confluence with the Nile up to Nagdier since the Turkish times (from 1821), found themselves fitted against the Dinka of Atar by the implementation of administrative decentralisation which placed the borders of Jonglei province and the Atar with the Upper Nile province and the Tonga Area Council, in the middle of both the Nile and Sobat rivers up to their confluence in Pijo (Jonglei canal mouth). In June 1981, this conflict extended to the use of firearms by the police of Jonglei province against the Shilluk villagers on orders of Mr Michael Mario, the Jonglei Provincial Commissioner, which resulted in the death of several innocent civilians, and the burning down of Shilluk villages on the east bank of the Nile starting from Obay up to Nyijwado in the South. The idea was to force the Shilluk to abandon their villages on the side of the Nile.

The politics of ' borders created such bitterness that it led to arms trafficking in Upper Nile and Jonglei provinces. Ethnic groups started arming themselves in preparation for wars or to resolve the question of these boundaries by physical means. The people had been completely disoriented and pitted against each other over issues that did not matter much in their lives. It was great luck that SPLM/A came up with a policy that sought to contain these conflicts. This is because many of the youths, who left their homes to join the SPLM/A, did so initially in the hope acquiring arms and come back to resolve the local conflict.

Initially, the political mobilisation for the SPLM/A in 1983/84 appeared to have gone along these lines mentioned above as a cheap means of getting recruits into the Movement. Thus, many of the Bor and the people of Kongor joined the SPLM/A in tens of thousands, hoping to acquire weapons they needed to fight back, or revenge the cattle rustling practiced against them by the Murle. It had nothing to do with a national agenda of liberation but to settle a local score with their neighbours, the Murle or the Nuers.

Similarly, in northern Bahr el Ghazal, the Malual, Twic and Abeyei Dinka initially in their tens of thousand established units of Anya-nya 2, and later joined the ranks of the SPLA, not because of national ideals, but because of their desire to avenge the raids of the Arab armed groups - Murahalieen - of southern Kordofan. The ecological disaster in western Sudan resulting from desertification have had serious socio-economic and political ramification, on the neighbouring nationalities and ethnic groups. The nomadic Arab tribes (Rezeighat and Messiriyah), looking for pastures for their livestock, were armed and encouraged by the central government in Khartoum to encroach and devastate the Dinka land in northern Bahr el Ghazal. The Nimeri government and the subsequent governments of Swar el Dahab, Sadiq el Mahdi and the present regime of the National Islamic Front are all guilty of this crime of arming the *Murahalieen* against their Dinka neighbours as a means of buying political support[7]. The result was a serious devastation of Northern Bahr el Ghazal, forcing many communities to migrate to the north, east to Ethiopia or farther south.

Having no government support, the people of northern Bahr el Ghazal joined the Anya-nya 2 or the SPLM/A in order to acquire the gun to defend their homes against the incursions from the Murahàlieen. This has been reflected in the songs they composed in the training camps, many speaking of their tribulations and how the 'home' or 'bai' has been devastated by the Murahalieen. Some of these songs are very moving that people shed tears as they sang them.

Another factor that embittered the people and pushed them to the ranks of the rebel movement, Anya-nya 2 or the SPLM/A, was Nimeri's policy (*kasha*) of selective and forceful return from Khartoum, back to their homes of origin, of the people of South and West Sudan, implemented by the regime in the last three years of its life. Many of the victims of *kasha*, and later the implementation of Islamic Sharia laws, swelled the ranks and file of SPLA as many South Sudanese, forced to return to the South in this manner, found it more expedient and morally right to join the armed struggle against the regime that has denied them citizenship. Many youths from the west, significantly the Nuba and people from central Sudan, like the Ingessina, who also have suffered oppression in the hands of the Arab North, joined the ranks and file of SPLM/A. The programmes on radio SPLA beamed out from Ethiopia, encouraging the poor, the dispossessed and the oppressed to join its ranks, accentuated the flow of the people into the SPLM/A training camps. Many black people in the country exasperated by the attitude of the Arab ruling circles over the years identified themselves the SPLA as the only way to their salvation.

The majority of people who joined the ranks and file of SPLM/A did so not necessarily out of political awareness or revolutionary zeal alone but mainly out of anger with the regime. This brought many of the pastoralists, students, workers, youth, women, peasants, and intellectuals, etc., into the ranks and file of SPLA. The insurrection served as the only convenient venue for channelling their anger and frustration against the regime. The school children and their teachers, university students, office workers, and other members of the armed forces, voluntarily left their stations to join the ranks of the armed struggle partly against of the division of the Southern Region and because of the imposition of the Islamic Sharia laws in 1983. Yet many others left because of the acute economic crisis into which the country was plunged, afflicting every sector of the national life and paralysing the state machinery in the southern regions.

The spontaneous manner in which the various ethnic groups and sections of the people of South Sudan joined the ranks of the liberation struggle assisted in eschewing many of the contradictions instigated and nurtured by successive regimes in Khartoum. In fact, the formation of the SPLM/A absorbed these secondary contradictions, enabling the people to forge a unity among themselves.

The SPLM/A, therefore, became a melting pot for all these ethnic differences and contradictions giving them a political and national content and form for the first time. They were able to coalesce around a national objective, whether expressed in the form of one united Sudan or New Sudan did not matter much to them. In terms of political and military organisation and articulation of the political question, SPLM/A was a better 'organised' political and military instrument compared to Anya-nya 2, the first armed groups to be established by the people against the regime but which maintained deep ethnic and sectional cleavages within its ranks.

The Southern Sudan Liberation Front (SSLF), a small group of leftist intellectuals, mostly students who left their universities to start a Che Gevara type guerrilla movement in the early eighties voluntarily dissolved their leadership structures and join the SPLM/A. Although the SSLF was armed with quasi-revolutionary and Marxist ideology, it poorly organised and had no experience to enable them undertake such a task. They did not differ much from the Anya-nya 2 in terms of their objective. What they espoused was an ideology that envisaged a separate and sovereign South Sudan. However, when SPLM/A emerged with high-sounding Marxist phraseology, the SSLF acquiesced and joined ranks.

Initially, in Equatoria Region there was marked hostility towards the SPLM/A, especially at the level of its political leadership because that organisation was perceived to be a Nilotic or Dinka movement, for that matter, whose objective was to reverse Nimeri's division of the Southern Region. Apart from that, it was assumed that the SPLM/A was bent on the destruction of the 'Equatoria Region' in order to impose Dinka hegemony. Nevertheless, the SPLM/A received support, especially among the people of East Bank, Juba and Yei counties. The Equatorians joined the SPLA in tens of thousands. There was no way a government in Juba could have stopped the wave of patriots leaving their homes to join the national liberation movement.

Thus, by the time Nimeri decreed the division of the Southern Region and imposed the 'Islamic Sharia laws', he had offended nearly all the sections of the South Sudanese society and had prepared a fertile ground for the war of national liberation. In fact, many South Sudanese joined the SPLA to complete what the South Sudan Liberation Movement (SSLM) and the Anya-nya had left unfinished, which is the independence of South Sudan. By the turn of 1983, the dice was already cast and many South Sudanese of different walks of life had already made their decision to join the liberation struggle.

The Bor mutiny and the establishment of the SPLM/A.

Against this historical background, and the deepening political and economic crisis of the Nimeri regime, the situation in the South was becoming more volatile. The people of the South were in mood to return to arms. It only needed a spark and the whole place would be up in flames. This was provided by the mutiny in Bor and Pochalla on 16 May, and in Ayod on 6 June 1983, led by Major Kerubino Kuanyin Bol and Major William Nyuon Bany, respectively.

In response to a call to arms South Sudanese of all walks of life trekked all the way to the Ethiopian border where the first SPLM/A camps were established. Even the question of the name of the Movement, its political direction and leadership were only resolved after arrival in western Ethiopia of the politicians, military officers, men, students, farmers, cattle herders, workers and others who comprised the rank and file of the Movement. Many of the politicians who joined the armed struggle did so not as a result of party decision, because there were no party organisations in the Southern Region then although many people pretended to have been members clandestine members of the Southern Front and SANU referred to above.

There were claims then that there existed a clandestine military organisation comprising former Anya-nya officers and men and that this organisation intended to capture power from the regional government in Juba[8]. This has been contested and I believe that if there were anything like that, it could not have been effected by those very close to the system and the military leadership, especially people like Major Kerubino Kuanyin Bol and Major William Nyuon Bany. In view of their respective political awareness and commitment to the cause of the people of South Sudan, it is very unlikely that they could have started the insurrection. When the political unrest commenced in Upper Nile and Bahr el Ghazal in the wake of the military activities of the Anya-nya 2, the military leadership and political establishment used Major Kerubino and Major William to hunt down the Anya-nya 2 fighters. In fact, they owed their promotions in the army ranks to the ruthless and treacherous actions against their compatriots.

It is unthinkable that the same people who were used ruthlessly by the regime to crush their fellow South Sudanese freedom fighters, could turn out to spearhead a revolutionary armed struggle, leave alone its socialist orientation. Major Kerubino and Major William were great friends. Major General Saddiq el Bana (a close relative of Nimeri), exploited their weaknesses[9] to amass for himself wealth in the form of money, gold, cattle and wildlife trophies: elephant tusks, leopard skins, etc.

In return, Kerubino and William were allowed to do whatever they wanted with the funds of their respective units. This is how the problem of the salary for the Battalion 105 under the command of Kerubino surfaced in November and December 1982, precipitating indiscipline in the ranks and file and eventually mutinies in May 1983. The military leadership in Khartoum resolved to crush Kerubino and his troops in Bor. Nimeri saw the mutiny as an opportunity to decree the re-division of the southern region and the imposition of the 'Islamic Sharia laws'.

So the assertion that there was a clandestine military organisation with such designs which involved Kerubino and William really boggles the mind. However, if it were true that there was an attempt to capture Juba and take over the Southern regional government, what was the agenda? Did it have anything to do with the re-division of the southern region? And why is it that it was not preceded by political agitation and mobilisation of the people as a precursor for an eventual military action by these officers? How many of the members of the clandestine movement eventually joined the insurrection? Why is it that many senior former Anya- nya officers elected not to join the SPLM/A? These and many other questions cast serious doubts on the claim published in the SPLM manifesto 1983.

Alternatively, if that version remained true, then that clandestine military organisation trailed behind the political events in the South and, therefore, would not have caught up with those events because Nimeri had taken the initiative. He ordered the attack on Bor before the one on Juba. He immediately decreed the re-division of the southern Region, which he engineered through political trickery of the Southern elite. In this respect then, the action of Kerubino was a case of 'jumping the events' which made the whole episode absurd and adventurous.

This is proved by the difficulty of deciding the political leadership and direction of the movement in Itang in July 1983; the discontent displayed by Major Arok Thon Arok, when he arrived late to the movement and found that his former junior officer, Captain Salva Kiir Mayardiit, had been promoted over and above him in the military hierarchy; the reckless behaviour of Kerubino towards the leadership of John Garang and many other incidences that occurred question the credulity of the clandestine military organisation. Many of these should have been decided long back before the insurrection began.

The SPLM/A emerged spontaneously. It was not something the people of South Sudan has prepared themselves for and it had no acceptable leadership. This manifested itself in struggles mentioned above; absence of an organisational structure capable of mobilising, galvanising and transforming this mass anger into a political force; and a concrete political agenda and ideology capable of being translated into social and economic realities for the people in South Sudan. This omission was to be the source of the initial conflict and power struggle and friction between the politicians and the military officers in the infant movement in July 1983 which precipitated the break with Anya-nya 2.

Unlike many liberation movements the world over, SPLM/A formation did not pass through a period of political incubation of considerable duration. This would have allowed for the evolution of a clear political line and ideological orientation. The political leadership of the movement would have been determined in a democratic manner according to the wish and will of the people. The structural organisation of the Movement capable of leading the struggle and absorbing all the various political and ideological hues would have emerged without the pains of bitter military confrontation with Anya-nya 2, which marked its birth in 1983.

The political situation in the southern region then was really volatile and could have led to an armed insurrection. But this required a clear political agenda, which could not have been articulated within the context of the SSU politics to which the southern political elite were glued. The struggle waged by most of the political elite was a struggle for positions in the system, articulated as a 'sharing of the national cake' which obviously had little link with the destiny of the people of the South. They did not pay attention to the issues that precipitated the mutinies among the Anya-nya forces. It was utterly impossible to unite this elite around a common national agenda. Perhaps the following quotation illustrates pretty well the situation in the southern region in the early eighties:

> ... constrain them to join in building a tower, and thou shall make them like brothers. But if you would have them hate each other, throw food amongst them. A civilisation is made of what is required of men, not on what is provided for them...[10]

It is because of this division and bitter struggles among the political elite that we find the military insurrections taking the central place in the struggle in the South Sudan, including the Torit rebellion in 1955. The rebellions and mutinies, (and they were many) were something executed by military officers and men obviously to push for limited economic and social demands in their barracks. Little did they impact the political situation, except for that of the Juba Airport 1977, which had clear political overtones, but were watered down by the politicians who did not want to sacrifice their privileged positions in government. In the absence of conscious mass political support a military mutiny amounts to nothing and this explains why the mutinies in the Anyanya garrisons fizzled away without impact and they were soon forgotten.

To illustrate this further the developments in Bor and Pochalla in mid 1983 had their roots in financial embezzlement and other administrative matters in the garrisons associated with the personality of Major Kerubino Kuanyin Bol. The uprisings were triggered off by a volatile political situation, emanating from the general crisis of the regime. Furthermore, those who ignited the fire in Bor were those very close to the army leadership in Southern Region - Major General Saddiq el Bana, a very close relative of General Nimeri.

This gives credence to the version that the mutiny was planned and instigated by Nimeri himself as a stratagem for speeding up the process of re-division of the southern region and the imposition of Islamic Sharia laws. In fact when the problem of army salaries in Bor started in late 1982, it was the regional government that ordered the released of money from the coffers of the regional Ministry of Finance to resolve the crisis. Nimeri, the bully, now blackmailed the southern politicians, in the regional government and the regional assembly into resolving the problem if they wanted to continue receiving his favours. Perhaps the motives behind all this would have been exposed had the regional government refused to foot the bill or had left the issue to the army command.

The point being emphasised here is that the SPLM/A's birth was spontaneous and many of its early political ailments can be attributed to those factors and more. The spontaneity of the insurrection has been emphasised only to underline one fact regarding the leadership question or the subjective factors of the liberation struggle in South Sudan. This is because most of the time, political actions in South Sudan are reactions to events triggered by policies of the northern political establishment. It underscores the point that the southern political elite, in spite of their involvement in government, has not made politics, political organisation, and the struggle for the political rights of their constituents a full-time occupation. This has its roots in our recent and contemporary history where organised political activity and discipline has been alien and wanting in South Sudan. This could be attributed to the Christian legacy, notwithstanding the contribution of the Christian priests to the struggle and the ultimate price they paid, combined with the deliberate colonial policy of isolating and insulating South Sudan from outside political ideas and influences.

The developments in the South Sudan during the forties and fifties, even up to the sixties could be blame for omission. But what about the generation of South Sudanese elite which had better opportunities and acquired the political skills necessary for leading and articulating the cause of South Sudanese people? Why is it that they have fallen into the footpath of the 'old school' politicians? This baffles me further because there is a replication of this phenomenon in the SPLM/A, which emerged with a political ideology, which was not a summation of the political struggle in the southern region, nor reflected the real interests and aspirations of the people of South Sudan. It looked like its leaders came from another planet unfamiliar with the reality of South Sudan.

There is a marked tendency on the part of the South Sudanese political elite to shy away from clearly naming what they and the people wanted. There is always a tendency to hide behind a facade suggestive of some degree of lack self confidence in the cause being undertaken. More attention was paid to what others will say about us than what we want ourselves. The question of United Socialist Sudan has before not been in the literature and vocabulary of the political struggle in South Sudan. It just appeared out of the blues as if it was meant or intended to blend with the international currents dictated by cold war politics. This proves one fact: That the programmes of this political elite are always formulated on ad hoc basis without long term strategic significance related the destiny of their constituents.

In fact, the southern political elite, by their greed for power, have sacrificed the future three to four generations of South Sudanese in order either to survive in the present indignities and infamy of serving the Arab dominated regimes, which have continued to butcher South Sudan or maintain an oppressive military machine to buttress their highly personalised authority. If that is not the case, then how can we explain the behaviour of Mulana Abel Alier, the veteran South Sudanese politician of such high standing and esteem among southerners and northerners alike, be explained.

Mulana Abel Alier was the first South Sudanese Judge, and he worked in the Judiciary until March 1965. The 'Round Table Conference on the Southern Problem' found him in this respectable profession. The Southern Front selected the learned judge to be a member of its delegation to the conference. He made a rare and patriotic decision to resign his position in the Judiciary when the then Chief Justice denied him participation in a political conference. Mulana Abel and the rest of his colleagues articulated the position of the Southern Front which centered on the question of self-determination and the holding of a plebiscite in the southern provinces as a step towards the resolution of the problem. His resignation was a question of principle to defend the rights of his people.

But look, when Mulana Abel became the President of the High Executive Council of the southern region, he threw overboard the question of self determination. Not only that, he resisted with force the holding of a referendum in Abeyei and Kurmuk areas as stipulated in the Addis Ababa Agreement and threw into jail some of the politicians who agitated for that in the southern regional people's assembly. In fact, Mulana Abel became the torch bearer of the slogan of the 'unity of Sudan', which won him Nimeri's honour of being *Ibn el Sudan el bar*, which translates into the *loyal son of the Sudan*, but with which the regional authorities sent the people of South Sudan to a deep sleep.

The political developments in South Sudan in the 1970s and the manner in which Nimeri played around with the southern politicians leaders, Mulana Abel, General Lagu and others showed marked political weakness and unprincipled loyalty to the dictator. Had these politicians conducted the affairs of the regional government in a manner commensurate with the wishes and aspirations of the people, the southern region would have became so strong that Nimeri would not have dared to manipulate and interfere in its affairs without the risk of provoking another round of war. In fact, the war would have erupted either in 1975 or 1976 instead of 1983. It is, therefore, the political weakness of this elite in the South that has paved the way for the present war.

From the outside, it appears the SPLM manifesto of 1983 was not intended for the people of South Sudan, which should mobilise and rally them behind the programme of the Movement, but rather to gain acceptability in the eyes of outsiders. It seems in its manifesto the SPLM/A was endeavouring to convince the northern Sudanese elite that a new brand of socialist South Sudanese, who believed in unity of the Sudan, had emerged. The barrage of tirade and vilification of the Anya-nya leaders depicting them as only interested in ministerial positions proves this. But the northern elite did not accept this quickly; they remained suspicious of the intentions of the South, as they will always be. Even the Communist Party of the Sudan, which should have been a close ally of the SPLM from the very beginning, did not shift from this out-South Sudanese stance seriously. So the SPLM and the people of South Sudan lost out twice, not winning the confidence and trust of the northern elite. And at the same time engendered divisions and fighting among themselves over whether the objective of the movement should be that of 'unity of the Sudan', or secession of South Sudan. It has come out clearly now that it was just to cloak a hidden agenda of personalised leadership.

The break with Anya-nya 2 revolved around the question of objective of the Movement. Many lives were lost because of this fighting and it diverted much of the political and military energy of the SPLM/A, whose leaders even proudly claim that the first bullet in the SPLA was shot against the separatist. And yet, to date, few people (mainly from the north) in the SPLM/A believe in the unity of the country. Now, more than before, the South Sudanese have become vocal about separation of the South Sudan from the rest of Sudan. They want what has been dubbed the New Sudan to be free and independent. This is better that pretending to be a unionist and cause the death of many people for no good reason. It is always more politically rewarding to be clear and open to the people in articulating their aspirations than to act to please or impress outsiders.

For example, the Eritrean leaders from day one told their people and the world they wanted their independence from Ethiopia because Emperor Haile Sellassie had abrogated the federation that formed the basis of their relations from 1952 unilaterally in 1961. They did not have to wait until the international political and ideological environment changed to enable them to put forward their actual objective. In fact, many people in Africa struggling for statehood owe it to the sacrifices of the Eritrean people that the Organisation for African Unity's Charter, which the stipulates the inviolability of the colonial borders, has now become redundant.

This ambiguity on the part of the South Sudanese political elite is responsible for lack of consistency, continuity of a national objective and evolution of a acceptable political leadership to spearhead the struggle of the people. Not only that, it has sufficiently dulled the consciousness of the people and made them passive spectators in their own cause. At every turn of events in the Sudan, leaders emerge who tend to promote the political interests of some particular northern groups in South Sudan and they usually got away with it. The cumulative effect of all this ambiguity and obscurantism on the part of southern elite, weigh more in favour of the development and progressive radicalisation of Islam and promotion of Arab culture in the Sudan, including the South, at the expense of the preservation and development of African heritage and culture. This is because in every round of fighting with the North, the South always emerged weakened as a result of betrayal by its sons and daughters.

Thus, while Islam in the Sudan, political or otherwise, is a factor in the present conflict in the South, the SPLM tends to promote the establishment of the so-called New Sudan Islamic Council to represent the interest of a tiny Muslim group - a group that does not exist in the Movement except for a few individuals. In whose interest, given the demographic characteristic of the South, will the manufacture of an Islamic council be or whom does the SPLM intend to impress or please with something which might prove dangerous in the long run?

It is not only the political bankruptcy of this elite that constitutes a dangerous pill which, if allowed to continue, will finally and irreversibly kill the spirit of resistance in the people who has kept the flame of the struggle burning up to this moment. It is this weakness and political pretensions of the South Sudanese elite that has resulted in divisions, like the 'kokra', during the early eighties, in which this elite group turned the struggle against themselves and divided the people or in what Riek Machar now calls 'parallel existence' of the liberation movements. It is the same weakness that has led to the signing of the 'Political Charter' with the NIF government. Until recently, Dr Riek Machar would split hairs with people over phrases, which did not reflect the separation and independence of the South Sudan, but see what has happened. He has travelled to Khartoum, embraced Omer el Beshir and Hassan el Turabi, saying: 'I have come looking for peace'.

In the defence of the 'Unity of Sudan' as per article two of the Political Charter, Riek Machar is sending his own people to go and die trying to recapture towns captured by SPLA from the NIF government. The people of South Sudan took up arms, and will continue to take up arms, not to fight and die in their tens of thousands just to maintain the unity of the Sudan, but to realise their self identity, freedom and social justice. This is what the political leadership should emphasise and nothing more or less. The minds and hearts of the people of South Sudan and their compatriots in the marginalised areas will only be stirred into action by fundamental ideas, images and feelings rooted deeply in their past struggles for freedom. It was utterly wrong to have swayed them from that.

The Ethiopian regime - the *Dergue*, was another factor that accelerated formation of the SPLM/A, but which also contributed to veering it in a course that precipitated internal contradictions. The Dergue regime, pinned down by war in Eritrea and Tigray and the numerous other internal contradictions, desired some counter forces to the Nimeri regime in the Sudan. This is on account of these dissidents having received substantial material, moral and political support from the Sudanese political establishment. The Sudanese and Arab support for the Eritreans and Tigray was out of strategic consideration related to Arab expansion in Africa. It had nothing to do with freedom struggle of these people. In fact, every regime that came to power in Khartoum supported the Eritrean cause for independence from Ethiopia since the days of Emperor Haile Sellassie out of this consideration and strategy.

The revolution in Tigray was just an additional dimension which compounded Mengistu's problems. To counter Sudan's support for the Eritreans and other rebel groups fighting the regime in Ethiopia, Mengistu supported Sudanese dissidents both materially and politically. However, this support was predicated on what was perceived to be the Ethiopian national interest of preserving its territorial integrity and unity. Thus, when the Anya-nya 2 founded their camps inside Ethiopia in 1975, the support they got from the authorities was something that could keep them going, but not to have an impact on the situation in South Sudan, leading to its independence or separation from the North. It was obvious the Mengistu regime, like the Imperial regime, would not countenance any separatist movement in South Sudan without embarrassing itself.

When SPLM/A raised the façade of 'United Socialist Sudan' as its objective, it found a ready and willing ally in the Ethiopian regime. Since Mengistu and his generals were interested, from the beginning, in supporting an armed resistance against Khartoum, the emergence of SPLA brandishing socialism blended well into their strategic calculations. The support by the Ethiopian regime to the military officers, as opposed to the politicians, and the subsequent emergence of a political-military High Command, the highest organ of the SPLM/A, comprising solely former military officers of the Sudanese army was evident enough of the militarist trend Mengistu had wanted of the infant Movement to follow.

The politicians who came to join the armed struggle found themselves ignored, marginalised and persecuted. They were branded as bourgeoisie' and, therefore, were perceived as either 'potential' or 'real' enemies of the people[11]. Thus, the seeds of division and dichotomy between the military officers, the politicians and the intellectuals, in general, were sown. Since it was an armed struggle and a 'revolutionary' one for that matter, a 'competent' military officer must lead it, so flowed the logic and that appealed to the Ethiopians and some South Sudanese. This is how the ascension of Col. Dr John Garang de Mabior to the leadership of the SPLM/A came about. His academic and military credentials combined to make him the best-qualified and suitable candidate for the leadership of this 'revolutionary' armed struggle. Although the High Command of the SPLM/A was presumed to represent the political and the military groups that dominated the scene and contested the leadership then, the latter developments in Movement together with the assistance of the Ethiopian regime tilted the balance of forces, and eventually enabled the military officers to gain dominance in the leadership.

The Ethiopian generals had their own calculations based on their perception of the strategic balance of forces in the region; their experience with the northern Sudanese opposition to Nimeri, fronted by the National Front of the Umma Party and the Democratic Party[12], and the elements of the Anya-nya 2[13] which they had tried to support as a counterbalance to the Sudanese and Arab support for the Eritrean revolution.

Whatever the significance of the assistance rendered to the infant movement, the involvement of the Ethiopian regime in the affairs of the SPLM/A from the very beginning seriously injured and distorted its growth and development. It prevented the emergence of an internal political and democratic culture, nurtured by an internal political debate and ideological struggle that could have cleansed the infant Movement and its combatants of the filth of the 'old Sudan'[14].

The evolution of a genuinely clear political line and programme representing and reflecting the ideological position of the dominant social forces in the Movement would have removed the contradictions which afflicted the SPLM/A before 1991. What unfortunately emerged was a militarist, putschist instrument intolerant, and averse to democratic principles and methods. The infant Movement was stifled of democratic discourse from the start. Differing political views were completely suppressed and a campaign of vilification, marginalisation and alienation began in earnest against the politicians and the intellectuals.

It should be stated clearly that the Ethiopian regime was dictated by its national interest rather than revolutionary or ideological solidarity with the people of South Sudan in the way, for instance, the Cubans supported the MPLA in Angola during the war of independence or against South Africa-sponsored UNITA. It is this national interest that prevented them from supporting a secessionist movement like the Anya-nya 2. The support for SPLM/A's call for a united socialist Sudan was worth undertaking without creating diplomatic backlash for the Ethiopian regime in the OAU and other international fora.

It was necessary to make this rather lengthy digression to illustrate the historicity of poverty of political organisation and tradition among South Sudanese political elite and how it influenced later developments in the national liberation struggle. The fact that the younger generation of this elite, who have had greater opportunity of acquiring political skills, have not deviated much from this trait is evidenced by what happened in Itang, the first refugee camp established in western Ethiopia in July 1983, when the leaders, both military and political, congregated to constitute the SPLM/A. Coming from totally different and variegated political and professional backgrounds, the only common agenda was the question of the leadership of the Movement, and secession of South Sudan.

The attempt to forge a common forum was frustrated; hence, each leader would gather his supporters and seek the endorsement of the Ethiopian generals. These manoeuvres ended up in bloodshed, which saw the retreat of Samuel Gai Tut, Akuot Atem and William Abdalla Chuol back into the Sudan. The dice was cast and Dr John Garang de Mabior emerged the leader of the SPLM/A. The support of the Ethiopian regime was, therefore, crucial to the outcome of this power struggle.

The fighting erupted between the supporters of Dr John Garang with the support of Ethiopian army, on the one hand and those of Samuel Gai Tut, Akwot Atem and William Abdalla Chuol, on the other hand, leading to many death. According to eyewitnesses, the Ethiopians precipitated the fighting themselves because of their impatience with the process the Sudanese adopted to choose their leaders. The Anya-nya 2 and their leaders withdrew back into Sudan. Their alliance with Nimeri was made much later when attempts at reconciliation were frustrated and Samuel Gai Tut was killed in March 1984. He was trying to come back and reconcile with the SPLA leaders. Kerubino's Jamus battalion in Thiajak on the border with Ethiopia ambushed him.

The first task, after the resolution of the leadership contest in the SPLM/A, was the reorganisation and rearming of the remnants of the battalions 104 and 105 and the elements of Anya-nya 2 which now formed the nucleus of the SPLA. The first wave of the recruits, mostly secondary, university students and office workers which joined, were given intensive training to form the Jamus (Buffalo) battalion (1983). As time went by and the insurrection gained momentum, the Jarad (Locus) division was graduated (1984), followed by Mour Mour division (1985), Kazuk (1986), Zalzal (1987) Intifadha (1988) and Intisar (1989). These were big divisions of SPLA, composed of more than fifteen thousand officers and men. Unlike the normal army formation, SPLA squad consisted of seventeen men; a platoon consisted of fifty one, a company made up of two hundred and twenty four while a battalion consisted of one thousand three hundred and forty four men. This constituted an enormous volume of fire. So when we talked of one SPLA battalion, it was something near to a Sudanese Army brigade. The divisions mentioned above, were those trained and graduated from the SPLA training camp in Bonga. There were auxiliary training camps in Bilpam, Dima, and Buma, besides the mobile ones.

The SPLA rapidly grew in numerical and military strength. By 1991, when it split following the Nasir attempted coup, it was between 100,000 to 120,000 men strong, almost the size of the Sudanese Armed Forces, less the Air force and the navy. SPLA engaged the Sudanese army and its militia and scored remarkable victories. By 1990, the stretch of territory east of the river Nile from the international borders with Kenya and Uganda up to the mouth of Sobat river was under the control of SPLA. The whole of western Equatoria with the exception of Yei, Rokon, Terrikeka and Juba towns, which remained under the government control, was administered by SPLA. In rural Bahr el Ghazal, SPLA controlled all the land routes.

The SPLA by its definition is a peasant army made up of volunteers. Apart from the initial ethnic and other contradictions, the members of the SPLM/A were propelled into action by nationalist and patriotic sentiments. Its training was rigorous and the conditions in the training camps were severe and harsh, to say the least. Nevertheless, the soldiers and men persevered till the end of their training sessions when they would be graduated and deployed in the fronts. The morale of the SPLA men and officers was very high and this grew with every operational victory scored and its coverage by the international media, especially the BBC[15]. The frequency and pace of its military victories against the Nimeri regime, whose image and credibility was on the decline internationally as a result of the imposition of Islamic Sharia laws and more oppressive laws, boosted the image and credibility of the SPLA.

This positive image of the SPLA projected by its military victories did not last long before it was tarnished by behaviour and acts of some of its reckless officers and men. By the middle of 1984, many of the cattle herders and peasants and lumpen from the towns had graduated and were now armed with AKM rifles. The pride of carrying a gun and being part of a victorious army, made many of these fighters forget the purpose for which they were fighting and turned their guns on the unarmed civilian population. It was not uncommon to find an SPLA trail littered with serious and horrendous human rights abuses and violations: murder, rape, looting and irrational waste of resources mainly grain and livestock. The arrogance of power acquired from carrying an AKM rifle made them wasteful and brutal to the civilian population whom they intimidated into submission.

Initial welcoming parties turned into tragic episodes, as the villagers and the civilians rose against the SPLA to protect their dignity, the honour and integrity of their families and their property. A case in point is what happened in the area of Terrikeka in December 1984. A small contingent of Zindiya battalion, made up of officers and men from Bor Dinka crossed into the Mandari area. They were welcome by the Mandari who lavishly served the soldiers with beef, grain, sorghum beer, alcohol and tobacco that were collected to serve the soldiers with. Three days of feasting and merriment turned into a nightmare. The SPLA soldiers went on a drunken looting and raping spree, which resulted in several murders forcing the poor Mandari to protest. The Mandari chief put it eloquently to the commander of this force:

> ... Commander Nyankot...we were told to raise food rations for your army. We knew our bulls, rams, grain, groundnuts etc., were going to be your food. This, because you are our sons, our army. Now see what your soldiers have done to my people... Have the private parts of our daughters, our wives also become rations for your army? You have betrayed and abused our generosity...[16]

This incident, which represented a common feature of the initial interaction between the SPLA and the civil population, alienated the Mandari who changed sides and allied with the Sudan government. The Khartoum regime was quick to exploit any crack between the SPLA and the civilian population. Not only did the Mandari migrate to Juba *en masse*, they were armed and recruited into the government militia by their leaders in Juba who exploited this situation for their own social and economic benefits with the regime.

This unfortunate episode repeated itself in many other places in South Sudan, wherever SPLA ventured to set its foot, without being corrected or the perpetrators punished. It occurred in Taposa and Didinga areas of the Kapoeta district in 1985 and 1986. The SPLA battalions of 'Bee' and 'Niran', mostly from Bahr el Ghazal, found it impossible to operate against the enemy garrison town of Kapoeta because of rear attacks by the Taposa tribesmen. The acts of some soldiers had turned some of the Taposa against SPLA in alliance with the Sudanese army. The Didinga, however, behaved differently. Although they had fought, ambushed and killed many SPLA soldiers in their villages, they collected the guns and brought them to the commander of the force, Late Cdr Martin Manyiel, who was so much embarrassed by the action of his army that he had to ask for their withdrawal and transfer to Bahr el Ghazal.

Initially, in spite of the fact that they had sided with Khartoum government, the Murle people supported and joined the SPLA in large numbers following the 'liberation' of Pibor, their district headquarters, in February 1987. However, the Murle quickly turned against the SPLA when some officers and soldiers began to take cattle by force. These people refused to acquiesce to the SPLA administration and fought its battalions in 1989 and in 1990.

Similarly fighting occurred between the SPLA and the Gaajak and Lou sections of the Nuer but in a different context of the war with Anya-nya 2. This rift was only healed after the agreement of reconciliation and unity 1988 between the two forces which saw the absorption of some elements of Anya-nya 2 into the SPLA.

In August 1989, it became the turn of the Ethiopian Anyuak to suffer the brutality of the SPLA. For reasons and motives, which could not be established, a contingent of SPLA went into action against the Anyuak, both civilians and Ethiopian government militia in Itang and Piny-udo, in which nearly two hundred people including women and children were massacred to the embarrassment of the Ethiopian government. In fact, many Anyuak intellectuals, both Sudanese and Ethiopians were outraged by this massacred and have not since forgiven the SPLA leadership for that crime[17].

What had happened to SPLA, an Army of volunteers and freedom fighters, whose soldiers fought with valour against the enemy, that its members turned easily to criminal action or brutalised the civilian population for whom they had taken arms in the first place? SPLA by its composition is a people's army, but its action was against the people. The SPLA was dubbed a revolutionary army but their actions against the people were reactionary and sometimes criminal. What had happened and why? The genesis of this un-revolutionary behaviour of the SPLA officers and men can be traced to the nature of their training. Although the factor of social background of a prospective SPLA soldier is of importance in this respect, it was rather the condition of formation of the SPLA soldier itself, the environment of his training and the development of his combat awareness which resulted from this training experience, that determined the overall behaviour of these soldiers and their interaction with the civil population. The neglect of political education in the course of military training is another important factor that contributed to this unfortunate behaviour and we shall to analyse this in the coming pages.

The objectives and leadership of the SPLM/A

The war spearheaded by the SPLM/A was characterised as a 'revolutionary armed struggle' whose main objective was the ' liberation' of the Sudan and the establishment of a united socialist Sudan. This marked a clear departure, at least theoretically, from the traditional articulation by South Sudanese political elite of the so-called problem of Southern Sudan. But represented in practice a dichotomy of goals and aspirations of the Movement from the masses of South Sudanese. While the leadership was talking of a united socialist Sudan, the people were talking of secession of South Sudan. For the people the enemy was the 'Arab North', while at the leadership level the enemy 'real' or 'potential' blended with the cold-war political propaganda jargons. 'Bourgeoisie', 'reactionary', 'revolutionary', 'comrade' were the vocabulary of the SPLA officers and men, and even among the civilian population behind the SPLA lines. Perhaps, the people at the base were truthful about what they wanted and why they came in large numbers, but this Marxist sloganeering was a political game whose centre laid outside the reality in South Sudan. It is easy to impress and win friends by using slogans, and revolutionary sounding propaganda. Indeed, until the split of SPLA in 1991, it was not uncommon for a young instructor in a SPLA training camp to call former government officials, teachers, politicians, etc. who came to join the Movement, 'bourgeoisien' or 'mahrasieen' or any other derogatory names associated with the 'old Sudan.'

Many members of the SPLM/A were not socialist, even many in the highest echelon of its leadership did not really believe that the problem they were fighting for was struggle between capitalism and socialism. In fact many of them with a peasant[18] background were quite averse to socialism. Yet socialism was adopted as the guiding ideology of the SPLM/A. Even the Sudan Communist Party was stunned by this and dismissed it as a cloak for Southern secessionism. The Communist Party never took the SPLM/A's claim to socialist orientation seriously; nevertheless, in 1983 - 1984/5, it supported the SPLM/A tactically as a means of destroying the Nimeri regime. When Nimeri was overthrown in a popular uprising in April 1985, the Communist Party, like other Northern parties, took an opposite position and started to condemn the SPLM/A for its continued armed struggle and 'taking the war away from its traditional place in the south to the North'[19].

Was the SPLM/A, in its composition, then a force capable of building socialism in the Sudan? Positively no. SPLM/A strove to capture the state power and then use that to build socialism. But this experiment, started by Nimeri has just disgracefully failed, and in fact in the eighties, the socialist system headed by the Soviet Union was beginning to show signs that it was not going to last. The SPLM/A experiment with 'socialism' was just an exercise in sloganeering. There was really nothing serious about it ; some of its leaders were convinced it was not their ultimate goal. It was an expedient to gain access to material support from the socialist camp. If it were not a matter of copying what Mao Tse Tung did in China or Fidel Castro in Cuba, as examples of raising a peasant army for social transformation, then the experience the SPLM/A and the people of South Sudan went through was completely an unnecessary exercise in self-delusion. No wonder that eight years latter no one talked again of socialism, worst still the SPLM Manifesto itself was thrown away without ceremony.

Socialism is always perceived to be the ideology of or supported by the poorer section of the society. It was, therefore, thought that once socialist slogans were raised, the people will come running to join the struggle. This was transparent and superficial. Many of the people who responded were South Sudanese and very few of them, if not a completely negligible number, were socialists or professed socialist tendency way back in the Sudan. It was not the socialist slogans that rallied these South Sudanese behind the SPLM/A, but its perceived nationalist ideals and perceptions. It would have been permissible to rally the masses of the people on something very close to their inner feelings than some far-fetched ideas which had no appeal to them.

The SPLM/A leaders wanted to build a powerful military machine which could have immediate impact, not on the socio-economic situation of the people, but on the political situation both inside the country and internationally. This military machine was, therefore, not a means for social transformation but for impressing friends and foes alike and winning material support. Social background was not made a criterion for the selection of the combatants and, accordingly, people of all walks of life flocked into the SPLM/A. Thieves, murders, rapists and fugitives from the Sudanese justice system found a safe haven in the SPLA and, when opportunity was there, they easily relapsed into their old practices. Many of the criminal and horrendous crimes committed against the civilian population were attributed to some of these social misfits masquerading as 'revolutionaries'.

The experiences of the seventeen years war (1955 - 1972) and the scramble for leadership among the South Sudanese leaders abroad, the proliferation of governments in exile and their lack of organic link with the freedom fighters in the field, all these must have given Dr John Garang reasons enough to have contempt of the politicians who joined the Movement. Not only had most of these politicians betrayed the confidence the people but they have also even turned the ten years of regional self-rule in the southern region into a nightmare. These politicians were spineless, self-seeking, docile lots who have made themselves tools in the hands of Nimeri against the people of South Sudan. They represented forces of division and tribalism in the South which eventually led to the 'kokra' and the destruction of the southern region by Nimeri. Garang was right, in a way, to assume that many of these politicians who later turned up to join the Movement were driven by personal ambition for power and not as a result of their conversion to the people's cause.

The struggle for power and the hairsplitting, which led to the break with the Anya-nya 2, bear witness to this and tend to vindicate Dr John Garang. However, there was room for metamorphosis to transform many of them, who were genuine freedom fighters, through political education and military discipline. Participation in the liberation struggle is the right, duty and honour of every patriot. The outright and indiscriminate ostracisation of the politicians and the intellectuals who joined the ranks was unfortunate as well as it was unjustified.

Nobody who volunteered to join the armed struggle was required to declare what he/she was before. No criterion, social or political or standard was set for anybody joining the ranks of the Movement. Many inflated their professional and occupational grades in the hope of being rated highly in the SPLA. There were instances when people claimed to have been directors, director generals in the former Regional Government in Juba, or university graduates etc., when, in fact they were just secondary school fall-outs. These were people who wanted to start a new and a different life on a clean slate and at a higher social level. The SPLM/A was a new world, separate and different from the 'old Sudan' where no one except perhaps those who had met before knew another's background.

There were those who claimed they were members of the Communist Party of the Sudan when they were not or who knew Dr John Garang from school days or who helped him found the SPLA, etc. as if that was a warrant to a senior position in the SPLA. This meant that the concern and worries of many such types was not the liberation struggle but the possibility of self-promotion. In this sense, membership of the movement was perceived not as a position of sacrifice, but a political space for social and economic advancement.

However, who, in all honesty, should question one's sense of patriotism and who can prevent one from joining an army of volunteers in a national liberation movement? Nobody would dare, of course. Nevertheless, it was always imperative and significant that each and every combatant in the liberation movement should ascribe to a certain code of conduct and a certain level of political awareness was required. It was a serious mistake to assume that each and everybody who had joined the movement was a 'revolutionary' and thus accepted without scrutiny or deployed without having acquired the necessary training to raise awareness.

In the absence of political and ideological training among these volunteers, in the absence of challenging assignments which would differentiate and identify quality from quantity between them, it is difficult to discern the goat from the wolf, the innocent from the guilty or the criminal, the real revolutionary from the pseudo-revolutionary, the mediocre from the seasoned fighter. Everybody was taken for whatever he or she said about self and that was enough. In fact, at the height of SPLA victories over the Sudanese army, in those early days, many rushed to the bushes and took up arms in the hope that they would be back into Juba, Malakal, Wau and other towns in the South in a matter of six months parading as heroes. It was not the sense of patriotism and sacrifice for the people's cause that pushed them to the armed struggle, but to them it was an investment in time, political and military space created by the insurrection.

The SPLM manifesto (1983) speaks of an early determination of the leadership of the Movement such that it was not hijacked by counter-revolutionaries. Whether that leadership was in the person of Dr John Garang de Mabior or vested collectively in the SPLA High Command, was not clearly defined until the split in 1991. Normally, leadership, whether of a liberation movement, a political party, trade union etc., cannot be only defined in terms of a single person or a group of persons who are office bearers per se. It entails the organisational structure, the constitution and internal regulations of that particular organisation. The constitution together with the internal regulations define the offices, their functions and the relationship between them and the membership, the rights and duties of each and every member of the organisation whether at the leadership level or at the base. In many political and social organisations, the office bearers are elected by either universal suffrage or by colleges and for a defined period of time. Unless one considered it a personal affair, as in a monarchy or an oligarchy, there is always need to go back and seek the mandate of the people.

For sometime, the names of Col. Dr John Garang, Kerubino Kuanyin and William Nyuon were the only ones tagged to the leadership of the Movement in the poems and morale songs of the recruits and SPLA soldiers and in the administrative structure of the Movement. Then slowly the names of Salva

Kiir Mayardit and Arok Thon Arok were added as permanent members of the High Command of the Movement. The inclusion of Salva and Arok was on the grounds that they were in the clandestine cells back inside the Sudan, something that cannot be proved. Nonetheless, if it were so, then Arok Thon should have retained his seniority over Salva. The fact that he came latter than Salva should not have been a problem, because as a clandestine cell, which took over the leadership of the infant Movement, then each and every one of them would have retained his position in the hierarchy, especially when no one from outside that cell entered the leadership. The same argument could have easily held for Lt. Col. Francis Ngor who should have been the deputy to Dr John Garang, because of his seniority to both Kerubino and William Nyuon in the Sudanese army.

Although there were efforts from the very beginning to establish institutions and structures of the Movement, and actually various committees, e.g., Political and Foreign Affairs Committee headed by Mr Joseph Oduho, Judicial and Administrative Committee led by Judge Martin Majier Gai, no great importance was attached to their work and much of their recommendations were ignored by the military leadership. These structures eventually died a natural death. This explains why the basic documents of these committees, like the constitution of the Movement and its internal regulations, which would have given them legality, were not drafted. Over a period of time, and as a result of the contradictions that emerged, some of them out of personality clash, power struggle etc., the power and the leadership of the SPLM/A passed slowly into the hands of the military officers. Veteran politicians: Joseph Oduho, Martin Majier and other were arrested and detained on flimsy charges of staging a coup against the military leadership. It is difficult to imagine or substantiate that somebody who had little to do with the military under such conditions as that obtaining in Itang could have contemplated staging a coup without a command. However, as it turned out this was a stratagem to smoothen the process of usurpation of the power by the military officers.

The High Command was not a structure that was destined to form a coherent and collective leadership structure of the Movement. Shattered by serious internal contradictions arising out of lack of commitment to a common national political agenda and personal rivalry between its members, for instance between Kerubino and William, between Arok and the rest of the members, and between Kerubino and Dr John Garang, the efficient functioning of this body was seriously impaired by these quarrels which made it look like it was deliberate to pave way for personal rule because no attempts were made to correct these attitudes.

The personality clashes within the members of the top leadership of the Movement could be explained partly in terms of person ambitions and pride. Leadership position has been completely dissociated from its sacrifice content and made a stimulus for competition for personal glory and honour. For instance Cdr Arok Thon Arok considered himself the only successful career military officer in the SPLM/A, having graduated from the staff college, and better qualified than the others. Arok Thon, thus, never recognised the seniority of Kerubino, William or Salva Kiir and, because of his social background in Kongor, considered himself, and not Dr John Garang, better suited for the leadership of the Movement. He exhibited a high degree of insubordination, sometimes bordering on rebellion and mutiny against his senior colleagues, a thing that added to his eventual arrest and detention in March 1988. These petty contradictions and rivalry reinforced suspicion, hatred and lack of unity within the SPLM/A leadership which at times filtered down to the ranks and file.

Another important factor that contributed to the instability at the top echelon of the Movement occurred in Bor during the battle against the forces from Juba on 16 May 1983. If we have to lay credence to the story that there was a clandestine movement of former Anya-nya officers and men to take over the regional government in Juba, that must have meant that the clandestine movement had a hierarchy and there cannot be any explanation as to why Col. Dr John Garang de Mabior, the most senior officer present in Bor during the battle, did not take over the command of the troops from Major Kerubino, especially after he was wounded in action. The fighting was left to Kerubino, his men in Battalion 105, elements of the Wildlife wardens and some Policemen, who fought courageously until they withdrew to the Ethiopian borders. At times of his extreme frustration and weakness, Kerubino would make reference to this episode to challenge Garang's claim to the leadership of the Movement, a fact that heightened tension in the High Command.

All this must have contributed in one way or the other to Garang's lack of enthusiasm to build the leadership of the Movement, comprising such elements that could challenge his authority. Much of the Movement's leadership energy was absorbed in ensuring personal survival and hatching of conspiracies to elbow out of the Movement those recalcitrant officers like Kerubino and Arok Thon. The negative impact of such a situation in the leadership on the development of the SPLM/A and the conduct of the war cannot be over emphasised. For instance, to have allowed people like Kerubino, William, Arok and John Kulang to commit as many personal mistakes as possible to permit their removal from command is something that weighed down on the morale of the troops and the civil population, because the damage was already done. Some of these senior officers committed with impunity outrageous and horrendous crimes. They looted, raped, murdered without being made accountable. The officers and soldiers in the front for which there was no moral ground, on the part of the SPLM/A leadership, to punish these junior officers and men, also emulated these crimes committed by leaders.

Half-hearted attempts were made to resolve the contradictions in the High Command. One of these was the appointment of the so-called alternate members of the High Command who, ironically, became more in number than the permanent members. The appointments were a means to divert attention from the contradictions rather than enlarging the decision - making base of the Movement. It was the members of this group that in the end precipitated the demise of the High Command itself and its final dissolution in 1994. The effect caught up with the cause.

The deployment of the members of the High Command in the operational zones was another way of defusing the tension among them. The posting, therefore, of Kerubino Kuanyin Bol to Blue Nile, far away from the General H/Quarters of the SPLA, was to enable him commit as many mistakes as possible and that was what he did, including the attempt to lead a rebellion against Dr John Garang in 1987. This was due to the fact that the High Command was not functional enough to resolve some its own contradictions. The last time the five permanent members of this body came together in a meeting was in late 1985, early 1986, and that was only to confirm the position of Cdr William Nyuon Bany as SPLA Chief of Staff, Salva Kiir Mayardit as deputy Chief of Staff for Operations and Security and Arok Thon Arok as deputy Chief of Staff for Administration and Logistics. From then onwards no meeting of the SPLM/A High Command was heard of again until the well publicised meeting of the High Command in Torit in September 1991, in the wake of the Nasir coup attempt. In the interim, the onus of running the movement administratively and militarily fell on Dr John Garang. An enormous task indeed for one person.

The intriguing thing about the SPLM/A was that it managed to conceal its internal contradiction from the world. In fact, until the coup announcement in Nasir in August 1991, and the barrage of propaganda stories about human rights violations within the Movement that followed this announcement, very little was known to the outside world about the SPLA. But after that the question of political prisoners and the child soldiers was quickly picked up by the international mass media. It was equally amazing that such an open Movement like the SPLA, in which the combatants spoke freely to anybody about their problems, etc., could manage to keep its secrets to itself.

The leadership methods of the SPLM/A were akin to those of the Sudanese Army, and could have been even worst. As a national liberation movement, and a guerrilla force, the SPLM/A did not have to function like a professional standing army in terms of relation between officers and men and between the army and the civilian population, on the one hand, and in the involvement in political dialogue and debate on the other. It is a political Movement in which 'armed struggle' was not an end but only a means to achieving the objective of liberation. This is what multiplied the problems of the Movement and its leadership culminating in the split. These problems reflected the political crisis emanating from ignoring and bypassing the need to organise and democratise. As is always the case, establishing democracy in a liberation movement cannot be put off until the military confrontation with the enemy has been completed for the simple reason that military struggle against the enemy can only be won by political means and centralisation of the movement's affairs can only be effective to the extent that it is democratic.

Apart from the early skirmishes that led to the break with Anya-nya 2, the internal political crisis within the SPLM/A started off vaguely and very few could sense that something was wrong in the Movement. Its first warnings were barely imperceptible. The powerful euphoria of military victories scored by the SPLA falsely mirrored some uniformity. Nevertheless, there were signs indicating that SPLA militants, especially the intellectuals, no longer felt the same respect for and trust in the Movement's leadership. People were paying back in kind for the humiliation and marginalisation they experienced daily. It was a kind of feeling one would shyly hide in public and would find expressions only in gossips and private social gatherings.

The leadership methods of the SPLM/A generated serious internal contradictions. The refusal to recognise that social and political contradictions, some of them of secondary nature arising out of clash of personalities, can not dissolve themselves but have to be resolved, exasperated these contradictions and made them explosive. For instance, the removal of Dr Lam Akol from the office of foreign relations of the Movement in 1990 and his redeployment at the war front where he had miserably failed two years earlier, is exactly what fitted him against Dr John Garang.

Dr Lam Akol had run the show well and had succeeded in painting a good picture of the Movement in his capacity as responsible for foreign relations. He might have committed some excesses which led to the decision of removing him, but had he been subjected to disciplinary measures, and that fact widely known to the rank and file of the Movement, he would not have had the opportunity to mobilise support for himself at a time things were rapidly deteriorating in the Movement. The issue became a personal matter between him and Dr John Garang de Mabior. Thus, all his agitations, both verbal and in print, were directed at the person of the SPLA leader.

The split with Anya-nya2 and its ramifications

The formation of the SPLM/A in 1983, found the units of Anya-nya 2 already operating against the Sudanese army in military combat in South Sudan. Bilpam in western Ethiopia was the centre of Anya-nya 2 but there were also some units operating in western Upper Nile and in northern Bahr el Ghazal. The failure to unify the fighting forces and the split with Anya-nya 2, referred to above, was a costly one. It entailed the loss of many lives between 1983 and 1988. Although it started as a political contradiction and a power struggle in the beginning, the split took a Dinka - Nuer polarity and had serious repercussions on the civil population of the two tribes in Upper Nile. It also had serious repercussions on the growth, development and the military strategy of the SPLA.

First, the split deprived the SPLA of the manpower it needed. Many Nuers, in eastern or western Upper Nile preferred to join the ranks and file of Anya-nya 2. Furthermore, the failure of the reconciliation talks and the death of Mr Samuel Gai Tut in March 1984 pushed the Nuer, under the leadership of William Abdalla Chuol, more into alliance with Nimeri. Perhaps what incensed many Nuers and provoked their mass desertion to the Anya-nya 2 was Kerubino's decision to prevent the burial Samuel Gai Tut. The SPLA was depicted as a Dinka movement and that blended well with Nimeri's propaganda, enabling the Anya-nya 2 to receive generous supplies of armament from the Khartoum government under the guise of 'friendly forces'.

The Anya-nya 2 forces occupied the middle ground between the Ethiopian borders, where the SPLA had its camps, and many of its operational areas inside the country. Their forces way-laid any column of SPLA on their way back to the country and made their movements quite impossible. Many lives, both military and civilians, were lost as a result of this internecine fighting. The Anya-nya 2 became a real obstacle to the progress of the SPLA recruitment drive in Upper Nile and Bahr el Ghazal. Many of the recruits travelling to the training camps in western Ethiopia were ambushed and dispersed by Anya-nya 2.

In one such serious incident in May 1984, more than three thousand recruits, mainly young men and girls from northern Bahr el Ghazal were ambushed and massacred by the forces of William Abdalla Chuol in the area of Fangak. Many of them were drowned in the river Nile. This was one of the most horrendous crimes committed against humanity in the Sudanese war, as hundreds of corpses floated down the Nile in a manner equal to what was to occur in Rwanda ten years later in 1994. Very few survivors managed to reach the SPLA areas to relate the tragedy. This horrendous massacring of unsuspecting innocent people on their way to the SPLA training centres repeated itself in Lou area in 1986. Over two thousand recruits and former Police and Prison Warders from Rumbek were massacred by Anya-nya 2.

These massacres of the Dinka recruits by the Anya-nya 2 had provoked SPLA which in turn had serious repercussions on the Nuer civilian population. For instance, the SPLA forces on their way back into the Sudan devastated Lou and Jikany areas as they sought to avenge the death of their kith and kin. Whole villages were razed to the ground, grain destroyed and livestock looted, men and women and children were killed indiscriminately. The SPLA retaliation was always more severe and ruthless as they were better organised than Anya-nya 2. This cycle of violence triggered off more hostility and ethnic animosity as each massacre by either side was avenged without restrain or hesitation. Many lives were lost including the death of Lt. Col. Francis Ngor and twenty-four SPLA officers at the hands of armed Nuer civilians in 1985.

The Anya-nya 2 did not target only the moving SPLA contingents, but also their camps. For instance, in May 1986, the Anya-nya 2 attacked, captured and occupied Bukteng, the H/Qs of SPLA battalions 104/105 before they were routed out by SPLA. Mainly Nuer officers and men manned the camp. The capture of Bukteng later turned out to have been a conspiracy hatched by some Nuer officers, out of sympathy and solidarity with their fellow Nuers in Anya-nya 2. An attempt to punish this cowardly act triggered off violent reaction from the SPLA Chief of Staff, Cdr William Nyuon Bany. At the time, of its capture, Cdr John Kulang Pout, an alternate member of the High Command, was the most senior officer on the spot in Bukteng.

Military principles would demand he and the officers under his command, should have been reprimanded and court-martialed for cowardice. Instead the wrath of SPLA system fell on the junior officers, most of whom were from Lou Nuer. Major Nikanora Magar Aciek, the officer in charge of investigation was arrested and detained by the Chief of Staff in his effort to protect John Kulang, Elijah Hon Top, and others. It showed how strong ethnic sentiments were even at the level of leadership of the Movement. Ironically, it was Cdr Elijah Hon Top, siding with Riek Machar, who ordered the assassination of Cdr William Nyuon Bany in January 1996.

The contradictions between the SPLA and the Anya-nya 2 continued unabated even after the demise of Nimeri in 1985. The political establishment that took over power in Khartoum of course inherited the Anya-nya to fight the government's war against the SPLA. The Anya-nya 2 were now deployed in strategic areas; they created buffer zones between the government garrisons and the SPLA controlled rural areas. The buffer zones were created by burning of the villages of the communities perceived to be sympathetic to the SPLA and their inhabitants driven away. The burning of Shilluk villages[20] starting from Papwojo in the South to Padiet in the North in 1987 was part of Sadiq el Mahdi' strategy of denying the SPLA access to food and other resources in the area. This phenomenon took place also in Wau in which the Fertit groups were armed not only to fight against the SPLA, but also to route out the Dinka from around Wau, thus denying the SPLA access to resources in the area.

The split with Anya-nya 2 and the conflict that ensued had its psychological and moral dimensions. Internally, within the SPLA there was hysteria against the Nuer as a community. Many patriotic Nuer elements, who bravely sided with the SPLA position, were hunted down and many were murdered in cold blood in the training centres, supposedly to weed out 'potential' sympathizers of Anya-nya 2. There was a witch-hunt for the so-called 'counter-revolutionaries' and the agents of the Khartoum regime who might have infiltrated the Movement. In this process many were framed with flimsy charges and executed for being enemies of the people.

For instance, Dr Juac Erjok, a veterinary doctor, who hailed from Ngok Dinka, Mr Lakurnyang Lado, a leftist activist, and member of the Southern Sudan Patriotic Front, a group of leftist students already mentioned and a certain Yahyah, a northerner worker trade-unionist, one of the few northerners to join the ranks of the SPLA, were framed as agents of Nimeri and were executed by a firing squad during the graduation of the first brigade of Jarad division in 1985. The exact reason for their execution has never been established.

The period between 1983 and 1985 was the most critical period in the life of the SPLA. As a result of this wanton savagery against certain ethnic groups, many of those who survived and were deployed in the front were neither motivated nor enthusiastic to fight so they deserted either to the enemy or to Anya-nya 2. In fact, many Nuers who survived the tortures in the SPLA training camps went straight to join Anya-Nya 2 officers and men, who rejoined the SPLA after the reconciliation in 1988, responded positively to the Nasir Declaration in 1991, demonstrating that reconciliation was a matter of political and military expediency at the top of the both movements, but had not permeated to the base of the Anya-nya 2 organisation. Indeed, the divisions within the Anya-nya 2 camps and the refusal of some of its commanders to endorse the agreement with the SPLA are testimonies to that. As such, when contradictions within the SPLM/A arose again, triggered off by the Nasir attempted coup, many Nuers saw the split that ensued as a result of Nuer - Dinka tribal animosity as an opportunity to revenge against the Bor Dinka.

The de-revolutionisation of the liberation struggle.

The struggle for leadership, which marred the birth of the SPLM/A, was resolved by military means. However, no political and ideological lessons were drawn from that struggle so as to prepare the leadership of the Movement for future eventualities. Having succeeded in establishing itself as the dominant political and military power in the South, and instead of consolidating the desired internal unity, the SPLM/A became obsessed with real or imaginary enemies of the revolution among its membership, especially the politicians and the intellectuals. This resulted in their ostracisation, marginalisation, humiliation and imprisonment. Political activities and organisation within Movement, whether in support or opposition, were proscribed.

From the inception of the Movement in 1983 until the convening of the First National Convention in 1994, the SPLM/A was stifled. The security apparatus - the 'Combat Intelligence', an equivalent of the defunct Nimeri's 'State Security Organ', throttled independent and liberal political opinion. The SPLM/A, therefore, emerged as a mere military machine modelled and structured on the Sudanese Army, which it purported to destroy or supplant, in everything from its chain of command to the relationship between the officers and men, on the one hand, and the relationship between the Army and the civilian population on the other hand. This, perhaps, is what bedevilled the infant Movement and paralysed its natural growth as a national liberation movement whose mission was the social and economic transformation of the Sudanese reality.

The 'Combat Intelligence' in its ruthless 'anti-people' mentality and methods and in their drive to enforce strict military discipline and instantaneous obedience to the SPLM/A leadership, created, in the Movement in general, and among the combatants in particular, an atmosphere of mutual distrust, suspicion, fear, indifference, apathy and outright demoralisation.

This uncomradely attitude was manifest first in the training camps and then in areas that fell under SPLA administration. The SPLA training camps themselves resembled prison concentration camps in which the recruits and prospective SPLA soldiers are brutalised, de-humanised and de-revolutionised. It was their instructors and the Combat Intelligence officers to whom these recruits lost their 'manhood', 'dignity', 'self respect' and 'revolutionary zeal' they came with on joining the SPLM/A. It was here that the SPLA officers and men internalised the oppression and brutality. Once they were deployed in the war front, their first victims become the unarmed civilians whom they now terrorised, brutalised, raped, murdered and de-humanised. The SPLA soldiers committed these atrocities in their effort to regain their 'manhood', 'dignity', 'self-respect' and 'confidence' in themselves.

It was in the training camps that the 'cult of personality' around the SPLM/A top leadership was cultivated in the SPLA soldier. In the course of their training, the recruits would spend eight to ten hours a day, not receiving political education, but on songs of praise to the leaders of the Movement. In fact, instead of praising the revolution or liberation struggle, the leaders idolized and mystified the leaders. Even the support from friendly countries and governments was mistaken for a favour from Dr John Garang de Mabior whenever personally interviewed and accepted each and every recruit into the Movement, and distributed the weapons and uniform to them individually at the time of their graduation. This genera feeling was reinforced by Dr John Garang himself. Thus, after this experience, each SPLA soldier formed the idea in his mind that it was Dr John Garang who was the revolution, and as such, it was the duty of all the soldiers to pay allegiance to him. Not only that, but any criticism of the SPLM/A leader was considered a criticism directed against the Movement and vice versa.

Emphasis on militarism meant a neglect of the other social, economic and political functions of the Movement. Given the need to destroy the enemy, it was permissible to emphasise military competence at the beginning in order to defeat the enemy and capture as much territory from him as possible in which socio-economic activities and political work could be undertaken. However, once a territory has been 'liberated', the immediate task should have been to mitigate the effects of war. In fact, without justification, the SPLA turned their guns on the civilian population. They turned against the SPLA and migrated en masse to the government garrison towns, where many were conscripted into the government militias.

In view of all these factors, the SPLM/A, instead of conducting itself like a genuine national liberation movement, degenerated into an agent of plunder, pillage and destructive conquest. The strong link between being a soldier in a national liberation movement and the solidarity with the people, which could have been provided by political training and education of the SPLA combatants, was completely absent. The sad result was that an SPLA soldier operating in an area different from his own home saw no difference between the civil population, for whom he had taken up arms, and the enemy. The SPLA became like an army of occupation in areas it controlled and from which the people were running away. This happened in Yambio and Tambura, where instead of welcoming the SPLA, the Zande took to the bushes, leaving the towns to the 'liberators'. No war of liberation can be executed without the people. Nor are the people liberated, but they participate in the liberation process through their own conscientisation. There is nothing, like 'we are the liberators' as many SPLA officers and men claimed.

Militarism - that is military action executed outside the context of political purpose - in the SPLA, produced a subculture of lies, misinformation, cheap propaganda and exhibitionism in which small victories are magnified ten-times to win the praise of the leaders. This became rampant when Radio SPLA started broadcasting names of the officers and men who had carried out military missions whether successful or not. Political work within the army and among the civilian population was reduced to cheap tricks ostensibly to raise their morale or win them over. In many areas, the people came to call this method of morale boosting 'politi-kai' which in Nuer language translates to 'political lies'. This meant that the action of the political officers did not match their revolutionary rhetoric. In fact, the lives of the people started to deteriorate as soon as the SPLA took over the administration of the towns and villages because the physical and social infrastructure which existed before their 'liberation' were completely destroyed and SPLA had nothing to replace them.

Between 1983 and 1991, the SPLA gained control over many towns and villages. The most important among them being: Buma (1984), Yirol (1984), Pochalla (1986), Pibor (1987), Kapoeta (1987), Nasir (1989), Torit (1989), Nimuli (1989), Bor (1989), Akobo (1989), Kejo-Kaji (1990), Kaya (1990), Yambio (1990), Maridi (1990), Tambura (1990). Most of these were provincial administrative headquarters or garrison towns teeming with social services before the war began. Their physical infrastructure was destroyed by fighting or brought down deliberately by the government army to erect shelters and bunkers. However, a visit to any of these towns, like Nasir, Akobo and Torit, in 1992 one would be surprised to find that the towns looked like the battle for their capture had just ended a few hours ago[21]. Nothing was done to clear the rubble to encourage people to go about their business, and reconstruct their social and economic lives. In many of these garrisons, the anti-personnel mines remained in their places, long after the town had been captured from the enemy, claiming lives of both the civilians and SPLA soldiers alike.

The absence of a programme for reconstruction and rehabilitation and failure to convert military victories into political programmes for social and economic transformation was reflected in the continued dependence of the SPLA, as well as the civil population, on external resources provided by relief agencies. The asymmetrical interaction between the providers and the receivers of relief aid, in this humanitarian aid relationship, induced and reproduced the dependency 'syndrome' in many communities in South Sudan.

The complete neglect of social and economic functions of the liberation movement meant that the SPLA did not have to depend on the people. Resources had to be imported. This could only be done by the international humanitarian agencies, but since humanitarian assistance is only provided for the needy civilian population, the task of distribution of this assistance fell on specially selected SPLA officers and men who saw to it that the bulk of the supplies went to the army. Even in cases where the expatriate monitors were strict and only distributed relief to the civilians by day, the SPLA would retrieve that food by night. The result of this practice led to the absolute marginalisation and brutalisation of the civilian population.

The SPLA is largely a peasant army with low level of political consciousness. That explained why when placed in a position of responsibility, a SPLA soldier found it difficult to make correct analysis of the mechanism and dynamics of running state machinery. However, it is not possible to operate as an intelligent militant in a national liberation movement without a certain minimum of political education and ideological orientation. The Movement's attempt at political education was the wholesale imitation of the curriculum of Ethiopian political schools. Teaching Marxist philosophy and hard dialectics to peasants and secondary school dropouts was the surest way of creating counter-revolutionaries. It is no wonder that the people never had confidence in these manufactured Marxists. The frustration created by lack of the grasp of the Marxist theories quickly changed into hatred for the revolution itself. The assiduous reactionaries in the SPLA were those who passed through the SPLA school of political training.

The militarisation of all aspects of life in the SPLM/A, at the expense of political mobilisation and conscientisation led to institutionalised militarism, war-lordism, relegation of conscious political discipline and social harmony to brute forces, military authoritarianism and absolutism. SPLA officers became obsessed with military hierarchies and ranks even if that meant compromising the principles of liberation. Being appointed to the High Command, the highest organ in the Movement, was the cherished ideal of many officers. This had a negative impact in that this attitude promoted competition for promotion which sometimes boiled down to conspiracies among the combatants to undermine one another in the struggle for ascendancy in the military hierarchy.

The obsession with military discipline produced an elite High Command completely isolated from the masses of the people. This militarisation and dissociation from political functions led to the mutilation of both the political and military machines. This is because instead of both being a cumulative force, they cancelled each other. The initial wish to place the centre of gravity of the revolutionary armed struggle only on military effectiveness ignored the importance of popular participation. As a result, from 1985 until the High Command returned to Sudan in 1991, Itang and Dimma, the largest of the refugee camps in western Ethiopia, became mere logistical support centres for the SPLA instead of being transformed into the nuclei of the New Sudan. Much of what should have gone to the refugees were confiscated and sold to obtain money for SPLA logistics; this was not without resistance from the people. Had the authorities taken time to explain the need to contribute to the liberation process, the people would have done so without resistance.

This, in any case, would not have been necessary if the Movement released the instruments of production and promoted self-reliance. The absence of this made the SPLM/A vulnerable and dependent on Mengistu regime. Too much dependence on external support could not make up for the lack of mobilisation of the people. This continued for as long as SPLA remained in Ethiopia and for as long as Mengistu remained in power. The demise of Mengistu's regime in Addis Ababa sent shock waves into the spinal chord and nerve centres of the SPLA. This, coupled with the treacherous betrayal by some of its senior officers, the SPLA did not recover from the consequences of ignoring internal political organisation until after the convening of the first National Convention in 1994 which proves one salient fact that the decisive military factor in the national liberation is mass participation and the morale, both of the army and the people. Morale is inseparable from political and ideological education.

The militarisation of the liberation movement led imperceptibly to the armed struggle, changing in practice and theory from being a principal form of revolutionary struggle to being its only form. In the minds of the leaders, there was no way of participating in the liberation process except by enrolling and becoming a combatant in the SPLA. Once disabled by an enemy's bullet or became sick, one became useless and redundant without prospects for any other deployment. Worst still, those who had not formally joined the SPLM/A or had not been trained in any of its training centres, were not permitted into the SPLA administered areas. Thus, the militarisation of the SPLM/A from its early stages of life meant its de-revolutionisation. In fact, for many of its senior officers, SPLA was perceived as a military space for self promotion and wealth in form of livestock looted from the civilian population. This generated cut-throat competition between the senior commanders over the loots and war booty[22].

The militarisation of the Movement, whether deliberate or accidental, resulted in the emergence of an elitist vanguard, which on the other hand meant a shrinking of the decision making base and a consequent concentration of nearly all powers in the hands of the person at the top. In absence of collective leadership and individual responsibility, the SPLM/A was slowly transformed into an autocracy. The result of this was that persons with little or no administrative and managerial expertise, sychopants, and the indifferent surrounded the leadership or relatives and friends who did not dare to criticize the leadership for its shortcomings or mistakes in the Movement. One outcome of this situation was the gross mismanagement of the affairs of the Movement at every level.

Since the whole affair became a network of close confidants of the leaders, there was no accountability or responsibility for some of the most serious flaws in the administration of the camps and the 'liberated' areas. For instance, the officer responsible for Bilpam was not held accountable for the death from starvation and related diseases of nearly three thousand Nuba youths under training in Bilpam in 1988 even after it was revealed that their food was being sold on Gambella market and the proceeds appropriated by the commander. Similarly, the death from hunger and starvation of hundreds of recruits in Dimma refugee camp was not investigated.

The death from thirst and hunger of more than five hundred SPLA combatants and recruits from eastern Equatoria in early 1985 was never investigated. Arok Thon Arok, who commanded the SPLA expedition to Equatoria, was never asked to explain what happened and why he made the error of judgment leading to that disaster. The victims were never remembered except for the naming of one SPLA battalion - Tingili. To gloss over those mistakes in silence was a sure way of repeating them indefinitely. This has been characteristic of SPLA in which there was always a rush to forget, to erase, and to forge ahead. Serious mistakes have been fudged in the course of this 'forging ahead'; and these eventually reflected badly on the SPLA with devastating consequences.

The over-concentration of powers of the Movement (political, military or administrative) in one hand meant that there was little time for the leader to attend to all these problems nor did he have time for in-depth resolution of these issues which were sometimes neglected, adding to their complication.

In the absence of organisational structures, it also meant that those officers who were lucky enough to be assigned to specific administrative, political, administrative or economic tasks treated the assignment as a personal challenge to be tackled by themselves alone. In the course of time, many outrageous mistakes were committed. Since there was nobody to account to, these mistakes were just hidden away to the detriment of the Movement.

This method of work encouraged competition for favours with the leadership, as that was seen as the only way of rising in the political and military hierarchy of the Movement culminating into emergence of sycophants and leader-worshippers. Sycophancy and leader-worship invariably spoiled the leader himself. He became used to being praised to the extent that if one did not flatter him one was suspected to be an enemy and sometimes whatever important message one had was completely ignored. In the course of time, he became intolerant, paranoid and vindictive even to the personal level. Being promoted to the position of alternate member of the High Command, was what many senior SPLA officers aspired to, and in fact some, who thought had done much in the Movement, deserted it simply because they were not rewarded with that promotion. This seemed to fit in well with retaining the loyalty and obedience of the officers, because any officer who wanted promotion must of necessity be seen to support and defend the leadership. Jealousy, mudslinging and vilification became common features in the Movement to the point that some worked to foil the military successes of their colleagues.

Another consequence of excessive militarisation of the SPLM was the emergence of the so-called 'progressive officers', a loose group of combatants, many of whom claimed were in leftist movements inside the country. If the SPLM/A had the structures and fora for discussing political and ideological issues, it is possible that the issue of these officers would not have endured for long, simply because that group did not have functional existence. In the beginning, this group - mainly intellectuals - formed a small closed ring around the leadership of the Movement to the chagrin of other members.

Since in the SPLA the relations between men and officers and between officers themselves were determined by their position in the military hierarchy and rank, it so happened that this group of the so-called progressive officers enjoyed some degree of privileges, having very close relationship with the

Movement's leadership. This was not a politicised relationship. It was based on personal friendship and acquaintance which soon degenerated into unprincipled political patronage. With time and due to other contradictions, the group disintegrated under the pressure of personal rivalry and intrigues for ascendancy in the hierarchy of the Movement. As a matter of fact, the progressive officers did not exist as a coherent, organised group. The name endured because some of the SPLM/A leaders, notably, Arok Thon, had their own motives to challenge the leadership of Dr John Garang. In their effort to undermine the leadership of Dr John Garang, Cdrs Kerubino, Arok and Kulang victimised the so-called progressive officers and many were detained on flimsy charges.

Premature conventionalisation of the war

The objective of any war is to destroy the enemy and preserve one's forces. Encouraged by the large numbers of recruits that arrived its training centres, and the easy availability of armaments for them on graduation, the SPLA was immediately tempted to engage the enemy in a conventional manner. This has serious disadvantages. First, the quality of SPLA training was not to the level of the Sudanese army and their deployment to fight the enemy in defensive positions resulted in large numbers of SPLA being put out of action by small enemy detachments. For instance, the battles for the garrisons of Jekau and Malual Gaoth in eastern Upper Nile, in 1984/85, proved real disasters for SPLA.

The conventionalisation of the war at an early stage necessarily went against some of the basic peasant characteristics. The peasants, for instance, are by their very nature, not keen to move far away from their immediate material surroundings: their families, their livestock, the village environment, etc. As alluded to earlier, many of them came to join the armed struggle not because of the lofty nationalist ideals with which the intellectuals were imbued but had come only to get the gun in order to solve the local and immediate crises caused by the neighbours. Thus, the conventionalisation of the war meant, therefore, that many of these peasants were deployed in the war front far away from their homes. They responded to this by large-scale desertions back to their home areas. Most of 'Koryom' forces deployed in Bahr el Ghazal - the Rhino battalion for instance, deserted and moved back to their homes in Bor, paralysing the SPLA military plans and operations.

In order to correct or prevent desertions and defections, the SPLA put in place some stern measures that provoked more desertion. For instance, an SPLA soldier caught deserting was summarily executed, ostensibly as a deterrent measure, but sometimes it ended up triggering off further desertions and open rebellion. To avoid being caught on the way, each and every deserter had to stay clear of SPLA positions and interceptions. This meant moving in the forests and depopulated areas, often resulting in loss of lives from hunger, thirst or wild animals.

The desertions and 'going back home' prevalent among the newly graduated SPLA soldiers would have been avoided if these peasants - turned - guerrillas had been deployed in their home areas immediately after training. There, they would have served as guerrilla irregulars, engaging the enemy detachments at will, and spending their time showing off their newly acquired military attire, which would have served to motivate others to join the SPLA. Then, after this period it would have been necessary and advisable to take them back to the training camps for more specialised combat training and political education.

Having gained combat experience, they would have willingly agreed to be moved to serve in other locations after having undergone further military training, political and moral orientation. They, therefore, would have formed the nucleus of the people's revolutionary army, imbued with revolutionary and patriotic ideas, and ready to transform these ideas into material needs of the people. They would have implemented the democratic reforms necessary for building the 'New Sudan' and participated with the people in the creation of the new social and economic order.

Apart from the problems of arising from managing such a large army like the SPLA without the necessary political instruments of control in addition to the military routine and discipline, the premature conventionalisation of the war added another dimension. It accelerated the pace of the armed struggle, and the SPLA fought and won many battles over a short period bringing large territory under its control, without having developed its political and administrative capacity.

The rapid expansion of the SPLA out paced the growth and political and ideological development of the SPLM. This had serious repercussions for the over all development of the war and the social transformation in the 'liberated' areas. First, feeding the SPLA required enormous resources and, since no efforts were made at mobilising the internal resources, it had to depend on external ones. Secondly, the gap between the front and the General H/Quarters became very wide, making it difficult to follow up on what exactly was happening in the field (and vice versa) apart from the combat activities against the enemy.

Encouraged by the examples of grabbing, looting, murder and rape committed with impunity by some senior officers in the Movement, many of the commanders in the fronts turned their attention to amassing wealth looted from the civil population. Sometimes the people were requested to contribute food rations for the army in form of bulls and heifers, many of which are taken by the commanders for themselves, leading to dissatisfaction among the troops. The conventionalisation of the war, necessitating the presence of large numbers of troops roaming the countryside, led to depletion of the resources which culminated in the deterioration of the relationship between the army and the civilian population. In many places the civilians migrated away from the so-called 'liberated' areas which were nothing but ruins. Without laws regulating the conduct of a people's revolutionary war, the SPLA transformed itself into an army of occupation, behaving not very differently from the enemy's army.

The progress of the war should have gone hand in hand with the growing awareness of the SPLA soldier and the civil population about the war and its nature. It should have grown hand in hand with the building of the people capacity to sustain the war effort and their lives.

The conventionalisation of the war could be directly linked to the lack of concern for the lives of the people. I did mention above that the battles for Jekau and Malual Gaoth were major disasters for SPLA and the people of South Sudan. If the war was to be a protracted one[23], then what was the hurry to make it conventional prematurely? The irony of this flaw was that SPLA had later to recruit people forcefully into the army, something unheard of in a national liberation struggle. The membership of the liberation movement ceased to be a voluntary affair. These mistakes led to massive demoralisation among the troops and, hence, desertions from the SPLA.

On another plane, the contradictions that developed between the SPLA and the civilian population reflected the internal contradictions in the Movement and in fact contributed to them. In Equatoria, as well as other areas, many SPLA soldiers deserted their units and took to their homes in the mountains in disgust with the treatment meted out to the civilian population by their colleagues from Bahr el Ghazal and Upper Nile regions. There were instances in which the SPLA soldiers, and even officers, fought against their colleagues from other areas who had mistreated their people. This made it easy for them to desert or defect and join the enemy. The defection of Capt. Peter Lorot (1999) to the enemy in Kapoeta and the subsequent insecurity that resulted in Chukudum and Himan, leading to the cold blooded murder of Chief Joseph Nakwa and Peter Kidi Osman are cases in point.

External and internal factors that contributed to the split of the SPLM/A

In 1983, the SPLM/A started off as a socialist organisation championing a revolutionary armed struggle as a means for restructuring state power in the Sudan. Its objective was the creation of a 'united' socialist Sudan, based on multiplicity, diversity and commonalities of its cultures. Whether that was genuine aspiration of the combatants that made up the Movement or was meant to camouflage secessionist motives is just beside the point. However, after warding off much of the resistance to its expressed objective, it was able, in a short span of time, to galvanise the various groups into a mighty military force - SPLA. As early as 1984, the SPLA had started inflicting irreversible damage on the Nimeri regime.

Many of the Nimeri's prestigious projects in the southern region, notably the oil fields exploration and development in western Upper Nile undertaken by the Chevron Oil company of the Sudan, a subsidiary of the Chevron Oil of California, the Compaignie de Construction Internationale (CCI), a French construction company that was digging the Jonglei Canal and the Juba Airport were forced to close down their operations in February 1984, dealing an irreparable damage to Nimeri's image internationally and in the Sudan.

The SPLA military victories in the South, coupled with the growing acute political and economic crisis of the Nimeri regime, triggered off a popular uprising that overthrew Gaafar Mohammed Nimeri in April 1985. The reversal of the USA administration position vis à vis Nimeri leading to his fall prematurely before the SPLM/A had established its political and constitutional authenticity was perhaps an attempt to prevent its radicalisation[24] which would have made alliance with the leftist forces in the North more immanent, thus putting the country in a revolutionary situation. However, this professed political ideology of the SPLM - socialism[25] - was definitely provocative to and perceived by the West, especially the United States of America, as a threat to its interest in the Horn of Africa. The emergence of a powerful and radical military and political movement in South Sudan, allied to a totalitarian regime in Ethiopia was viewed as a threat to the established strategic balance of forces in the region of the Horn of Africa. The SPLM/A, therefore, found itself entangled in the super power rivalry in the region.

It is not clear whether there were efforts on the part of the different US administrations to counter SPLM/A's radicalisation and its development into a genuine national liberation movement with a leftist tendency that would jeopardise the American interests in the area. Why this did not happen in the context of the cold war politics and super power rivalry, especially when the SPLM/A was very close to Mengistu regime, is a very interesting anomaly, which requires some research. For instance, the US administration's support for Nimeri did not translate into hostility against the SPLA in spite of its professed socialist ideology. Perhaps the Americans knew well in advance that the SPLA claim was not serious or the US administration was having second thoughts about the usefulness of Nimeri. Nevertheless, the US administration supplied Nimeri with military hardware, trained his military and intelligence organs, etc. This was at a time when Operation Moses[26] was in full swing, when the SPLA closed down the Chevron petroleum development, which was an American interest, in western Upper Nile.

In spite of its serious internal contradictions, the SPLM/A has indeed waged a successful armed struggle; it had developed into a formidable military and political force which could not be ignored when considering the balance of forces in the Sudan political theatre and in the Horn of Africa. It, therefore, had real and potential enemies who could have had an interest in its destruction and who could have instigated the divisions and splits by widening the internal contradictions.

In the country, the NIF government stood to benefit from the demise of the SPLM/A. Having usurped power from the Umma and DUP coalition in a military coup, the NIF was an isolated force and could only maintain its grip on power by proving to the public opinion in the North that it was capable of stopping the war, and, hence, the suffering of the people by defeating the SPLA, not negotiating with it thus making it more credible to the northern public opinion more than the coalition of political parties it overthrew. It was, therefore, in the interest of the NIF to instigate and encourage rifts and cleavages which would eventually lead to the destruction of the Movement. To achieve this, Omer el Beshir, after seizing power in June 1989, started off immediately by dangling the possibility of the southern secession[27], efficaciously meant to test waters in the SPLM/A, as it created a feeling and hope among many of its members that an end to the war was in sight. He then proceeded to identify the opportunists, the ambitious and power hungry elements in the SPLM/A leadership who would be used to destroy the Movement. This was in addition to the long-term military, diplomatic and politic offensive that the NIF regime had embarked upon.

In NIF's strategic planning, the SPLM/A was to be destroyed by isolating it internationally by entering into alliance with the EPRDF to weaken and destroy the regime of Mengistu in Ethiopia which was the main supporter of SPLM/A. The diplomatic plank of this offensive against the SPLM/A was for the NIF to enter into agreements with the governments of the neighbouring countries, namely Uganda and Kenya to deny the SPLM/A any logistical support by placing monitors on the common borders with Uganda to oversee the movement of SPLA.

The opposition political forces in the North: the Umma Party, the Democratic Unionist Party, the Communist Party of the Sudan, the Trade Union Alliance, the Legitimate Command of the Sudanese Army, although allied with the SPLM/A in the National Democratic Alliance - NDA, had their own fears and suspicions about the SPLM/A and its strength. While they wanted the SPLA, they did not want it totally to destroy the Sudanese army and to emerge victorious, a fact that would shift the centre of power in the Sudan to the South.

The political forces in the North opposed to the NIF, therefore, wanted to use the SPLA to fight the war, weaken the NIF and create a political situation that will enable them to return to the helm of power in Khartoum. This can be proved from the experience with the northern opposition to Nimeri and the events which followed the popular uprising that brought down his regime, when they turned around to condemn and vilify the SPLM/A and its leader Dr John Garang between 1985 and 1989 for refusing to join the Intifadha government and the fact that while allied with the SPLA, parties like Umma and DUP took a long time to commit their forces to war against the NIF regime. When they did so, the numbers they mobilised could not compare with the SPLA (New Sudan Brigade) in the North.

The National Islamic Front was the only political force in the north that collaborated with Nimeri until his demise. The Umma, the Democratic Unionist Party, the Communist Party of Sudan, and a few South Sudanese individuals, were all in opposition to Nimeri when the March April uprising came. However, having overthrown Nimeri, the National Alliance for National Salvation[28], constituted from these parties and the trade unions, wanted the SPLM/A to lay down its arms, return to the country and participate as a junior partner in the transitional government of Gizuli Dafa'Ala[29]. Many of these northern leaders were incensed when the SPLA refused to join the new government. The northern parties had believed, albeit wrongly, that it was Nimeri who divided the southern region and hence caused the war, he, therefore, was the only problem, and since he has been overthrown, SPLA had no good reason to continue fighting[30]. On the other hand, many in the North felt that SPLA was a South Sudanese army and it was, therefore, necessary to curtail its growth and strength by inviting its leaders to participate in junior positions in the government which tacitly meant destruction of the SPLM/A as a military political movement.

Therefore, apart from the NIF, the major northern political parties in the NDA, especially the sectarian ones, namely the Umma and DUP, stood to benefit from the internal contradictions of the SPLM/A and actually must have worked to widened the gap by their support of individuals like Lam Akol and, perhaps, encouraged him to oppose Dr John Garang to foment the split, but later turned around to support the SPLM/A mainstream on the pretext that Garang fought for the unity of the Sudan. Going by the utterances of some of the NDA's leaders, the real motives for this support could be the destruction of the SPLM/A as a southern movement through its internal splits. The NDA's ambivalent position of wanting the continued existence of the SPLM/A but not as a credible power player is an obvious contradiction.

To comprehend this, it needs one to delve deeply into the complexity of the Sudanese society, the political history of the Sudan and the attitude of the northern political elite towards the South and South Sudanese. In early 1992 SPLA, following its split and infighting, suffered setbacks and reverses at the hands of the Sudanese army and lost several towns and villages. This was a source of happiness and celebration for some NDA leaders who were then meeting in Cairo. Some were reported to have uttered such remarks as ' it is good SPLA is defeated so that it is reduced to its actual size'[31]. This is coming from an SPLA ally and tells much not only about this alliance, but about the fact that many northerners have not shed their characteristic attitude of being *hazi fiak,* i.e. sons of the land.

The Pan-Arabists in the Sudan, and in the Arab world saw the strength of the SPLA and the possibility of its capture of power in the Sudan as an affront to its interest and, therefore, an obvious source of immense fear for their strategy of Arabising and Islamising Africa. To the pan-Arabist, therefore, the SPLM/A must be contained and frustrated from becoming a major player in the political theatre of the region. It is worth mentioning that, historically, when it came to the question of South Sudan, the political parties in the North were determined to maintain an northern domination of the South (whether or not by force of arms) in spite of their acute political and ideological differences. Whatever government came to power in Khartoum, whether it was an Islamic fundamentalist regime, like the present one, or that of the political parties it overthrew or military dictatorships of Ibrahim Abboud or Gaafar Nimeri before it, promoted the interests of the Arab North. That they continue to receive military, economic and political support from the Arab and Islamic countries goes to prove that northern Sudan fronts for the Arab and Islamic cause in black Africa. The NIF is, in fact, more vocal about this as we shall see in the later pages. It is worth mentioning that no Arab country or regime declared support for the SPLM/A. The earlier support given by Gadhafi had to do with his hostility to Nimeri and was, therefore, a case of the 'enemy of your enemy is your friend'.

Another potential enemy of the SPLM/A is Egypt. Apart from the general Arab and Islamic strategy and its contradictions with some Sudanese political parties like the Umma Party and the Communist Party, Egypt is weary and afraid of the SPLM/A strength. It's perception of the SPLM/A is conditioned by a consideration that SPLM/A is a counter power that is at variance with its strategic national interests because SPLM/A might call for the creation of a separate and independent state in South Sudan. Egypt's fears of the SPLM/A are, therefore, much more than the question of its share of the Nile waters and the extensive agricultural resources in the South[32]. As a regional power, it has not relinquished its colonial claims to the Sudan; this is over and above the fact that it has stakes in the Islamisation and Arabisation of black Africa. In fact Egypt will do anything in its power to undermine the strength and power of the SPLA. Despite Egypt's contradiction with Sadiq's government, in 1986/7 Egypt provided supplied weapons and ammunition to that government to arm the militia in Kordofan and Upper Nile in order to fight the SPLA.

The position of Egypt vis-à-vis the SPLM/A was put to test by the UN Security Council imposition of sanctions against the NIF regime following its refusal to repatriate to Ethiopia the three Egyptian terrorists who attempted to assassinate the Egyptian President Hosni Mubarak in Addis Ababa in June 1995. The Egyptian regime's arguments against imposition of economic sanctions on the grounds that they hurt the ordinary Sudanese people rather than NIF government was hardly convincing. However, President Mubarak's argument that imposition of arm embargo against the regime would strengthen the southern rebels (sic), speaks volumes of the intentions and motives of the Egyptians. It proves beyond reasonable doubt that to the Egyptian establishment the prospect of a strong SPLM/A seizing state power in the Sudan is too ghastly to contemplate. It was, therefore, in Egypt's strategic interest that its internal divisions and splits minimised the strength of SPLM/A.

Nigeria, a state with problems similar to those of the Sudan, is troubled by the power and possible success of the SPLM/A. Of all the countries opposed to question of secession of South Sudan from the North, Nigeria is perhaps the most vocal because, given its past Biafran experience and the latent sessionist tendencies in different parts of the country, it cannot encourage secession elsewhere in Africa. That is why President Ibrahim Babangida brokered the Sudanese peace talks to convince the SPLM/A to accept the NIF federal system modelled on that of Nigeria which had an interest in curtailing SPLA power.

The regime of Mengistu Haile Mariam was a generous friend of the SPLM/A. But the regime had many internal enemies. It is possible that, apart from the Ethiopian rebel groups, some of which had direct combat encounter with it, the SPLA must have rubbed shoulders with some internal forces opposed to the regime of Mengistu and, therefore, those forces could have worked for undermining the Movement[33] and its possible destruction.

Tiny Rowland, the British financial tycoon, could have exacerbated the internal differences in the SPLM/A. The role played by Tiny Rowland in the political arena in the Sudan ranged from being intermediary between the various governments in Khartoum and the SPLM/A. This role started in the 1984 when Nimeri, desperately in need of finding a quick a solution for the war, engaged Tiny Rowland to mediate between Khartoum and the SPLM/A. He later became a benefactor of SPLM/A, dishing out financial and other logistical support to the Movement. Tiny Rowland's financial assistance[34] to the Nasir faction leaders has contributed to widening the gap and making the split permanent. Rowland was motivated by business deals and profiteering. His relationship with the SPLM/A was to give him leverage in negotiating these business deals, especially the sugar industries in the Sudan. The NIF government made use of Tiny's relationship with those of Riek Machar, Lam Akol, Kerubino and Arok Thon to destroy Garang and the SPLM/A mainstream.

It is said that the NIF government channelled large amounts of money to some SPLM/A-United leaders for settling huge hotel and telephone bills, renting of luxurious houses and cars in Nairobi through Tiny Rowland's Lonrho office in Nairobi.

In April 1993, the SPLM/A-United's delegation to Abuja was carefully chosen by Tiny Rowland himself and, according to people close to Kerubino and Lam Akol, the going of the delegation to Abuja, uninvited by the Nigerian authorities, was meant to embarrass Garang and the Nigerians[35]. No one could tell how that could prove an embarrassment. However, the high-handedness with which that incident was handled led to a split within the ranks of SPLM/A-United which later gave birth to Patriotic Resistance Movement of South Sudan lead by Cdr Alfred Lado-Gore.

It would be wrong to say that in his support for the leaders of the Nasir coup, Tiny Rowland deliberately worked for the destruction of the SPLM/A. As a business tycoon interested in profits accruing from contacts and contracts from governments and liberation movements, definitely wanted to use his relations with the political movements in the South in order to strengthen his hold on the Kenana Sugar Company and, in fact, he wanted to edge out the Kuwaitis completely. Following the split within the Movement, he now invested in Dr Lam Akol and the Nasir faction to use as a counter weight to Dr John Garang, and make the SPLM/A leader accept whatever would have brought palatable returns from the government in Khartoum.

In this respect, Tiny Rowland could not have wanted an immediate disappearance of the SPLM/A. However, it is true that he was not at ease with the methods of the SPLM/A and its leadership, especially given the fact that the SPLM/A did not treat Tiny Rowland in the way other liberation Movements in Southern and central Africa who revered his financial handouts have done. Rowland, therefore, tried very hard to project Dr Lam Akol as a counter pressure on Dr John Garang in order to bring the SPLM/A to the negotiating table with the NIF regime. However, in the course of all these flirtations with Kerubino and Lam Akol[36], Rowland inadvertently destroyed what he wanted to build as a counter force.

The actions of Tiny Rowland, especially his direct involvement in the running of the faction, his preferential treatment of some members of the faction and others, represented by renting of luxurious houses, hotel suites and cars, and the speed with which he wanted the faction to operate to match the schedule of the NIF government, created the conditions for the disintegration of the SPLM/A - United.

Like a besieged castle, therefore, SPLM/A could endure external attacks if its house was in order and all its members lined up behind its leadership. What could have been extreme danger to the existence of the SPLM/A as a national liberation movement were the internal contradictions including the neglect of political work and democratic institutions which led to the split and the infighting that resulted in the tilting of the balance of forces in favour of the NIF government.

The SPLM/A internal contradictions

This preceding part of this chapter has dealt with the external factors or factors presumed to have been instigated by the potential or real adversaries of the SPLM/A, and which aimed at its disintegration, eventual defeat and destruction. There could still be so many of these intrigues, some of them very powerful catalysts. However, it is not enough, perhaps not even convincing at all, to speak of the external factors as causes of all the enormous problems in the Movement. As the old saying goes that 'a castle under siege, no matter how weak are its defenses, can only crumble from inside', that is to say, when it is overwhelmed by its internal contradictions. This is quite pertinent to the SPLM/A whose contradictions were more dangerous to its survival than the combined might of its many external enemies.

The trouble with the SPLM/A is that it made no efforts to learn from past experiences in the armed struggle in South Sudan. In fact, glossing over previous mistakes is a sure way of condemning oneself to repeating them indefinitely. Regis Debray put it brilliantly correct:

> ... A rush to forget, to erase, to forge ahead is certainly a move in the direction of the current, in the direction of life; but life leads to death, and swimming with the current leads to passivity. If a wound is gaping open, if the pus has produced a neurosis of compulsive repetition, then how can silence cure it...[37]

Many of the SPLM/A problems, which latter developed into serious crisis, resulted from the attitude of postponing solutions, of forging ahead, of not talking about the mistakes. Mistakes were not analysed and their roots causes established, crimes were committed and the perpetrators left unpunished, especially when they had relationship with those in position of power. In 1983, the Movement survived the difficult days of struggle against the forces of Anya-nya 2 although it was still resting on the support of the Nuer nationality which formed the bulk of both the Anya-nya 2 and the infant SPLA. In 1987, the episode of Kerubino Kuanyin Bol would have been another disastrous event. We were the tragedy of splits and collapse then because of the fact that tribal and sectional solidarity were not strong enough to overwhelm South Sudan nationalist instincts still powerful among nearly all the members of the Movement. It is this instinct that made the arrest and detentions of Kerubino Kuanyin and Arok Thon an easy affair in the SPLM/A[38].

There were so many incidences that would have caused splits and bloody confrontations like what happened in 1991 and after. But the SPLM/A internal cohesion was stronger, not because of political and ideological awareness, but rather because the contradiction between the South and the North was stronger than the internal contradictions. This is a clear case of external contradictions constituting a basis for internal cohesion and organisational unity of the Movement. Nevertheless, it should not have allowed much room for complacency in matters of organisation which could have been easily exploited by the enemy. That the SPLA spearheaded an armed struggle against a strong and powerful enemy should have been cause enough to strive for a high degree of organisation, unity, solidarity and discipline to counter the enemy's political and ideological strength.

In all these ambiguities bordering on confusion, SPLM/A seemed to have enjoyed some advantages. It was not very generous in divulging information about its internal dynamics. Much of what filtered out of the SPLM/A propaganda machinery, significantly radio SPLA, was about 90 percent disinformation or things concerned with the military combat, mainly news about the fighting which were always efficaciously exaggerated. The information department was weak and inefficient; the print media was not regular, even for internal consumption. That the Movement had succeeded in insulating itself was both a strength and a weakness. It was important, given the weak ideological and organisational base of the Movement, through which little information about its internal contradictions reached the enemy. But this was a major weakness in that it denied the Movement the opportunity of correcting or learning from its mistakes and some of the defeats it suffered. A defeat in the military front, like what occurred following the split in 1991, when the enemy regained an upper hand in the military front and recaptured some strategic garrisons from the SPLA, should form the basis for a political and diplomatic victory for the Movement.

There were ample opportunities for the Movement to resolve many of its internal contradictions and draw revolutionary lessons from that exercise. For instance, there was a golden opportunity for structural transformation, democratic and administrative reforms of the Movement, following the arrest and detention of Cdrs Kerubino and Arok[39]. Their removal from the position of authority should have been the basis for restructuring the political leadership of the Movement. This would have allowed political and ideological debate to permeate the ranks and file of the Movement. Unfortunately, this did not happen, and, like many other contradictions, the SPLM/A leadership played them down, allowing them to multiply and become more complex, rendering their resolution very difficult. According to Regis Debray:

... You cannot make the basis of a real contradiction magically disappear simply by leaving the contradiction unspoken... A debate evaded in the short term is in fact an inevitable crisis in the longer term, and a probable split in the end...[40]

This is precisely what happened. The contradictions in the High Command translated themselves into a split within the ranks and file at a time the SPLM/A was at it weakest moments. Having lost the support bases in Ethiopia due to the downfall of Mengistu, the SPLA was forced to retreat hastily back into the South Sudan. It was these factors which appeared to Riek Machar and Lam Akol spell to the doom for SPLA, something that encouraged them to embark on their treacherous Nasir adventure.

Given the politically suffocating environment in the SPLM/A, especially in its rear bases in the refugee camps in Ethiopia and in the 'liberated' areas, it would have been foolhardy to come to the open against the SPLM/A leadership, without exposing one to high risk. It was extremely dangerous and many lost their lives on flimsy charges of being against the leadership of Dr John Garang. The political work against the prevailing conditions and the struggle for reforms in the Movement had to be, of necessity, clandestine. The only time intellectuals and officers sat to debate the problems in the SPLM/A was in September 1987 in Itang; even that debate was not taken to its logical conclusion. It turned out later that what appeared like a return to a liberal and democratic atmosphere to the Movement was, indeed, a trap into which people were lured and some of those who spoke their minds were accused of staging a coup, were arrested and detained, and only saw the light of the day following the split of the Movement in 1992[41].

The 'Political Cadres Group'[42] came up with a political programme of debating what was called the creation of the 'New Sudan' in Itang refugee camp. The ensuing discussions and debate drew in many intellectuals and officers of the SPLA present in Itang then. It was, of course, not the creation of the 'New Sudan' in Itang which was the burning issue then; people were crying out for justice, parity in the distribution of the food rations and other commodities[43]. People wanted to know the general direction of the Movement after the arrest of Kerubino and his officers. This turned out to be an exercise in the raising of the awareness of the people who now started to speak out openly for their rights. The arrest and detention in October 1987 of over twenty SPLA officers in Itang on the flimsy charges of being members of 'progressive officers' organisation hostile to the leadership of the Movement was in fact precisely because of this level of agitation in the refugee camp which the Movement's leadership wanted to nip in the bud.

Following these oppressive measures and, more specifically, when rumours started circulating that those officers and men who were arrested and detained were subjected to torture and inhuman acts in which many of them were said to have died, the situation in the SPLM/A and in the refugee camps reverted to what it was in 1983/4. It was characterised by general fear, apathy, indifference and self-insurance. To stay alive became a cherished idea and this encouraged the culture of silence and insensitivity to all that was happening. The element of trust and mutual confidence that prevailed among the officers and men of the SPLA and between the people themselves was eroded and shattered fear of being arrested and subjected to humiliation.

So oppressive was the situation in the SPLM/A that the nationalist aspirations and solidarity that brought the combatants together in the national liberation struggle seemed to evaporate in the hot air of fear, suspicion, and conspiracies. In just systems, the greater the political or governmental responsibility one held, the greater the obligation to behave with dignity and honour, in both one's public and personal conduct. In the SPLM/A, the higher one was in the hierarchy the more was one feared. This was because by their very action, some of these leaders respected neither law nor morality, and some behaved as if they belonged to a caste above everyone and everything else.

The psychological and moral impact of the events in the Movement on the recruits and the civilians was heavier, because of the clash of this reality with the image of the prospective historical role of the SPLM/A. As a national liberation movement struggling for social justice and democracy, the SPLA had no justification for adopting oppressive methods in dealing with its subjects. It was all the indignities associated with such behaviour by the leaders that cowed the majority of people to docility and indifference. It is almost impossible to organise the people independently, for whatever purpose, without thinking of being arrested or harassed by the authorities.

The irony of the situation prevailing in the SPLM/A was that if one got arrested for any kind of political protest against injustice done to somebody, one got blamed for arousing the wrath of the SPLA authority. This did not invoke sympathy or solidarity but instead the people blamed the victim. The people would ask, 'why did he have to behave like that, didn't he know that everybody is aware of all that he was saying but were keeping their peace?'. Thus, when people came out of detention, they were extremely careful not to provoke another confrontation with the authorities. This was also not accidental, but the behaviour of some SPLA commanders and their exercise of power of death and life over their subjects reinforced this docility.

For instance, in 1985, at the height of his power madness, Kerubino Kuanyin Bol, the deputy chairman and deputy Commander in Chief of SPLM/A, on one of his visits to the General Headquarters in Bilpam ordered the execution by firing squad of a group of eight detainees who were waiting for the conformation of their sentences ranging from six months to a few years. Their crime did not warrant a death sentence but this showed how arbitrary and high-handed action without reference to the decisions of the Court Martial indicated that there was a matter of grave danger to the Movement and the people[44].

In a similar episode, fuelled by tribal, sectional hatred and animosity, Cdr Arok Thon Arok, a member of the High Command, in what amounted to a genocide in 1987, ordered the execution of a complete SPLA company[45] which had allegedly attempted to desert its position. This allegation was not proved but, nevertheless, people were summarily executed. This was a case of double standards. For in 1985 Cdr Arok did not find it necessary to sentence to death fellow Bor SPLA soldiers when they deserted him in the Lou area out of fear of the Anya-nya 2. The SPLA disciplinary and penal laws of 1984 provide for such executions. But death sentences were meted out after exhaustive investigations and were executed after obtaining permission of the commander in chief. However, in this case these provisions were deliberately ignored.

In early 1988 before his recall to the general headquarters, Dr Lam Akol, then alternate member of the High Command and zonal commander for northern Upper Nile, executed 7 Shilluk soldiers. Their crime, which was neither proved nor investigated, was an alleged mutiny. Lam Akol was noted for his rigidity and lack of concern for the welfare of men under his command. There were times they would go for days without food, as a result there was much heckling in the ranks which his informers, the combat intelligence officers, claimed was a mutiny brewing among the soldiers. The alleged ringleaders, therefore, were arrested and executed after subjecting them to some mock trial. It was a mixture of malice, fear and ignorance on the part of Lam that he never attached any importance to the lives of people.

There was nothing to hold anybody to such an organisation that had no concern for the lives of its members. As a result, there were desertions, assassinations within the ranks and outright surrender to the enemy. This was not a healthy environment for a liberation movement. In fact, the situation was so tense that it appeared as if it was going to explode. Fortunately, it did not explode. This could be attributed to the following reasons.

The majority of the members of the SPLM/A believed that the resolution of this contradiction should come after the immediate confrontation with the enemy was finished and the conflict with the North settled. This trend was right and wrong at the same time. Putting off the resolution of an internal contradiction, for whatever reason, was wrong because it caused much of the pain that would otherwise have been avoided. But the fear of those who favoured this position was well placed. In a situation like what prevailed in the SPLM/A, which was fuelled by tribal and sectional sentiments, and where political and ideological bonds were weak, it was possible that a slightest upheaval in the ranks and file would deal a deathblow to the Movement. It was, therefore, necessary to persevere in the face of all these difficulties and internal contradictions, lest the enemy took advantage of them. The events that followed the split of the Movement in 1991 vindicated that position. In fact, the majority remained in the SPLA mainstream because of this consideration. It is these feelings among the SPLA combatants that gave the impetus to the fighting between 1983 and 1991 leading to the capture of most of South Sudan by SPLA in spite of the fact that half the SPLM/A leadership and senior officers were in detention.

Second, the primary contradictions between the North and the South were very powerful and, in fact, were the motive force behind the SPLA strength and ability to mobilise the people in South Sudan. Many SPLA officers and men identified their enemy as the Arab Muslim North. Due to low level of political consciousness, they associated the internal contradictions not with some organisational or structural failure but with the particular individual. As a result of this attitude, any move to oust Dr John Garang from the leadership of the Movement was bound to have no essential support, especially in Bahr el Ghazal. Very few people saw the leadership dimensions of the contradictions within the SPLM/A and between the SPLA and the civil population.

This made the movement for reforms and democratisation of the SPLM/A a very difficult, if not an impossible, task. As a result, SPLM/A became an environment in which conspiracy and plots flourished and thrived. Many people were pushed to the extreme of thinking that only the removal of Dr John Garang de Mabior from the leadership that was the solution. As Debray correctly puts it:

> ...The absence of a profound ideological motivation in the members of a movement, even a few of them, even perhaps one is a time bomb planted among them. It can be detonated by personal rivalry, by frustration and by temporary setback and power struggle. In a sense it is no more than the literal truth to say that whenever the military training of the cadres takes priority over their political training, the lives of the militants are in danger....[45]

The SPLM/A internal political crises were in the beginning imperceptible except for a few people. However, they began to show slowly; first between the members of the High Command themselves. They started to erode the respect and trust for the leadership of Dr John Garang even among those whom he hand picked. It wouldn't be surprising that the nearer one was the more one understood the working of the leadership and the more it generated contempt. This was exactly the case with Dr Lam Akol and Dr Riek Machar who were close confidants of Dr John Garang. Hence, the crisis in the Movement diminished the authority, popularity and respect that Dr John Garang commanded among the ranks and file and in the international community, especially on the African continent.

The civil war in the Sudan has always attracted the attention of some African countries. When the SPLA started the war in high gear, inflicting serious defeat to the Sudanese army, it won respect and praise from a lot of quarters on the African continent, just short of full diplomatic recognition. The SPLA was seen rightly by many Africans in light of an African army defeating an Arab regime. Consequently, Dr John Garang de Mabior, the SPLM/A leader, was accorded the kind of respect enjoyed by a head of sovereign state whenever he visited some of these countries[46]. In him and the SPLA, they saw an opportunity to correct the prejudice of history and fate of the African people in the hands of the Arabs and the Europeans. That helped in boosting the awareness of the people about the cause and tribulations of the their fellow blacks in the Sudan.

Notes

[1] Patricia Mercer. 'The Shilluk Trade and Politics from the mid-seventeen century to 1861'. *Journal of African History*, XIII, 3 (1971) pp. 407 - 426.

[2] Late Father Saturnino Lohure, Joseph H Oduho and William Deng Nhial went to East Africa and founded the Sudan African National Union (SANU) in 1960.

[3] The National Unionist Party - NUP, led by Ismael el Azahri, and the People Democratic Party, led by Sheikh Ali Abdel Rahaman, were once one party but separated over the issue of unity with Egypt on independence of the Sudan. However, just before the death of Sayed Ali el Mirghani in October in 1967, the two parties merged to form what became known up to this moment as the Democratic Unionist Party - DUP.

[4] This included working in the Workers Trade Unions, Farmers Trade Unions, Students Unions, leading anti-regime strikes, some political others economic, which culminated in the civil disobedience of October 1964 which lead to the downfall of the Military regime. It is in these fora that the inter party struggles in the form of ideological struggles continued. It proved that the Leftist parties were more organised and they controlled the Unions.

[5] The Charter of the Professional Front which speared headed the October uprising and, hence formed the October Government following the collapse of the military regime, provided for political activities by civil servants. This was put to serious test in March 1965, during the Round Table Conference on the Problem of Southern Sudan, when Abel Alier, then a Judge, was forced to resign from the Judiciary on the ground that the Judiciary was independent and the Chief Justice would not allow him to participate as a delegate of Southern Front in the Round Table Conference.

[6] Mr. Santino Deng Teng was the Minister of Animal Resources in the regime of Ibrahim Abboud.

[7] David Keen (1994) *The Benefits of Famine*.

[8] The SPLM Manifesto July 1983.

[9] Majors Kerubino Kuanyin and William Nyuon were functional illiterates, who would not pass their examinations.

[10] An Arab saying quoted from Okot B'pitek in *The Poet as the Ruler* East African Publishers.

[11] SPLM Manifesto 1983.

[12] The National Front (Umma and DUP after the withdrawal of the Muslim Brotherhood) had attempted an armed invasion of the country from Libya in July 1976. Nimeri defeated this. Many coups they had fomented had equally be foiled. In 1977 the NIF reconciled with Nimeri in Port Sudan and they joined the Nimeri regime. This was short lived as they returned to

exile. Saddiq el Mahdi stayed in Ethiopia where he tried to raise an army from among the Ansar. The project did not take off because of the basic contradiction between the Ethiopian regime and Saddiq. This force later dispersed following the demise of the Nimeri regime in Sudan.

13 The Anya-nya 2 was formed in 1976 following the Akobo mutiny of 1975. Its political leadership was not defined although there were claims that Mr. Gordon Mortat was the President. The Anya-nya 2 programme was that of secession and formation of an independent and sovereign state in South Sudan. This did not go down well with the Ethiopian regime which was fighting a war against the Eritreans independence Movement.

14 'Old Sudan' has been repeatedly used to connote the corrupt and oppressive regime and the political environment in the country. SPLM/A was, therefore, struggling armed means to replace this with the 'New Sudan'.

15 BBC covered the attacked by SPLA on the Chevron Oil Company's camp in Rub Kona on February 4th 1984, Nile steamer between Malakal and Bor on February 4th, attack on CCI camp on the Jonglei Canal mouth on February 11th., and attack on Malakal on February 22nd. All these led to the closure of CCI and Chevron stopped the development of the oil fields. This was a big setback for Nimeri and his regime.

16 The Mandari and the Bor Dinka are neighbours and have a lot of cultural things in common. But when the politics of division set in 1981, the Equatorian intellectuals used the Mandari to fight and route the Bor Dinkas out of Juba town. Many Bor Dinkas have not forgiven the Mandari for this and when they had opportunity, like in the SPLA, they slipped into the Mandari land with the objective of revenging. The Mandari in the villages were not aware of what went on in Juba, so they did not suspect the intentions of the Bor SPLA men.

17 This was revenged by the GPLM, an Anyuak dominated political military movement which took power in Gambella following the demise of the Mengistu regime and ascension to power in Addis Ababa by the EPRDF in 1991. The GPLM together with EPRDF forces captured Pochalla from the SPLA in 1992 and handed it over to the Sudan Government.

18 The peasant is used here loosely to include the cattle owning communities who also practice agriculture.

19 These were the words of Brigadier Mohammed Osman Abdalla, the then Minister of Defence in the Transitional Military Council- TMC, when the SPLA forces attacked and overran Gardod in Southern Kordofan in 1986. But these were reverberated by the Medan, the mouthpiece of the Communist Party, when SPLA captured Kurmuk in November 1987. The paper perceived the SPLA as a stooge in the hands of Socialist Ethiopia.

20 At the beginning of the conflict, the Anya-nya 2 tended to discriminate in favour of Shilluks. They did not see the Shilluks as a threat to their quest for leadership of the South and their struggle against the Dinka. However, after the shooting down of a Sudan Airways Fokker Friendship passenger plane with more than sixty people on board in August 1986 by an SPLA contingent of Shilluks, there was now need to punish the Shilluks and this was done ruthlessly causing large scale migration of the Shilluks to the North.

21 This was my impression of the situation when I went to Nasir in January 1992. Even some of the enemy's military equipment, which could have been repaired and re-deployed, were still lying in waste.

22 It was a fashion between the Nilotic and other tribes in South Sudan to display ones wealth in the number of wives one married. In the SPLA and in the areas under its control, the commanders least the soldiers take them for their feeding quickly exchanged the cattle looted or confiscated from the civilians for wives.

23 SPLM Manifesto 1983, chapter 8, clearly speaks of the war being a protracted one.

24 Although the manifesto of SPLM 1983 clearly defines its political and ideological direction, the social and ideological composition of the SPLM did not really make a socialist Movement.

Background to the present war 75

25 The Manifesto of SPLM 1983.
26 The airlifting of Ethiopian Jews to Israel through and with the cooperation of the Sudanese government.
27 The first announcement of the regime, which was carried by a Kuwaiti News Agency was that the new regime was ready to consider the idea of secession of South Sudan. The SPLM/A responded negatively to this.
28 A coalition of the Political Parties, the Trade Unions and Popular Organisations like the Sudanese Women Union, The Sudanese Youth Union, etc.
29 The letter of Dr. Gizuli Dafalla to Dr. John Garang in May 1985.
30 This was out of the erroneous assumption that the war started because of the division of the South and the dismantling of the Addis Ababa Agreement.
31 Southern Sudan Vision No. 3 March 1992. Published by Department of Information and Culture, Nasir Faction of SPLM/A.
32 The digging of the Jonglei Canal was stopped by the war in 1984. Nimeri and the Egyptian had planned to used the Jonglei Canal Project to settle about two and half million Egyptians in Upper Nile against the wishes of the people of South Sudan.
33 SPLA had clashes with OLF, GPLM and other armed groups. In 1989, SPLA clashed with Anyuak militia in Itang and Piny-udo, although this proved very embarrassing for the Ethiopian regime, nothing was done to bring the perpetrators to books. The participation of the GPLM and EPRDF in 1992 in the capture of Pochalla must be seen in the light of punishing the SPLA for its excesses and support for Mengistu.
34 The Nasir faction was able to maintain a presence in Nairobi because of the intervention of Tiny Rowland. In fact after the failure of the peace and reconciliation talks in February 1992, there were moves to expel the Nasir leaders from Kenya.
35 In this round of talks arranged by the Nigerian government between the Government of Sudan and the SPLM/A, the SPLM/A - United was not invited to Abuja. SPLM/A-United conducted a parallel Peace talks with a junior Government delegation in Nairobi. However, before that started Tiny Rowland flew Cdrs Kerubino Kuanyin, Arok Thon Arok, Lam Akol, Faustino Atem Gualdit, John Luk and Taban Deng Gai to Abuja in his jet.
36 Until October 1993, when he came out to Nairobi, Riek Machar tactfully remained in South Sudan. The affairs of the faction was run by Kerubino Kuanyin Bol his deputy and Lam Akol his Secretary for External Relations and Peace.
37 *A critique of Arms: The Revolution on Trial.* (1974) Penguin Books.
38 Arok Thon Arok, Member of the SPLM/A Politico-Military High Command used to boast that he enjoyed the support of more than forty five percent of the SPLA officers corps. When he was arrested on March 8th. 1988, nobody protested or raised a issue against that.
39 Regis Debray (1974) A Critique of Arms. Penguin Books.
40 The Nasir faction raised the issue of release of the Political detainees in the jails of the SPLA during the Nairobi Peace talks and as a result many of those who languished in detention since 1987 were released.
41 A group of SPLA political commissars deployed in the refugee camp to undertake political enlightenment.
42 The practice was that rations were distributed according to ranks in the SPLA. This put the soldiers and junior officers at a disadvantage, leave alone the civilians who in order to survive in the camp were forced to buy back their rightful share of food rations by having to work as labourers in the houses of the senior officers and members of the High Command.
43 The incident was really unbelievable because although the case involved rape, which the SPLA Penal and Disciplinary Laws (1984) provided for such executions, there, among those executed was somebody who had fought the colleague and because he hailed from Bor, Kerubino just ordered him executed.

44 About 230 men
45 Regis Debray, op cit.
46 It is that in one of his meetings with Dr Garang the Zambian President Kenneth Kaunda shed tears of joy and pride when the heard that the blacks Africans were now ridding themselves of the yoke of Arab oppression and domination in the Sudan.

3

Hatching the Conspiracy

... It is admirable to give your life for a great ideal... and contemptible to use a great ideal for personal ambitions of glory and power...

Jose Marti

There is a general belief among South Sudanese that when a very important and magnificent event, say something that may result in a positive transformation in the lives of the people, who have been suffering, is about to happen, the devil will jump in to spoil that promising prospect. The people are thus left in a state of shock, hopelessness, apathy etc. This seems to have been the feelings prevalent among the majority of the people of South Sudan and in the SPLM/A following the announcement carried by the BBC Focus on Africa on August 30th 1991 that Dr John Garang de Mabior, chairman and Commander in Chief of SPLM/A, had been ousted from the leadership by a group of three commanders in Nasir.

In fact, the Nasir Declaration was carried earlier in a radio message from Cdr Riek Machar addressed to all units of the SPLA on August 28th. 1991. A message of that nature, addressed to all units from a commander other than the chairman and Commander in Chief of the SPLA, was bound to be badly received by the units which would count themselves still loyal. To make sure that their move received wider national and international coverage, and for the consumption of those in the SPLM/A with no access to radio messages, the Nasir leaders called on the BBC to make an information backup. In fact, many officers and men of the SPLA who heard of the coup from the BBC initially thought it was not serious.

Between 1989 and 1991, the SPLA had maintained an upper hand against the enemy with its capture of the whole of western Equatoria, the whole of eastern Equatoria with the exception of Juba and Yei garrisons, rural Bahr el Ghazal and the stretch of territory in Upper Nile south of river Sobat. The general feeling, therefore, among the SPLA officers and men and the people in South Sudan was that SPLA was poised on capturing Juba, bringing an end to the war and the suffering of the people. That is why the Nasir Declaration was a tragic blow to the hopes and aspirations of the people of South Sudan.

The Nasir adventure was a political and military move carefully calculated to snatch the leadership from Dr John Garang at one of the weakest moments in the Movement's history. The Movement had just retreated back into the country from its bases in Ethiopia following the demise of the Mengistu regime. Many SPLA units had not reached their destinations inside the Sudan and the Movement was still in a state of reorganisation and consolidating its positions in the liberated areas. The leadership and the ranks and file, at this stage, were more preoccupied with the question of survival of the Movement after such a temporary setback.

The Nasir Declaration, and the split that followed from it, resulted in the worst humanitarian disruption in the recent history of South Sudan. The political contradictions at the level of the SPLM/A High Command was resolved militarily and it spilled over to the civilian population, giving rise to tribal conflicts and killings on an unprecedented scale as well as massive displacements, looting of livestock, abduction of women and children and burning of homes. The internecine fighting between the SPLM/A mainstream and the Nasir faction that followed the split played well into the hands of the NIF regime which regained initiative on the military front, recapturing from the SPLA such strategic towns like Pochalla (April 1992), Kapoeta (June 1992), Torit (1993) among others.

The Nasir adventure and the changes it created in the strategic balance of forces, even at the level of the Horn of Africa, is such important an event that it cannot be ignored. Why did it happen? Did the SPLM/A supreme leadership, know of the planned coup in advance and, if so, what steps were taken to avert it? It is imperative that the facts about the whole affair be unearthed. It is incumbent on those who supported the adventure for genuine reasons and who have recovered their mental stability and social reality to honestly recount what happened in order to give credence to our existence as revolutionaries ready to learn from our mistakes and errors of judgment. This is of paramount importance in view of the developments that caused the disintegration of the Nasir faction and its vain efforts to survive on the massive financial and military injection from the enemy and through the formation of fake alliances. This should constitute a public and a general self-criticism on the part of the author for his active support to the Nasir Declaration between August 1991 and October 1994 which was inspired by nothing but naivety and parochialism. It should help soothe the passions.

My personal contribution in the SPLM/A

I joined the ranks of the SPLM/A formally in April 1986, flying straight from Khartoum to Addis Ababa, after casting my vote in the 'Graduates Constituency' in the general elections for the Constituent Assembly elections. It is perhaps necessary to add that it was the first time I voted in parliamentary elections. I had been in the trade union movement for sometime, and had been serving as secretary for foreign relations in the Juba University Sudanese Staff Association -JUSSA, a position that placed me on the political scene of the National Alliance for National Salvation, and which made me frequently shuttle between Juba and Khartoum during 1985 in the wake of Nimeri's downfall following a popular uprising in April. I had the privilege and honour of placing JUSSA on the map of the Sudan Rural Solidarity (SRS)[1] in its formation in Medani in November 1985 during the conference of the National Alliance for National Salvation.

My decision to join the Movement at that time was precipitated by two significant developments. During the Medani conference of the National Alliance, I had a sharp disagreement with the way Mr Ibrahim Nugud, the General Secretary of the Communist Party of the Sudan, articulated his views on the SPLM/A. In spite of the SPLM/A coming out as a 'socialist' movement struggling for one United Socialist Sudan, the Communist Party still viewed the Sudan People's Liberation Movement and Dr John Garang merely as a southern movement and leader respectively, whose objective was secession of the South.

Not only that, it was assumed that the SPLM/A and Dr John Garang were serving not the interests of the Sudanese people, but of the Ethiopian regime and the western imperialism. I dismissed these allegations, but they had a profound impact on me. I began to recall an Arab saying that runs; 'a slave, no matter how long his turban has lengthened is still a slave'. Which literally meant that the SPLM/A and Dr John Garang, no matter how much they may developed politically and ideologically, remain what they were - southerners who should not be trusted at all.

I could not draw a parallel between socialist Ethiopia and imperialism, but that made me to conclude that northern Sudanese, propelled by their superiority complex, will never appreciate any initiative from South Sudan. Even the building of 'socialism' must of necessity by a North Sudanese enterprise, which the South Sudanese must only be accommodated in.

My decision was further accelerated by the proposed partial parliamentary elections[2]. Given the fact that the mass movement which resulted in the demise of the Nimeri regime, was irreversibly on the decline, and the traditional sectarian parties in vying for state power were to likely repeat once more the events that occurred in South Sudan following the overthrow of Abboud in 1964, it appeared to me that the 1986 elections, like those of 1965, were bound to escalate the war. The euphoria of the popular uprising that ended the sixteen years of autocracy and dictatorship had fizzled away in a matter of one year. It was like the post October 1964 scenario was being recreated by the events unfolding in the country following the fall of Nimeri.

There was bound to be an escalation in this war whose victims were usually the unarmed civilian population. It appeared to me that the proposed partial elections for the Constituent Assembly in 1986 had some striking resemblance to those of 1965 which was held at a time war was ragging unabated in the South. When South Sudanese intellectuals and government officials were being murdered in cold blood in the towns by the Sudanese army[3], villages were being burnt and people were forced into the bushes or across the borders into the neighbouring countries for refuge. The government of Mohammed Ahmed Maghoub (Umma Party) embarked on cold blood massacre of southern intellectuals in the false belief that that would weaken the Anya-nya. The prospects for the repeat of these atrocities in the South loomed now that the war had broken out again and escalated.

These atrocities were of no great concern to the northern and southern politicians alike. The major sectarian parties, like hungry wolves, were only interested in how to retake the state power after sixteen years of exclusion. They frustrated the efforts to rid the country of the legacy of Nimeri regime, and effect reforms. This reinforced my resolve to join the armed struggle and the SPLM/A.

I had participated in the first war during the struggle for the freedom. This is because I believed in independence of the oppressed people of South Sudan as a matter of principle. This is not peculiar to me alone, but something every South Sudanese kept secretly in his/her chest. This freedom and independence cannot be won by the tactics of passive resistance along the lines of the class struggle drawn and waged by the Communist Party of the Sudan. Although there is a class dimension in the contradiction between North and South Sudan, the driving force was not the class contradictions and the notion of the proletariat class wining state power in a revolution.

The driving force for the rebellion and revolution in South Sudan is South Sudanese nationalism and the will to be free and independent. It is still primordial and vague, but it is there. It has only been shattered by Khartoum's policy of 'divide and rule' and subjected to serious tests by the experience of the ten years of southern regional government in Juba which made tribalism, sectionalism and regionalism[4] a strong counter force. Coming from a background of progressive political ideology to join the armed movement was a question of raising myself to the highest method of struggle where maximum sacrifice is required.

I underwent general and officers' training and graduated as a captain in the SPLA, became commander of Daniel Chwogo Task Force and went into combat. It was only unfortunate that my first combat exercise was my last one. I am however, happy that I have survived it in order to continue the struggle by 'other methods'. These other methods were difficult to come by given the situation in the Movement then. I was not given another assignment in spite of the fact that I was physically and intellectually fit to undertake any duty on behalf of the Movement. I found myself with others in a clandestine activity to raise the awareness of the people for effecting changes, reforms, democratisation, respect for human rights and civil liberties etc. The result was the heightening of our marginalisation and ostracisation in the Movement. Nevertheless, I refused to submit or accept the fate of becoming a 'semi retired veteran musing over the past'[54]. While the SPLM/A leadership did not see any use of an amputee like myself, since combat was the only preoccupation of the Movement then, I struggled to keep myself alive physically, psychologically and intellectually. I did not want to become a 'limping corpse' wasting away in Itang refugee camp where alcoholism was the only peaceful exit route out of political inaction, apathy and frustration which took grip of many intellectuals that joined the SPLM/A and who were lingering without deployment in the refugee camps. I migrated to the city looking for intellectual opportunities, and to re-establish my relation with the academia.

Thus, between September 1989 and August 1991, I was forced to suffer the indignity of having to look after my own personal affairs instead of what I had come out to do in the struggle for liberation. Nevertheless, I insisted on maintaining my revolutionary links with the people's cause. I knew it was a temporary situation which was bound to change sooner or latter. My revolutionary zeal and enthusiasm for participation in the activities of the Movement never grew grey hair. I must be honest and fair; it was not just Adwok in me making these decisions. I thought and still think I was inspired by something much deeper. In all my tribulations, I was reminded and inspired by those intelligent words of Mao Tse Tung that:

> ... When forced into a passive position through incorrect appraisal and disposition or through overwhelming pressure, a guerilla unit must strive to extricate itself. How this is done depends on the circumstances. In many cases, it is necessary to 'move away' ... To 'move away' is the principal method for getting out of a passive position and regaining initiative... [6].

These words kept ringing in my mind and they were a constant source of inspiration.

In order to change the sense of alienation and 'marginalisation' that I was forced into and suffered into, I used Mao's wisdom to move away from that passive position by exploiting the freedom and opportunity it created for me to engage myself in gainful employment, something which kept me alive intellectually, physically and spiritually. It was by relying on this dialectical way of thinking that I was able to survive and later regain my rightful place in the revolutionary struggle, in the SPLM/A. Short of that, surely, I would have, like many others, surrendered to the enemy or sought resettlement in other parts of the world. The temptation, coupled with other factors of real life, was great. It, however, took a long time and route to come back in high spirits and to contribute to the struggle by the 'other means'.

At the height of emotional stress, it is possible that one's mental faculties and capacity for objectivity become impaired. It is then that unprincipled alliances are struck. No human being is immune to such fits and I consider myself the weakest. I am highly sensitive and emotional and easily become victim to those who use my emotions for their sinister plans. When we agitated for democratic reforms in the SPLM/A, we believed some members of the High Command, with whom we had friendly relations, would join us in the struggle for reforms in the Movement. It was a simplicity that ignored social and class factors. It was out of this that I committed one of the gravest mistakes of my life - supporting the Nasir Declaration.

How the conspiracy began.

The SPLM/A as an organisation has a reputation for keeping its secrets. At one time this was a source of jealousy for some quarters outside it. Nevertheless, there were times when some information, especially from the higher echelons, leaked out forming occasional subject for gossip among the rank and file and other disgruntled people. For instance, it became an open secret in mid 1990 that there was a serious quarrel between Dr John Garang on the one hand, and Dr Riek Machar and Dr Lam Akol on the other hand, arising out of the insistence of the two engineers to force Dr John Garang to call a meeting of the High Command of which technically they were not members[7].

Dr Riek Machar had just come back from a working holiday which took him to east Africa and Europe. Having spent more than five years in the bush - western Upper Nile where he was zonal commander – he needed some rest and had to be flown out of Leer. Dr Lam Akol had then just been reassigned to the military front after spending three years as Director for External Relations Department of the Movement. The two engineers made a troublesome combination. Although the two were alternate members of the High Command, they considered themselves 'equals' of Dr John Garang and were more than ready, at least for Dr Lam Akol, to rub shoulders with him over political, organisational and other internal matters of the Movement. This was unusual in a military organisation like the SPLM/A. Dr Garang must have been highly surprised by this behaviour on the part of his officers. The fact that they were both PhD holders like him did not warrant such a behaviour which in the army is called insubordination that may lead to the court martial of the offender.

It was also an open secret that Dr Lam Akol, who in 1986 was somersaulted in the SPLM/A hierarchy (over and above many officers who had been in the Movement since 1983) and assigned the command of northern Upper Nile zone without undergoing military training and who had been favoured with comfortable assignments, had finally fallen out with Dr Garang because of his arrogance and fiery ambition. Many of these so-called open secrets in Movement filtered out as rumours. Rumours have a penchant for enriching themselves through addition and subtraction to the extent that the original story may be altered beyond recognition. Perhaps it must have been thought that posting Lam Akol to a military front would bring into focus some of these simmering contradictions and, hence, speed up their resolution. The Nasir coup and the subsequent developments must have vindicated these speculations.

By the middle of 1990, both Riek Machar and Lam Akol were posted in Northern Upper Nile. Riek was in Melut area where he carried out successful operations against the enemy. Lam Akol was in Maban area where he was almost captured by the enemy. Lam Akol's political and academic talents could not match well with his military and tactical knowledge. He was more of a political activist than a military officer and it is unfortunate that his skills and strength here did not compensate for other weaknesses. As an upstart military commander, he should have used his political and organisation skills to motivate his subordinates whose military skills could have compensated for his weaknesses. No, Lam Akol would not do that; he is rigidly single minded in whatever he decide to do, whether correct or wrong, and found it difficult to change. His near capture by the enemy storming out of Maban was due to the fact that the advance SPLA column, commanded by an officer not happy with Lam Akol's command, opened a bridge, so they say, which allowed the enemy troops to advance to his tactical headquarters.

In spite of all these bad feelings with one another, Dr John Garang still could send Lam Akol on some international errands for the Movement. In December 1990, Lam Akol was dispatched to Cairo to attend the meeting marking the establishment of the National Democratic Alliance - NDA. I got that information when I passed that afternoon through the SPLA office[8] to Debri Zeit where I lived with my family. However, that Lam Akol would call me was something I had not contemplated because I had not been on talking terms with him for quite sometimes owing to the manner he treated people, even his own colleagues, with contempt[9].

The car that came to pick me reached the house at about quarter past nine in the evening. I had just finish tutoring my children and we were preparing to go to sleep, when the gatekeeper came with a two lines note signed by Lam requesting me to come to see him in Addis Ababa.

There was commotion in the house, the people[10] there were quite reluctant to permit me to travel to Addis Ababa by night. They were worried because that was how late Joseph Oduho had been taken and arrested by SPLA on the 8 April 1988. I assured them that nothing was going to happen to me and that I would definitely be with them the following day.

The road to Addis Ababa was empty and made the driver speed like a jet. I sat in the front seat wondering what the contact with Dr Lam Akol for the first time in three years was going to be. My mind ran through all kinds of scenarios. 'He must be in serious trouble', I thought, 'and in that case, he should be looking for some support from me'. Lam Akol is a very pompous and a self sufficient person; his character is such that he will not look for one or anybody, unless he was in need or wanted some assistance. 'But what kind of assistance did he want from me and how would I deliver it', I thought to myself as the car cruised through the streets. All these thoughts were terminated by our sudden arrival at the gate of the guesthouse.

After exchanging greetings I could notice that Lam Akol was warm, so excited, in high spirits and behaved as if there was no problem between us. This artificial show was perhaps because I had accepted to come and the opportunity was now open for him to convince me to join him in his political adventure. Shortly after my arrival, we were left alone in the room to start our business.

My meeting with Lam Akol took almost three hours before we finally went to sleep. He did not beat around the bush, as he wanted his point brought home immediately. 'Garang has taken us all for a ride. He has proved to be a dictator. Time has come that he must be told that enough is enough', he emphasised and continued to talk as I listened carefully to his rhetoric, debating in my mind what serious rift must have occurred between the two men to warrant Lam Akol's venom against Garang; I wondered whether all his descriptions of Garang did not also apply to Lam Akol himself.

Knowing how eccentric Lam Akol is and his attitude of not listening to others, a fact that alienated many of his friend and colleagues both in school and elsewhere, I held my peace listening to his sermon. However, I could sense from his facial expression that something haunted him. He must have feared that in case I did not support him, I could divulge all that he was telling me to the SPLM/A authorities. Dr Lam Akol is a very discreet person who prefers to do his things alone without witnesses. So I had to assure him that he could count on me that most of what we were going to discuss would remain within our chests.

When he finished talking, I took my turn.

'I am happy that you have come to vindicate what we were talking about over the years and have proved for yourself', I said. 'No Movement can progress without organisation, without internal democracy, a defined political ideology and direction and without respect for civil liberties and human rights including the right to life. But Lam you must be careful. Dr Garang is very powerful at the moment and so powerful that he can break your neck now and nobody will dare to question him. Those who would have questioned him in any eventuality are those whom you have alienated through your own arrogance. You have scattered the forces that you could have counted on in the eventuality of confrontation with Garang; who will not hesitate to crush a weakling like you if you showed dissidence, and that will definitely add to his strength. After the arrest and detention of Kerubino and Arok, there is nobody in the SPLA who can dare to challenge Garang. The only person I see who can pose a challenge to Garang is Dr Riek Machar and for obvious reasons. He can put together a large Nuer following, he has managed to unite and organise them, he is a good SPLA commander and has scored victories against the enemy; he, unlike you, has no problems with the intellectuals and officers in the SPLA and so in my opinion if there is a movement for reforms of the SPLM/A, I see him the only person who can or should be in the centre of things,' I continued to tell him.

'Riek is weak politically, how can he lead such a movement?' Lam Akol interjected.

'Yes, he is weak politically, that I know', I replied. 'But leaders are made by people. Nobody is born a leader and I see that Riek has some qualities of leadership which in my opinion should only be assisted to develop them'[11].

Lam was not pleased with my opinion. What he had expected was that I would give him unqualified support based on ethnic solidarity. However, before we parted, I advise him that if he was seriously contemplating a political or military move against Garang, he needed first to mobilise and consolidate the support of the Shilluks behind him, and in that respect I would assist him in creating the necessary conditions for reconciliation with many of the officers and men he had alienated when he was zonal commander of northern Upper Nile. Dr Lam Akol's rigid, sometimes mechanical, leadership methods, coupled with his arrogance and lack of concern for the feelings of others, have put him at odds with many people who have done business with him.

This made his deployment as zonal commander of the Shilluk area (1987 -1988) an utter failure. He failed to build himself a political base in his own homeland. Failed to win over the Reth of the Shilluks who would have made it easy for him to mobilise the Shilluk youth and their recruitment into the SPLA. Dr Lam Akol bitterly disagreed with Reth Ayang over the way the SPLA soldiers were treating the civilian population; looting their food, raping their women and girls and stealing their livestock. As a Shilluk himself, he should have had respect for the Shilluk tradition which revered the king. One day, while Reth Ayang Kur Nyidhok was travelling from his home in Owikyel to Kodok (a government garrison), Lam Akol ordered that the king should be ambushed, returned to his home and killed if he resisted. The Shilluk officers and men in the ambush refused to execute Lam Akol's order and the Reth went to Kodok. However, the damage had already been down. This was an incident that sent many Shilluk soldiers deserting their positions and marked the mass migration of the Shilluk civilian population of 'Gar' to northern Sudan. Indeed, later in 1988, Reth Ayang was still apprehensive about the SPLA and it took him time to change his attitude. When the late Cdr Martin Manyiel came to take over the command of the area from Dr Lam Akol, Reth Ayang asked whether Cdr Manyiel hailed from the same SPLA as Dr Lam Akol. Of course there was a big difference. As a professional army officer; Martin Manyiel was more courteous, he was well versed in management of his troops and their affairs.

At that material time, the idea was to support in unequivocal terms any efforts towards the democratic reforms and democratisation in the SPLM/A. It was also more of a question of building enough pressure on Dr John Garang to accept the demand for these reforms in order to build a strong Movement, i.e. to make the SPLM a genuine national liberation movement, and the SPLA a genuine people's army. This was an enormous task which involved many sacrifices and much longer planning and perseverance. I did not realise that Dr Lam Akol wanted a quick result which bordered on nothing short of destroying the Movement if it became difficult to remove Garang from power. Dr Lam Akol knew there was a general dissatisfaction and opposition within the rank and file of the Movement and he saw himself as well placed to lead it. For this reason, he downplayed the qualities of Dr Riek Machar in order to tilt the balance in his own favour.

Challenging the leadership of Dr John Garang at that time was not an easy task. In the final analysis, it meant a military confrontation with him. In this respect, it was Riek Machar who had a military command capable of resisting Garang. Lam Akol, therefore, acquiesced to my suggestions and immediately started courting Riek Machar although in the SPLM/A hierarchy Riek Machar was senior to Lam Akol. Dazzled with the possibility of becoming the leader of South Sudan, and aware that he would command the support of the Nuers in the contest for the leadership of the South, Riek Machar was persuaded to join this political adventure to oust Dr John Garang from the leadership of the Movement. The duo shuffled their cards and Riek Machar became the leader of the clandestine move not to reform and democratise the SPLM/A, but to oust Garang from the leadership of the Movement.

Riek Machar had harboured some wild illusions that he was destined by some divine will to lead the people of South Sudan. This is based on nothing but a legend that the Nuer prophet, Ngundeng, is said to have prophesied that a leader of South Sudan would come from the descendants of Teny-Dhurgon[12]. Authentic versions of the legend don't mention anything of Riek Machar being the leader of the South although the legend is told and retold on a version palatable to Riek's ego. On the contrary, it appears that Ngundeng was very angry with Teny, Riek's grandfather. He had come to visit the prophet, and, as custom, he had to bring some bulls for the prophet. Teny hid the rest of the bulls in Gawaar and came with only one bull to report to the prophet who by then was in Waat (Lou area). The prophet knew Teny was lying and named him 'Dhurgon' literally meaning a liar.

The beginning of 1991 was not a very good time for the regime of Mengistu Haile Mariam. It was a time the Ethiopian army was suffering serious defeats everywhere at the hands of the rebel groups, chiefly the EPLF and the EPRDF. Garrisons fell to the rebels one after the other, especially in the western front, where whole battalions and divisions surrendered without firing a bullet. In what looked like mock solidarity with Mengistu, the SPLA sent some battalions into action against the OLF and GPLM in the area of Assossa which turned out to be a fiasco. The military situation in Ethiopia was deteriorating so fast that there was no way the SPLA would have changed it in favour of Mengistu.

In March, I paid a visit to Itang refugee camp at the height of mobilisation to defend the western front. The SPLA commanders were swearing that what happen in Assossa[13] in 1990, whereby thousand of refugees were massacred by a joint Sudanese army, OLF and GPLM, in the wake of their recapture of Kurmuk would not be repeated in Itang and Piny-udo refugee camps. President Mengistu had just finished his tour of the Gambella region to assess the situation for himself. The writing on the wall was very clear the regime was about to crumble.

A discussion with the Gambella regional secretary of the Ethiopian Workers Party revealed something which made me believe that a conspiracy was brewing against the SPLM/A leadership. I was informed that the political leadership of Ethiopia was convinced that Dr John Garang de Mabior was not a true 'comrade' and ally of the Ethiopian Regime. He had taken them for a long ride. In fact, the party secretary was so bitter with Dr John Garang that I felt very embarrassed.

Mr Thowath Pal is an Ethiopian Nuer hailing from Lare. He was a secondary school drop out, and was a captain in the security/intelligence unit of the army. He was die-hard supporter of the regime for obvious reasons. But there was something else; he was a Nuer and the regime used him or he used the regime's power to suppress the Anyuak people, the second largest and politically dominant ethnic group in Gambella, forcing many of them into opposition against the regime. During our discussion, he use a language that smacked of Lam Akol's verbiage. I knew for sure that the Nuer factor was at work. Riek Machar is a Nuer and definitely the Ethiopian Nuers would support his bid for leadership in South Sudan. A ground was now being prepared for ousting Dr John Garang with the help of the Ethiopian authorities through Mr Thowath Pal[14]. I became interested in knowing more, but his analysis would not go further than that Garang had betrayed the confidence of the Ethiopian people and that he was a dictator oppressing his own people.

The events in Gambella would have been very dramatic and sad had the regime of Mengistu not fallen in time. It was clear that Riek Machar and Lam Akol had convinced Thowath and the local Nuer administration of the Gambella region that Garang must be overthrown and the way to do it was to have him arrested with the assistance of the Ethiopian army if he came to Gambella. There were people in the regime who were definitely not happy with the SPLM/A and Dr Garang.

After the fall of the Mengistu regime, Lam Akol produced a document raised some valid issues and reflected approximately the situation in the Movement then. It had nothing new because this was exactly what the people were talking about. In any case, as an alternate member of the highest political military organ of the Movement, nothing prevented Lam Akol from raising all these issues in a memorandum to his colleagues, especially at a time when the focus of everybody was how to maintain the existence of the SPLM/A after losing its rear bases in Ethiopia. This document, like its sister document 'Why Garang Must Go Now', which circulated immediately before the coup announcement was meant really to discredit the SPLM/A leadership in the person of Dr John Garang. For instance, the document starts off as follows:

> ... The political upheavals and convulsions in Ethiopia that led to the demise and collapse of the regime of Mengistu Haile Mariam late this May .... Not only triggered off major and dramatic changes in the alignment and balance of forces in the region- Horn of Africa - but has set in motion deep and profound socio-political and military revulsion for the SPLM/SPLA ...

The document goes on to give reasons for this revulsion as the total dependence of the SPLM/A on the Ethiopian regime and dictatorial leadership Garang provided in the 'last eight years', and continues:

> ... In this context, the geo-political changes, brought about by the events in Ethiopia, do not only pose as a reverse or setback in the political and military sense but a blessing in disguise for the SPLM/A in that it has brought to the fore some of the basic and fundamental internal contradictions whose resolution are crucial for the survival and viability of the SPLM/A and its forward progress...

Yes, a crisis in the Ethiopian regime was definitely bound to have repercussions on the internal situation in the SPLM/A. But it was sheer opportunism, one that borders on treason, for a leader to circulate such literature in a clandestine manner when he had the opportunity to discuss it with his colleagues in the High Command. In eloquent verbosity the document comes to the conclusion that:

> ... There can be no way for fundamental changes and democratisation of the movement as long as Garang retains the leadership of this popular movement. The only clear and straightforward sensible way out of this impasse is for Dr John Garang to resign unconditionally and perhaps honourably if he elects to do on his own accord. Otherwise, Garang has reached the terminal stage of his megalomania and has been tolerated too much and for too long...

The objective, therefore, of the exercise was really not to reform the Movement as many of us had wanted and worked for. In the plan of Riek and Lam Akol, the dice was already cast. Later, it became evident in their other document 'Why Garang must go now', which appeared a few weeks before the Nasir Declaration. Hence, according to the logic of Lam Akol's initial document, the events in Ethiopia for reform supposedly provided the impetus for internal changes in the SPLM/A. It did not mention the struggles which had been going on inside the Movement long before he had fallen out with Dr John Garang.

This enlivened opportunism based on was two false readings of the situation in the Movement. The first was that, having lost external support as a result of the demise of the Ethiopia regime, and having lost its bases in western Ethiopia, the SPLM/A was doomed and was not going to survive. That is why the importance of external resources and the support of Mengistu were emphasised in the document, implying that the SPLM/A could not survive without external support.

The second false reading was that Riek Machar and Lam Akol believed that, given the widespread discontent and dissatisfaction with the leadership among the rank and file, and because of the general contradictions in the Movement, any move against the leadership of Dr John Garang was going to translate itself in an uprising against him. The two men were convinced that their anti-Garang plot would carry the support of each and every SPLA officer and man.

Immediately after the sudden withdrawal from western Ethiopia, the SPLM/A leadership was faced with a very serious political, military and humanitarian situation, which no patriot should have exploited for personal benefits. The resettlement of the returnees, and the mobilisation for international humanitarian assistance to relieve them was not an easy task. The Sudan government air force was bombing the camps for the returnees in the Sobat basin area.

The SPLA had not reorganised itself in order to meet any threat from the enemy which, of course, wanted to take advantage of the situation. Indeed Omer el Beshir had announced over radio Omdurman in June 1991 that it was just a 'matter of a few weeks and SPLA will be finished'. This was a time every patriot should have rededicated himself to the political and military survival of the Movement. As a matter of fact, many of the officers, including some members of the High Command who had been in contact with Riek Machar and Lam Akol, changed their minds and argued that the question of the leadership was not the most urgent problem in the wake of the new political and military situation in the Movement. It appeared that it was not the SPLM/A which was doomed on account of losing its bases in western Ethiopia, but it was the move itself to change the leadership of the Movement which was doomed to failure. Perhaps Riek and Lam Akol did not realise that under such circumstances real patriots behave differently and they may suppress or postpone resolving the contradiction to a later date in order to secure their mutual survival.

When the intentions of Dr Riek Machar and Dr Lam Akol through their publication and open agitation in Itang and Gambella became clear, many of those who initially supported the idea were taken aback. The general intelligence service (GIS) men of the SPLA were following them and were reporting these subversive activities to the SPLM/A leadership. Such were too high the risks involved in this anti-Garang adventure that many, under the perceived weight of its consequences, dissociated themselves. Those who stuck with the group were either officers who had been disgruntled by lack of promotion in the hierarchy. As mentioned earlier, many officers in the SPLA were more preoccupied with hierarchies and ranks than their functions.

Thus, there were those who had never been to the frontline, but wanted their names appearing in the officers' list with all its implications. There were also those self-seekers who wanted a space for self-aggrandizement. There were those wanted to use the opportunity for personal vendetta or grievances. A case in point is that of a certain medical doctor who was deeply incensed by his being transferred from a certain vantage point to another location. The losing of the few privileges he was enjoying was reason enough for him to declare his membership of the Nasir faction. These were the type of people who ended up being staunch supporters of Lam Akol.

As it turned out later, many of the officers and men of the SPLM/A, apart from those who out of tribal solidarity supported the Nasir coup, did so out of fear for their lives or had their vendetta against the leadership of Dr John Garang or out of sheer opportunism. Many of them defected back to SPLM/A. As a result, the mobilisation for the support of the coup failed. This explains why the coup itself could not expand and gain support outside the Nuer and Shilluk districts in Upper Nile. The Equatorians who joined to support the Nasir faction or the SPLM/A - United in 1992 and 1993 did so out frustration with the SPLA's prosecution of the war in east bank Equatoria. Many of them have since deserted the rank and file of the SPLA and have gone back to their villages in the mountains.

The Nasir Declaration, 28 August 1991

August 28th 1991 will go down in the history of South Sudan as the most important single day when the people's aspiration for freedom and justice suffered a serious blow at the hands of its own sons. The Movement's weakest moment was turned into an incentive for power struggle by some of its ablest sons. It was a power struggle that was driven by wishful thinking and possible encouragement by the enemy rather than meticulous political and social engineering. The radio message sent by Dr Riek Machar to all SPLA units was done without prior knowledge or consent of the targeted units. It was made in the ' hope' that those dissatisfied with Garang's leadership would join and support the coup.

This was a funny way of implementing a military coup leave alone the fact that the SPLM/A, in spite of its growth and strength was still a guerilla force without a permanent base or seat which would have been targeted by the coup plotters like in a conventional military coup. The coup would have been effective only if the coup plotters had succeeded in apprehending Garang and his headquarters. Had the announcement also come when Garang was in Europe and America during the months of June and July, perhaps they would have succeeded in creating confusion among the troops and it would have been possible that some in the High Command, who had initially promised their support, would have gone in with the coup leaders.

However, there was no immediate response from the SPLA units to the radio message sent on 28 August, except understandably from the western Upper Nile zone (Bentiu), where Riek Machar hails from and where, until July 1989, he was zonal commander. It cannot be said that the SPLA radio operators had been ordered by Garang not to receive the message of Riek Machar[16]. The message was received, but what happened is that many of the units were taken by surprise; they were being informed for the first time. A military coup could only be successful if the prospective participants and supporters had seen aware well in advance. This was not the case. Riek Machar and Lam Akol had expected a spontaneous uprising against Garang because, as they maintained, he was a dictator and the ground in the Movement was fertile for his removal.

That was the most unlikely way of garnering support for a coup under the circumstances. The coup came at a time when many SPLA officers and men were still going to their new areas of deployment and, even if there were officers and men who might have supported Riek and Lam in the preparatory days, there was no way they would have participated because they were either still fresh in their new locations or had not arrived. So this could have been a contributory factor for the lack of response and support for the coup. At least there should have been a feed back from the units before the coup announcement to ascertain whether or not the supporters were in place and what kind of support was there to enable the coup to be declared.

The only preparations for the coup that seemed to have been made by the leaders in Nasir was the consultation they made with the NIF government. In August 1991, before announcing the coup, Riek Machar made sure first to send commander James Biel Jok to Malakal garrison, Mr Gatluak Deng, to brief the NIF governor for Upper Nile State and the commander of Malakal garrison about the plan and to get assurances of the NIF support. The government's response was prompt and positive and, therefore, the coup was declared. The NIF government accepted to supply military logistics in the form of ammunition[17], and turn over the command of the Anya-nya 2 and government militia to the Nasir leaders. This comes out forcefully in point no. 13 of the document 'Why Garang must go now'.

The coup leaders also contacted the outside world to enlist international support and publicity for the Nasir Declaration. Dr Lam Akol knew very well that the coup had not garnered sufficient support and that if it did not succeed in other parts of the South, it must succeed abroad. He, therefore, paid more attention to the external propaganda. Helped by the army of relief and humanitarian workers who flew in and out of Nasir, Dr Lam Akol, while in Nasir, was able to send and receive mail from Europe, America and other parts of the world. To illustrate this point I reproduce here the letter that Dr Lam Akol wrote to me while I was in Berlin, Germany, in August 1991. It reads:

Nasir
6/8/91

Dear Gindwong (Peter Adwok)

I hope you are doing fine. Rebecca brought your envelope containing the two documents but there was no letter from you; much to my disappointment. The documents are very much appreciated.

Following the last developments in Ethiopia, events here in the field have been moving very fast. The struggle for democracy within the Movement has intensified and we have decided to jettison Garang out of the leadership of our Movement. The necessary steps on the ground have been undertaken and it will not be long before the whole thing gets into the open. I had wanted to write to you earlier but when Rebecca came on 2/7/91 she did not have your address in Germany.

I, however, sent to Dr Peter Nyot Kok a document entitled 'Why Garang must go now'. The letter to Nyot should have been posted to him from England in the last week of July. I have specifically asked him to share it with you. So if you have not yet received a copy it must be on the way. On your side you can send him a copy of our 'Towards the organisation of the SPLM'.

Garang has been exploiting the nationalism of our people for his parochial ends. It is time to tell him enough is enough. Dictators of his ilk learn the hardest way. Since the fall of Mengistu up to the time of writing Garang never set foot into Southern Sudan. As usual he is trying to play tricks. Recently he secretly summoned his stooges William Nyuon and Salva Kiir to Nairobi where they held secret meetings. The plan they came up with was to isolate us from our forces and then arrest us (Dr. RIEK MACHAR, Gordon Kong and myself). To execute the plan he called for a meeting of the High Command in Kidepo on 21/8/91 and the three of us are to be picked up by a plane from Nasir to Kapoeta. There and then we will be arrested; a desperate plan. Needless to say we will not be fooled. The three of us and Martin Manyiel are the members of the so-called High Command they identify with opposition and the discontent now simmering in the rank and file. Martin is still in Nairobi and we have not heard from him since 3/7/91. Whether his exclusion from detention is because he is commanding no troops now or for another reason I do not know. Try your best to locate him.

The other point of paramount importance is the question of contacting our people inside towns in Sudan and those abroad. Lt. Col. Gatluak Deng, the Governor of Upper Nile, is said to be in Germany for medical treatment. If he is still there find him out and talk to him frankly in the spirit of the document and tell him that the three of us have asked you to contact him. We know him very well so do not feel inhibited.

Best of wishes and regards.

(Signed)
Lam Akol

From this letter, which I have to reproduce in full to put the record straight, it is obvious the relationship between the group in Nasir and the NIF regime was well established. The assertion that 'we know him very well do not feel inhibited', was not a joke. In their preparation for the coup, both Riek and Lam had made extensive contacts and that is why they were so confident.

A few days later after receiving this letter, on 30 August, BBC Focus on Africa carried the news of the coup in Nasir. That Garang had been overthrown by the group of three commanders in Nasir was efficaciously orchestrated to capture the headlines. This is what initially gave the coup a boost - external factors conspiring to consolidate, into permanent split in the ranks and file of the SPLM/A and the establishment of the Nasir faction, what would have been an isolated political stratagem. It was a kind of a phenomenon in which the cause had to catch up with its effects. But what Lam Akol mentioned and emphasised in his letter as the 'necessary steps on the ground have been undertaken' turned out to be a farce and a deceitful manoeuvre to draw the people into his conspiracy. Perhaps what he really meant must have been the steps undertaken jointly with the NIF regime for the complete destruction of the SPLM/A.

In fact, the coup plot had been discovered earlier and, definitely, the leadership had taken precautionary measures. Their advances to some Shilluk and Nuer officers, most of whom were in the SPLM/A intelligence organisation and were already deployed in east bank Equatoria, to join the adventure were rebuffed. They were properly advised against this adventure. This raised a lot of worries in both Riek Machar and Lam Akol, who started to panic. This explains the hurry to announce the coup without a feed back from some of their supporters in the military front. In itself, it was a kind of blackmail for some of the officers with whom they had contacts before the coup. For instance, in the letter, Dr. Lam states that they had not heard from Cdr Martin Manyiel, which proves the point that they should not have declared the coup without examining the balance of forces between themselves in Nasir and the rest of SPLA. In fact, it was a malicious act arising out a sort of convoluted logic that 'he who has had himself soaked should now swim'. All the correspondence to the people abroad was meant to clear their conscience disturbed now that the conspiracy had been uncovered.

Without the BBC announcement and the international interest in the Nasir Declaration it aroused, especially over the question of human rights and 'child soldier', many people in South Sudan, including SPLA officers and men not directly involved in intelligence and security matters, and the world at large, would not have heard about the coup. They would have learnt of it after much time had elapsed. Therefore, it is clear the Nasir coup makers had not made enough political preparations to win popular support within the SPLA and the people of South Sudan. Although there were divisions within every SPLA unit over the Declaration against Garang, the most decisive factor in any military action is not the general discontent but the factor of the unit commander. This means that unless the officers and the NCOs have been sufficiently politicised and their support mobilised, there is no way a military unit can engage in a coup plot. That is why some of the units under the command of Riek and Lam Akol in Maban, Shilluk Mid West, Pan Aru and many other units, did not support the Nasir Declaration.

The coup endured more due to external factors than to internal support. That is why it failed to achieve its objective immediately. For instance, in Agworo, the headquarters of north west Upper Nile zone, Captain Marconi Okuch Aba attacked and overtook the command from alternate commander Akwoc Mayong on 4 September because Akwoc had inclinations towards the coup leaders. The officers and men in Maban area, under the immediate command of Lam Akol, refused to take orders from him and they withdrew to the Shilluk Mid West. In Pariang, Captain Mayik Jaw arrested the area commander and some of the officers who had shown some signs of support for the coup. In Lou area (Waat and Akobo), the support for the coup picked up slowly as result of the tribal appeal made by Riek Machar and that is how

Waat and Akobo belatedly came under the command of the coup leaders on 10 and 15 September, respectively.

The international humanitarian intervention and the relief operations in the Sobat river basin undertaken by the Operation Life Sudan and a host of NGOs which flocked there to relieve the returnees from Ethiopia assisted the coup leaders to consolidate their move. The relief planes and personnel flying in and out of Nasir became the mailbag for the coup leaders. Much of the information flowing in and out of Nasir then would not have been possible without the relief planes and personnel, some of who were very sympathetic to the political cause espoused by the coup leaders who also exploited this opportunity to the maximum.

For instance, Riek Machar's marriage to a British relief worker was calculated to exploit her potential among the relief community. This bore fruits immediately. The question of human rights was high on the agenda of the international community. The late Emma McCune, Dr Riek Machar's wife, who worked for Street Kids International, used her position she used to depict the SPLA's 'Face Foundation'[17] as a kind of child labour project. This together with the unanswered question of the 'unaccompanied minors' in Pochalla and Nasir provoked the visit of the French minister Kuchnar to Pochalla, coinciding with the BBC announcement. All these moves were intended to put the SPLM/A and its leader Dr John Garang de Mabior in a bad publicity light which in turn made the Nasir coup leaders an alternative leadership for the SPLM/A.

The BBC announcement of the coup caused mixed reactions. There were those who genuinely believed that the internal contradiction should not lead to a split and placed their good auspices in the service of reconciliation. The 'People for Peace in Africa', a church based peace group in Nairobi; the former Permanent Secretary in the Ministry of Foreign Affairs and International Cooperation, Mr Bathuel Kiplagat; the National Council of Churches of Kenya; the New Sudan Council of Churches; a group of concerned South Sudanese meeting in Adare, Ireland, and many other individuals, worked diligently to prevent a split in the SPLM/A. It was recognised that there could be genuine reasons for the coup but the coup itself was not a solution. It was, therefore, imperative for the two sides sit down and negotiate a reconciliation.

There was nothing wrong or outrageous in reconciling two opposed groups and all the efforts and resources that were made available for this process were in good faith. But this, ironically, resulted in the very opposite of what the peace mediators wanted. It created a de facto recognition of the coup and consolidated the split. This happened in a way which nobody ever contemplated in the rush for reconciliation of the SPLM/A factions. The peace and reconciliation talks were scheduled to take place in Nairobi which meant the two SPLM/A factions had to send their delegations to that city. The 'People for Peace in Africa' made the necessary arrangements for bringing the delegations to Nairobi. The Nasir delegation led by the architect of the coup and Secretary for External Affairs and Peace in the Interim National Executive Committee, Cdr Lam Akol, arrived Nairobi on 29 September and was accommodated in Hotel PanAfrique.

The 'Nairobi Peace and Reconciliation Talks', as they were later known, did not take off until 20 November, almost two months after the arrival of the Nasir group. This was perhaps one of the tactical mistakes committed by the mainstream SPLM/A. They had not realised that any procrastination worked in favour of the Nasir group. Once mediation was accepted, any delay in the convening of talks worked exactly in favour of the Nasir faction. It enabled them to make the necessary political and diplomatic contacts in the Kenyan capital. Despite the failure of the coup, Dr Lam Akol got an opportunity to fight Garang by political and diplomatic means[18].

He almost succeeded in this diplomatic offensive with the financial assistance of the NIF siphoned through Tiny Rowland. During this long period of stay in Nairobi, Lam Akol was also able to establish contacts with the NIF government in a place outside the country. A delegation led by Dr Ali el Hag Mohammed came to Nairobi in October, specifically to meet with LamAkol. It was in this meeting that they agreed to further consolidate the military cooperation started in the field. Mr Taban Deng Gai was sent to Khartoum by air to supervise the delivery of the ammunition and armament.

Furthermore, the delay in the peace talks on account of SPLM/A mainstream delegation having not arrived put the Nasir group in a better publicity light. They were now projected as ready for peace and reconciliation while the SPLM/A was accused of war mongering, especially after the SPLA attack and capture of Adok and Leer in western Upper Nile in early November. Many in the NGOs community and the rest of the world changed their attitude towards the SPLM/A only after the collaboration between the Nasir faction and the NIF, especially its military aspects which resulted in massive humanitarian disruption and human rights abuses unprecedented before in SPLA-controlled areas became too obvious to ignore or contradict. The Nasir move to oust Dr Garang from the leadership of the SPLM/A, therefore, flopped, giving rise to the internecine fratricidal war in the South which lasted until 1995.

The creeping revolution and the SPLA in fighting

The Nasir coup leaders behaved as if they had blackmailed the people of South Sudan. Either they got the support they wanted to overthrow Dr John Garang or else they would unleash a reign of terror and lawlessness in the South. Whether these were orders from Riek Machar or not, many summary executions of Dinka officers and men who did not support the coup, were carried out in all the areas that fell under the control of Riek Machar. Some SPLA commanders reciprocated and ordered the cold-blooded murder of Nuer and Shilluk officers and men found by the coup in Equatoria and Bahr el Ghazal. Dinka areas bordering Nuerland were raided and people, especially the elderly, were killed, cattle looted, women and children abducted in the same manner the Murahalieen did in northern Bahr el Ghazal.

In September 1991, when Ayod, Waat and Akobo came under his control, Riek Machar ordered a large contingent of troops made up of his SPLA elements of Anya-nya 2 from Dolieb Hill and heavily armed Nuer civilians - Jiech Mabor, or white army, mainly from Lou and Gawaar, to invade Bor and Kongor districts. In the thinking of Dr Riek Machar, Garang could be defeated either by destroying his home area or by destroying his SPLA troops. Initially, the involvement of the armed civilians was due to the fact that he did not have enough forces, but it was also to whet their appetite for wealth -Dinka cattle, women and children captives. As a result, thousands of people perished directly or indirectly due to secondary causes of hunger and disease, thousands of heads of cattle looted, hundreds of women and children abducted, and as many as tens of thousands displaced.

The use of 'Jiech Mabor' for operations against the SPLA in Bor area had serious difficulties. After this looting spree, there now arose the need to take the loot back home in Nuerlan. Since they obeyed no military orders, the marauding forces decided to return to central Upper Nile falling short of pursuing Riek Machar's objective of capturing Torit, the presumed SPLA headquarters from where Garang was said to be issuing orders.

Nothing can demonstrate the devastation of Bor area more than a story told by one of the Nasir forces officers who witnessed the return of the Anya-nya 2 to Dolieb Hill and the way they distributed their loot. When the news of the destruction of Bor reached Malakal, the Bor Dinka officials in the town organised themselves to rescue the women and children who had been abducted and to return them to their relatives through negotiations with the leaders of Anya-nya 2. But as soon as the rescue team arrived at Dohlieb Hill as agreed, one young girl, already married by one Nuer officer, in a dramatic show of anger, took exception of this and refused to go with her relative. She had this to say:

> ... My father, mother and sisters were murdered in front of me. The man who killed my relatives was himself killed by the man who has now taken me his wife. The Nuers captured me because they have power. He who wants to take me back can only do so by force and nothing more...

Until the Waat meeting of the Nasir faction leaders in December 1992, and even up to September 1994, during the Akobo conference, many of the abducted women and children were still being traced by their relatives in parts of Lou and Gawaar areas. The conference was informed that some of the abductors were refusing to hand over their captured women and children, especially the girls, some of whom had already been married. The devastation of Bor and Kongor was almost total and the civilians who survived had to trek many hundred of kilometers into Equatoria for safety where they established camps for the 'displaced people' with the assistance of the international community.

The struggle to defeat the SPLA could not have been the grand reason for staging the coup. Riek Machar had to bluff the people of South Sudan by pretending to mobilise the Nuer population for the capture of Malakal. A comprehensive plan was laid down in which Malakal was to be attacked and captured from the 'Arabs'. Riek used to tell anybody visiting his headquarters in Ketbek, near Nasir, that he had made agreement with the NIF governor of Upper Nile, Lt. Col. Gatluak Deng that the police, prison warders, wildlife forces and southern elements in the Sudanese army would participate in the attack and capture of Malakal. The time for the operations was set to be just after the beginning of the rains in July 1992. The spiritual leader for the Bor expedition, Mr. Gatkek Wutnyang was summoned back to Nasir to participate in the military preparations and planning. The Jikany people were told that Gatluak Deng was their son and they should support him because they stood to benefit when the 'Jelaba' were chased away from Malakal.

However, the supposed attack on Malakal was, in fact, a diversionary ploy designed to play with the minds of the Nuers. In reality, Riek Machar had no intention of attacking or capturing Malakal; he did not know how to explain this apparent change of his mind to the people. Once the Frankfurt Agreement was signed with the NIF regime, coupled with the failure of Dr Lam Akol to secure military supplies, any military action against the NIF government was out of question. This wheeling and dealing precipitated a crisis with the Jikany who thought the Malakal operation was being put off because it was they who would have benefited from its success. In the course of time, Wutnyang became bored by idleness in Nasir and so he led an offensive against the GPLM government in Gambella, burning down Itang and Anyuak villages on the way before he was repulsed back by the EPRDF force.

This did not prevent the spiritual leader from pursuing the agenda of capturing Malakal, even when Riek Machar had shown a complete reluctance. In October 1992, Wutnyang with his 'Jiech Mabor' attacked and captured parts of Malakal before being repulsed back by the army. Emboldened by the Wutnyang's attack, Riek Machar ordered a fresh attack by his troops and elements of Anya-nya 2 in November, resulting in a disaster.

Riek Machar's leadership methods did not depart much from Garang's methods, if not worse. He perfected the use of lies and disinformation as weapons for political survival. Thus, while he engaged the minds of his supporters in the Malakal project, he was secretly piecing together another expedition force to be sent to Equatoria. Though Riek Machar was convinced that there was no way he would defeat the SPLA and take over the leadership from Dr John Garang, the strategic alliance with the NIF rekindled his whims and dreams of becoming the leader of South Sudan. The force he pieced together in Nasir, christened 'Block Busters', was, therefore, part of the implementation of the Frankfurt Agreement signed on 25 January, 1992 by Dr Lam Akol and Dr Ali el Hag Mohammed. In fact, this agreement was a formalisation of collaboration between the Nasir faction and the NIF government that started in Nairobi in October 1991 when A/Cdr Taban Deng Gai was dispatched to Khartoum to procure military logistics in the wake of the inter-SPLA fighting in central and western Upper Nile.

Taban's mission was to go and meet President Beshir personally on Riek's behalf and to seek his support both militarily and financially. A/Cdr Taban, after being debriefed by President Beshir, Dr Hassan Al Turabi and army generals in the General Headquarters in Khartoum, was flown to Malakal in an Antenov plane which was put at his own disposal for operations against SPLA forces. His first trip was to Leer and Duar in western Upper Nile where ammunition was air-dropped. Taban Deng was on board the Antenov with a long-range communication radio set through which he maintained contact with the forces being supplied on the ground and, most importantly, with Dr Riek Machar, the leader of the coup, who monitored the operations from Ketbek near Nasir town. The Nasir forces using the ammunition air-dropped by A/Cdr Taban Deng from Sudan Army Antenov plane repulsed Cdr William Nyuon of SPLA who commanded an attack on Adok and Leer. Commander William Nyuon and his forces were forced to withdraw to the Yirol area of Bahr el Ghazal. It was at this time that forces from Waat, Ayod, Akobo and Nasir were ordered by Dr Riek Machar to launch their attack into Bor area after they had received loads of ammunition from the Sudan army. The internecine fighting had begun in earnest.

The 'Block Busters' were commissioned and flagged off from Nasir in June 1992. This was against the background of some bitter disputes with the spiritual leader Wutnyang and the Jikany people who did not see any logic of fighting in Equatoria. Riek Machar sent off his forces to fight SPLA in Equatoria at a time when the Nairobi Peace Group, who had gone to meet the two leaders over the formation of one SPLM/A delegation to the Abuja peace talks brokered by Nigerian President Ibrahim Babangida, depicted him as conciliatory dove because he accepted their proposal while Garang was portrayed as a hawk because he rejected the idea of a joint delegation. The SPLM/A had genuine reasons for rejecting the idea of a joint delegation. This is because, apart from the inter-SPLA fighting, the Nasir faction was busy facilitating the movement of the government forces through the areas it purported to be controlling. For instance, in April- May 1992, when the government military convoy broke out from Malakal south-wards through Nasir faction-controlled areas to recapture towns held by SPLA, Riek Machar made no effort to stop it though he sent misleading information to Nairobi claiming that the convoy had fought in Chuilbuong and Magough.

The other objective the 'Block Busters' was to lend support to Cdr William Nyuon Bany whom Dr Lam Akol and the NIF government had tried to persuade to defect from the SPLM/A. The contacts were started in Nairobi and then completed in Abuja exploiting Cdr William's weakness for money and other material incentives. By luring him out of the SPLM/A, the Nasir leaders and the NIF believed they had inflicted a final death blow to the SPLA. This exposed the half-heartedness of the Nasir leaders over the formation of only one delegation to negotiate with the NIF government.

The SPLA in-fighting played havoc with the lives of the people of South Sudan as well as with their destiny. The fundamental issues of liberation were eclipsed behind military grandeur of the combatants. But in all this Riek Machar and the Nasir leaders carry the blame for having started something whose negative implications they did not envisage. There is a basic fault with Riek Machar's logic. The objective of the coup was to wrest the leadership of the SPLM/A from Dr Garang. That meant that the survival of the Movement was equally important to Riek Machar. But, having failed to oust Garang, he then turned around to work with the common enemy for the destruction of the SPLM/A.

Pig-headed obstinacy and insistence on his position would have been permissible only if the South was an independent country and the main issue was an internal power struggle between the leader of such country. But even so, there are times when national interest takes precedence over narrow party objectives. It was more pertinent in the situation where the immediate military confrontation with the NIF regime had not yet been resolved. The contradiction between the NIF regime and the people of South Sudan remained the primary contradiction. That which emerged between Riek Machar and John Garang was a secondary contradiction which should have been resolved politically and not militarily.

Riek Machar and Lam Akol's arguments for the coup: democracy, institution respect for human rights and civil liberties were all bogus. They did not institute in Nasir and all the areas that came under their control a better-structured organisation exercising the democratic principles with respect to human rights, and other issues they raised for staging the coup. In this way, they would have garnered the support of the bulk of South Sudanese and the SPLM/A officers and men. But they did not do this.

The SPLA in-fighting continued unabated in different parts of Equatoria and Upper Nile with few skirmishes into Bahr el Ghazal throughout 1993 and 1994. Riek Machar continued dispatching forces, serialised as 'Block Busters' II and III etc., from Upper Nile to east bank Equatoria. Forces were mobilised to western Upper Nile, Shilluk Midwest and other areas. The justification for shifting the war front to east bank Equatoria was to gain access to the international borders with Kenya and Uganda in order to procure military logistics. This provoked serious contradictions within the Nasir faction between the supporters and opponents of this strategy. Questions were raised as to whether Nasir faction really had military supplies at the borders ready to be picked to warrant the enormous lost life in the process. And, in that case, why couldn't these supplies be airlifted in the same way relief food was being airlifted to Nasir and other locations in Upper Nile. Nothing could prove the Nasir collaboration with the common enemy more than this fighting which Riek Machar unleashed on the SPLA in order to fulfil his dreams of becoming the leader of South Sudan.

The insistence of Riek Machar to fight his way to the borders, at a high cost in human lives, was designed to secure those borders for the NIF regime in accordance with the Frankfurt Agreement. The way he surrendered Nasir town the NIF army in April 1995 vindicates this point. However, Riek's adventurous effort to secure the Sudan's southern international borders was not realistic for the following reasons: First, these borders were too far from the Nasir faction bases in Upper Nile and this posed serious difficulties for the Nasir forces in terms of supplies and reinforcements. Secondly, the Nasir supply lines were vulnerable to the SPLA military pressure since it controlled the territory between Upper Nile and the southern international borders[20].

Indeed, the SPLA put up stiff resistance and defeated Riek Machar's forces in east bank Equatoria, denying them permanent bases. The only beneficiary of the fighting between mainstream SPLA and the Nasir faction was the NIF government which took advantage of the situation to regain territory in the Juba - Nimuli axis unleashing a new wave of human displacement and suffering. These NIF successes, reversing the liberation process, could not have come about without this strategic collaboration with the Nasir traitors.

The war unleashed by Riek Machar not only physically weakened the SPLA and exhausted its finite resources, shifting the balance of forces in favour of the enemy, it also had a psychological impact on the SPLA forces, resulting in widespread desertions among the officers and men. This fighting demoralised many combatants on both sides to the point of quitting the struggle on the ground that it had become a tribal war that served no useful purpose. It was the biggest advantage the enemy reaped from its collaboration with the Nasir leaders, depicting the whole conflict as a South–South contradiction.

Further, Riek Machar and the Nasir leaders justified the fight-to-the-borders in terms of what they called a 'creeping revolution' which in itself was an open admission of the failure of the Nasir coup to achieve its objective of ousting Dr John Garang from the leadership of SPLM/A. It was a mixture of obscurantism and opportunism, underpinning the desperate search for allies in the Kenyan capital which Dr Lam Akol set himself to achieve between 1991 and 1993, culminating in the formation of the SPLM/A - United in March 1993.

In view of the facts enumerated above, the logical questions to ask at this juncture are: Was the Nasir coup an act of capitulation from the onset, in which case the flirtation and collaboration between the Nasir faction and the NIF government was not a tactical exercise but a strategic objective of the coup? Or was it because of the failure of the coup to achieve its objective of placing Riek Machar and Lam Akol at the top leadership of the SPLM/A that the Nasir leaders, out of desperation for political and military survival, developed the flirtation and collaboration with the enemy into an outright capitulation, as consummated on 10 April 1996 in the form of 'Political Charter' between Riek Machar and his deputy Kerubino Kuanyin Bol and the NIF government?

To answer some of these pertinent questions, it is imperative to analyse the internal dynamics and development of the Nasir faction from the day of the Nasir Declaration until the split between Riek Machar and Lam Akol in February 1994. Of course the failure of the Nasir coup to achieve its desired objective and the collapse of the Nairobi peace talks in February 1992 created a de facto recognition of the existence of two factions in the SPLM/A - the Nasir and Torit factions.

In retrospect, it is hardly surprising that the transformation of the Nasir faction of the SPLM (August 1991 to March 1993)[21] into SPLM/A - United and finally into SSIM/A (September 1994), in the wake of the failure of the coup due to lack of support from the vast majority of SPLM/A members was bound to culminate into the capitalisation of the Nasir leaders to the NIF regime. I am convinced that if the coup had succeeded Riek Machar and Lam Akol definitely would have stopped the tactical collaboration with the NIF enemy which started in Malakal in July 1991 and would have rallied the rest of the South behind them. But once the coup failed, the effectiveness of the Nasir faction as a political and military force was restricted only to the Nuer and Shilluk districts of Upper Nile and the coup leaders were pushed towards more collaboration with the enemy for political and military survival.

The year 1992 was an eventful year. Cdr William Nyuon, the SPLA Chief of Staff mutinied and deserted the SPLA on 27 September. Soon after the capture and execution of Mr Malath Joseph, a group of political detainees escaped and fled to Uganda. The year ended with increased fighting between the Nasir forces and those of William Nyuon on the one hand, and those of the SPLA, on the other. In Waat, the Nasir leadership met amid serious recriminations over the events in Malakal, but resolved that Riek Machar should lead the troops to eastern Equatoria. Lam Akol returned to lead the diplomatic work in Nairobi.

The escape of Kerubino Kuanyin Bol, Arok Thon Arok, Faustino Atem Gualdit and others from detention centres inside the Sudan and their appearance in Kampala where they established contact with NIF government on the one hand, and the Nasir faction on the other hand, gave an impetus to the collaboration with the enemy. The escapees were rushed to Nairobi where they were accommodated in Hotel 680. In fact, the conference in Nairobi (March 1993), which culminated in the formation of the SPLM/A-United, was financed by the NIF government with funds channelled through Lonrho's office.

So what started as a tactical move ended up as a strategy and finally an end in itself. Although the coup failed to change the SPLM/A leadership, it split the national liberation of movement in South Sudan and led to the emergence of the two rival factions. This came about against a background of bitter internal contradictions within the Nasir faction and later in the SPLM/A United which precipitated several defections and desertions within the ranks, including some of its top leadership. The Nasir faction was in a highly unstable state and this prevented the formation of coherent leadership, explaining in a way the desperate search for allies undertaken by Dr Lam Akol in Nairobi and abroad, no matter whether or not they existed as a force on the ground.

The first alliance that Nasir faction made was with an obscure group called Imatong Liberation Front (ILF) led by Peter Abdalla Sule and pieced together from elements known to have strong ties with the Sudan embassy's intelligence service in Nairobi. The merger was effected in April 1992 and some of the senior ILF personnel were absorbed into the Nasir faction.

The second alliance was the formation of the SPLM/A-United from the Nasir faction led by Riek Machar, the SPLM/A Forces of Unity and Democracy led by Cdr William Nyuon and the group of ex-political detainees led by Cdr Kerubino Kuanyin Bol. It was at this juncture that Joseph Oduho, the veteran South Sudanese politician, was slain in Kongor where the leaders of the groups had gone to meet and finalise the merger with Riek Machar.

No sooner was the formation of SPLM/A-United announced than Cdr Alfred Lado-Gore, Cdr Barri Wanji and other members of what was formerly SPLM/A Forces of Unity and Democracy broke away to form the Patriotic Resistance Movement/ Army of Southern Sudan. This group was dissatisfied with the portfolios given to them in the Interim National Executive Council, but it was more out of fear of Kerubino and Arok whose presence in powerful positions rekindled old memories of the SPLM/A High Command. In fact, from that time, the SPLM/A - United went through serious internal convulsions which saw shifting of positions, alliances and emergence of power centres revolving around Riek Machar.

The contradictions at the political level had serious repercussions and ramifications on the rank of the army file as well as the civilian population in the areas under the control of SPLM/A United. This manifested itself in a general break down in law and order culminating in the Lou - Jikany conflict which Riek Machar failed to control for nearly three years. This conflict claimed more than two thousand lives including women, the elderly and the children, tens of thousand of heads of cattle stolen, villages, including Nasir town, the factions H/Qs was burnt down by Riek Machar's own officers and men[22].

There was also a complete breakdown in discipline among the troops of the SPLM/A-United. In fact, there were really no troops. The bulk of Riek Machar's army were officers with no soldiers to command, and the armed civilians - Jiech Mabor, supplemented that. Commanders and officers openly disobeyed Riek Machar's orders and, as result of this insubordination, rebellion and mutinies within the ranks were common occurrence. For instance, in June 1993 two officers mutinied in Akobo and when they were about to be overcome, they withdrew and ran to Ethiopia from where they found their way to Gambella and to Khartoum. Again in October 1994, there was an attempt on the life of Riek Machar himself which he survived narrowly. Commanders and their men travelled to Malakal to make their own contacts with the enemy without the permission of Riek Machar and they returned to the ranks without being reproached[23].

Riek Machar had on many occasions admitted the fact that Cdr William Nyuon had gone to Juba or Khartoum without his knowledge. Although this was a blatant lie, it also reflected Riek Machar's weakness and lack of tact for administering the faction which, in fact, contributed more to the faction's gravitation towards anarchy. He had a penchant for quickly changing his mind, even over issues, which people had laboured hard on. This, coupled with lack of forcefulness in his leadership style, eroded the confidence of his commanders and leadership cadres.

The dismissal of Dr Lam Akol from the powerful post of Secretary for External Affairs and Peace in the INEC in February 1994 came against a background of quarrels and disputes over Riek Machar's lack of commitment to a consistent policy guidelines. That was a natural consequence of an unprincipled and treacherous alliance in which, having failed to achieve the desired objective, they become embroiled in recriminations and personal vendetta.

Unlike Riek Machar, who most of time depended on chances, Lam Akol was a meticulous schemer who would calculate every step he took. He had discovered that Riek Machar was a hopeless leader and, therefore, needed to be removed from the faction's leadership. Riek Machar got wind of the conspiracy to oust him, but instead of resolving such brewing leadership crisis involving some other commanders politically, he unilaterally dismissed Lam Akol who was accused him of collaboration with the NIF government. This was a hypocritical accusation since the collaboration with the NIF had all along taken place with the knowledge and blessing of Riek Machar himself. But he could blame it on Lam Akol who was in charge of external relations and had stayed abroad to drum up diplomatic support for the Nasir faction. This Machiavellian approach precipitated the rift between Riek Machar and Lam Akol and the split of the SPLM/A-United.

Collaboration with the NIF government was the one single factor that sufficiently discredited the SPLM/A-United and its leadership in the eyes of the people of South Sudan and the international community. At the level of the Horn of Africa, Riek Machar and the SPLM/A-United were not taken seriously as a part of the national liberation struggle. With the emergence of power centres around Riek Machar's leadership, this added to the internal contradictions within the faction. At least there were three such centres competing for Riek Machar's attention and the position of the Secretary for External Affairs and Peace. The Bahr el Ghazal group in the SPLM/A - United, led by Dhol Acuil, demanded this powerful position as a price for their continued support. Riek Machar had to bend this demand and sacrifice Lam Akol. Being the architect for the policy of collaboration was, therefore, a convenient pretext for his dismissal.

In his continuous effort to discredit Riek Machar, Lam Akol submitted a memorandum to the INEC of SPLM/A-United in December 1993 in which he analysed the political and military situation of the faction in which he came out with a suggestion that the SPLM/A-United should reunite with SPLM/A mainstream, and Riek Machar to become the deputy to Dr John Garang in a reunited Movement. As it appeared, it was just another political gimmick calculated to infuriate Riek Machar. Dr Lam Akol was not honest about that presentation nor did he really mean business. He knew very well that Dr Riek Machar would not accept that suggestion. Nevertheless, he proceeded to circulate that document widely in the diplomatic circles in Nairobi to expose Riek Machar as the main obstacle to the unity of the Movement.

This was immediately after the sad events in Washington DC, where Riek Machar refused to sign the Harry Johnston document with Dr John Garang over a very trivial point which could have been amicably resolved. The consultations for the IGAD peace initiative on the conflict in the Sudan had just begun. The trip to Washington by the two rebel leaders was made in that context and the US administration was working on bringing the two closer to an agenda.

Had Riek Machar accepted that proposal, Dr Lam Akol and his group within the faction would have found it an opportune moment to discredit him among the Nuers as a weak leader and, by so doing, to pave the way for his removal from the leadership of the faction. All in all, Lam Akol and his protégés in the INEC were not sincere about the reunification of the SPLM/A-United with the mainstream SPLM/A led by John Garang.

If Dr Lam Akol was honest and really desired the reunification of the SPLM/A, then what prevented Lam Akol from pursuing that conciliatory gesture and the agenda of reunification with the SPLM/A after his dismissal from the SPLM/A-United, especially after he took over the command of the Shilluk Mid West? That could have been an opportunity for him to establish contacts with the SPLM/A in the spirit he wrote to Riek Machar. But instead Lam Akol engaged in more treacherous contacts with the enemy, meeting Zubier Mohammed Salih in Atar garrison in March 1994, enabling him to receive military logistics and a farm tractor from the NIF government. He joined forces with Gabriel Tang-ginya, the NIF government militia commander, against the SPLA, and SPLA-United, culminating in the murder of Cdr Peter Panom Thanypiny, deputy governor of Riek Machar's Phow state in March 1995.

Viewed against these internal contradictions and developments, Riek Machar's eventual capitulation to the NIF government in the form of the 'Political Charter' he signed with Zubier Mohammed Salih was a radical departure from his original plan. Propelled by his blind ambition for leadership, which does not match with his personal leadership qualities, Riek Machar worked himself into a point of no return, typical of a person who has no original ideas of his own. This, coupled with a baseless self-confidence, sometimes bordering on childishness, was responsible for Riek Machar's inability to see reason and to change course whenever opportunities for such action presented themselves.

One such opportunity was provided by the failure of the Nasir coup itself which transformed a political and military contradiction at the level of the SPLM/A leadership into a Dinka - Nuer conflict. It was this distortion which complicated the conflict and made its resolution very difficult. The other opportunity was provided by the events in Lafon in April 1995. Riek Machar's acceptance of one aspect of the Lafon Declaration which dealt with peace and reconciliation and his rejection of the reunification and reintegration with the SPLM/A precipitated another split within the ranks of his movement which escalated the conflict in central Upper Nile that finally pushed Riek Machar to the point of signing the 'Political Charter' with the NIF government as a bait for maintaining a political space in South Sudan.

To put the record straight, the SPLA in-fighting was precipitated by the actions of the Nasir leaders and they bear the full responsibility. The staging of a coup itself was high treason and that is how it is viewed around the world. It was a futile and costly attempt to change a situation in a guerrilla army without presenting a credible alternative leadership. The Nasir coup boiled down to a conspiracy which, according to Dr Garang, did not need to be rewarded. This constituted a dilemma for the liberation movement as the Nasir group became a major setback. It was impossible to ignore its activities, especially once Riek decided to aim his guns at his compatriots instead of the enemy.

Riek Machar's inability to impose his authority on the Nuer people and to establish law and order in central Upper Nile gave rise to the Lou-Jikany conflict which continued unabated for three years. There is no doubt that, under the circumstances obtaining in South Sudan, the Nasir coup constituted a major set back for the SPLM/A struggle in South Sudan. Dr John Garang de Mabior, the target of the coup, has himself accepted the fact that Riek Machar was an important player in the politics of South Sudan who could not be ignored. Accordingly, there would not have been any quarrel with Riek Machar had he turned his guns against the common enemy. The cold-blooded murder of officers and men of the SPLA between 1991 and 1995, whether committed by the forces of Dr Riek Machar or those of Dr John Garang, came as a by-product of the Nasir coup and the responsibility for triggering that lies with Dr Machar and Dr Akol.

The lawlessness that reigned in Nuer land culminating in the Lou - Jikany conflict is attributable to the weak leadership Dr Riek Machar provided following the attempted coup, and his inability to impose his authority on the Nuer people. One old man in Nasir warned Riek Machar against what he termed feminine attitude of talking to people with his head bowed down.

> ... My son, if this is how you plan to lead the Nuer people, you are going to fail. The Nuers were led by powerful leaders when they crossed the Nile to come to the east, that is why they succeeded to have this land and to assimilate other tribes..

Riek definitely failed because the project was not originally his own. He was just brought on board on account of the Nuer factor in the leadership contest. It is usually dangerous to jump into situations one has not fully prepared for. It is his impulsive decisions that have landed him straight in Khartoum– straight into the hands of the NIF government.

Notes

1. This was a coalition of regional political parties and social groups originating from the peripheral areas of the Sudan: South West (mainly Dar Fur), East (the Beja Congress) and a very few from the central Sudan (the Funj and southern Blue Nile). In November 1985 in Wad Medani, these groups came together to form the Sudan Rural Solidarity in order to forge their unity and articulate the concerns and worries of their constituents in face of the domination by the major northern parties.
2. Elections could not be conducted in many territorial constituencies in South Sudan because of the state of war and emergency.
3. There is a long list of atrocities and crimes committed against the people of South Sudan by the government army between June 1965 when the elected government of Mohammed Ahmed Maghoub (Umma Party) took over from the transitional government of Sir el Khatim el Khalifa in January 1966. e.g., the massacre of 76 officials in a wedding party in Wau, the massacre of Watajwok, the massacre of Juba, and so many individual eliminations in different parts of the South.
4. This was strong among the elite in Equatoria. Overwhelmed by the hegemony of the Nilotic from Bahr el Ghazal and Upper Nile, the Equatorian elites sought for regionalisation of the Southern Region to enable them gain access to the 'national cake'.
5. Albie Sachs *The soft vengeance of a freedom fighter.* David Philip, Cape Town. 1989
6. Mao Tse Tung. *Six Essays on Military Affairs.*
7. An alternate member of an organisation is usually not a full member, and although such member may attend the meetings of that body, does not have a voting right and, hence, he has no right to ask the chairman to call the meeting of that body. More over the SPLM/A High Command had not internal regulations entitling a member to require of its Chairman to call a meeting.
8. I was then teaching in Asmara University, but because of the escalation of the war in Eritrea, the University was transferred to Addis Ababa.
9. As Director of External Relations Department of the SPLM/A, the office in Addis Ababa fell under his authority. One day Lam Akol came into the office to find more than six SPLA officers chatting and in a very contemptuous manner ordered them out. I was so much offended by his attitude that I disobeyed the ordered. I left in disgust and since then we have not talked to one another.
10. There were three SPLA families in the compound at the time. My wife was away in Itang refugee camp attending to some family matters.
11. I was really serious in saying that. But this was based on an experience when we were in the University of Khartoum together in early seventies. Many things had changed about Riek Machar which I had not known since we never met again since I left the University.
12. This was enriched with modern additions, which the Nuer kept upgrading as being Ngundeng's prophecies. That the prophesied Nuer leader, or the man who will deliver the black people of the South Sudan, would be 'unmarked', or 'unscarcified' left-handed, and with a gap in between his upper canine teeth, a description that fitted Riek Machar so well that he believed it was him described by Ngundeng. During his time there was nothing called South Sudan as a political entity, but the black people in South Sudan were battling with the foreign invaders: Turks, Arabs and Europeans slavers. Some of these additions include the role Cdr William Nyuon Bany was going to play in the struggle and how he was going to die etc., thus, it therefore, became a mixture of myths, politics of tribalism and sheer ambition to lead, that propelled Dr Riek Machar into the adventure. Dr Lam Akol became the architect, main thinker and the spokesman of the Nasir move.
13. In September 1990 the SPLA suffered a reversal at the hands of a combined force Sudanese army, Gambella People's Liberation Movement and Oromo Liberation Front in which the

refugee camp housing tens of thousands of Sudanese refugees was burnt down resulting in several thousands death and SPLA had to relocate to Gambella region from Wallega.

14 Mr. Thowath later joined the Nasir faction of the SPLM, but developed that relation to become a direct ally of the NIF against the Ethiopian regime.

15 *Southern Sudan Vision*. Special Anniversary Issue No. 12 September 1992. Published by the Department of Information & Culture, INEC, SPLM/A (Nasir faction).

16 The SPLA In-fighting: What are the facts? Department of Information and Culture, INEC of SPLM/A (Nasir Faction) Press Statement, December 15th, 1991. Published in *Southern Sudan Vision* No. September 1992.

17 The fighting against the SPLA (forces against the coup) in central and western, and Shilluk area of Upper Nile in September and October 1991, following the coup, was effected with the ammunition dropped by air from the Government of Sudan Air force Antenov planes, directed by Riek Machar himself by radio from his H/Qs in Ketback, near Nasir.

18 In Nairobi, Dr Lam Akol was able to make extensive diplomatic work, meeting Ambassadors, Foreign government representatives and ministers. To illustrate this, the telephone bill for his suite in Pan Afrique for the months of October and November 1991 topped one million Kenyan Shillings

19 'War, Children, Traditional Values and the International Humanitarian Principles' (1996). A research into the link between the South Sudanese Traditional values and the International Humanitarian Principles in respect to rights of Children and other vulnerable groups in situations of conflict, undertaken by Larjour Consultancy and the South Sudan Law Society.

20 Cdr William Nyuon and his entourage was ambushed by SPLA twice on this route in which he lost many men and materials including vehicles.

21 From the announcement of the coup in Nasir up to the time of the formation of the SPLM/A United.

22 Proceedings of the conference on Peace and reconciliation between the Lou and Jikany sections of Eastern Nuer, September Akobo 1994. (unpublished)

23 Cdr Simon Gatwich Dual on the pretext of fighting Garang and the SPLA was able to meet Zubier Mohammed Salih, the Vice President of the Republic in March 1994. He was issued with ammunition, which was later used in the fight against the Jikany. In fact, officers from Jikany also made their way to Malakal to procure military logistics.

Announcing the Nasir Move in August, 1991. The Nasir leaders left to right: Riek Machar, Lam Akol and Gordon Koang Chol.

Meeting of the Interim National Executive Committee of the SPLM/A Nasir faction in Waat, December 1992. 1st row: Lam Akol, Riek Machar and Gordon Koang Chol. 2nd row: John Luk, Simon Mori Didumo and Peter Abdalla Sule. The author appears in the third row (he was the Secretary to that INEC meeting).

A pose after the meeting. Left to right: Riek Machar; Lam Akol and Gordon Koang Chol, John Luk, Simon Mori Didumo and Peter Abdalla Sule

Announcing the ouster of Riek Machar from the leadership of SSIM/A, Chester House Nairobi, Kenya August 14th, 1995. John Luk and Peter Adwok Nyaba (the author) flanked by Ben Rubin Oduho (right) and George Maker Benjamin (left).

John Garang, Leader of the SPLA.

Politics of Liberation in South Sudan

Remains of a Sudan Government convoy destroyed in March 1997 between Yei and Morobo in an SPLA ambush in which more than two and a half thousand Sudan troops, elements of the West Nile Bank Front, women and children were killed and many were captured alive.

A Sudan Government Howitzer captured during the ambush.

Sudan Government Soldiers captured alive near Yei. The man seated first from the right is Col. El. Tayeb el Hussein, the Commander of the Sudan forces in Morobo who was ordered by the Military H/Qs in Juba and Khartoum to proceed to Yei when it was already in the hands of SPLA. He ordered the blowing up of the bridge 17 miles from Yei, ostensibly to deny the SPLA hot pursuit but unfortunate walked into a deliberate SPLA ambush just outside Yei.

Uganda child soldiers of the Sudan based Lord's Resistance Army (LRA commanded by Kony, captured at the Uganda – Sudan border following SPL offensive in Southern Sudan.

Politics of Liberation in South Sudan 115

West Nile Bank Front officers and men captured in the ambush by the SPLA. The elderly man on the right was the deputy of Juma Oris.

Sudan refugees in Koboko. They have been frequent targets of the West Nile Bank Front attacks from Zaire and Sudan.

4
Between Guilt and Shame

... Let those to whom the heavens grant such opportunities reflect that two courses are open to them: Either so to behave that in life they rest secure and in death become renowned, or so to behave that in life they are in continual straits, and in death leave behind an imperishable record of their infamy...

Niccoló Machiavelli –
The Prince

It goes without saying that the SPLM/A started off on a false foundation not based on the reality of South Sudan. That is why it suffered a lot of infantile ailments culminating in the Nasir coup. After the resolution of the initial hiccoughs in 1984, what it needed urgently was structural and democratic reforms that would enable its leadership to build it into a genuine national liberation movement capable of answering the fundamental problems of the Sudanese state.

It also goes without saying that the SPLA, no matter how much it had grown in numerical strength and the size of territory it controlled, was essentially a guerrilla army. Its main characteristics were mobility and absence of a defined front. Unlike a standing army of a state, it did not have to have a known permanent headquarters or a permanent base, housing its senior most officers. It is perhaps what underpinned Dr Garang's reply to a question about his headquarters by a BBC correspondent in June 1989, when he said, 'as we talk in Bush House, it is here'. Therefore, staging a military coup in a guerrilla army like the SPLA with the view of ousting its leader was tantamount to wishful thinking. In fact, the coup was promptly termed a 'theoretical or theatrical coup', which implied its practical impossibility.

The nature of a guerrilla army is such that it can move with freedom and once it cannot have freedom of movement, then it is in trouble. Thus, a small guerrilla force is capable of pinning down a large enemy army contingent. It has been proved by experience that it is virtually impossible to crush a guerrilla contingent if it is well organised and disciplined, no matter how small or poorly armed it may be. Right near home, Riek Machar found it difficult to subdue Cdr George Athur who operated a small SPLA force in central Upper Nile, sometimes causing havoc on Nasir forces in the area. George Athur attacked and burnt down Baliet in April 1992, sending Riek Machar men to flee in disarray despite the fact that his was a very tiny force compared to Riek Machar's followers. Indeed, George Athur was able to resist the Nasir forces for two years until he was able to link up with the main SPLA force in Kongor in 1993.

In retrospect, what Riek Machar and Lam Akol caused by their action in the most irresponsible manner in Nasir was a split within the ranks of the SPLM/A at a time when it urgently needed unity and solidarity. Given the circumstances then, what the duo were desperately trying to do was to make the reality of the SPLM/A submit to their imagination. As meticulous as they were, the two engineers-turned-guerrilla commanders sat in Nasir and programmed their action on false premises that since Garang was dictatorial, autocratic etc., and because of the simmering discontent and dissatisfaction within, any announcement about his demise would be applauded and supported by the rank and file. The reality was different. Dr Garang took the political initiative leaving the Nasir leaders to catch up with the consequences of their treacherous action.

On the other hand, what unfolded in Nasir did not reflect in any sense the slogans which were used to rationalise the coup. The reasons for staging the coup were given as: democratisation and establishment of structures in the SPLM/A; self-determination leading to separation of South Sudan from the North; respect for human rights and civil liberties; release of political detainees; conventionalisation of the SPLA ranking system etc. However, until the Nasir faction disintegrated none of the issues raised above had been implemented. The Nasir faction did not fulfil the task which it set itself to undertake. The coup, therefore, became an unwarranted adventure. The Nasir leaders embarked on the most vicious crimes never committed in the SPLM/A. This poses the question: How did the leaders in Nasir expect to supplant the SPLM/A leadership without a more advanced political and military organisation?

The Nasir faction and its leadership.

At the time of the Nasir coup announcement in August 1991, the SPLM/A had the High Command as its highest organ of power comprising the Chairman and Commander in Chief and 12 other members. There was also the Chief of Staff of the army. Although this was not a functional structure *sensu stricto*, there was no clear definition of functions. Each and every officer interpreted his duties according to his understanding and reading of the political situation. Some of the so-called alternate members of the High Command did not have specific functions. In fact, Riek Machar and Lam Akol wielded inordinate power in the Movement because of their respective abilities to exploit their positions. What is important to note here is that at no stage did Riek Machar and Lam Akol use their influence to change things in their units.

The structure established following the failed Nasir coup was the Interim National Executive Committee - INEC, with Riek Machar as its chairman and Commander in Chief and Lam Akol as its Secretary for External Affairs and Peace. They were the only two in the Nasir faction's leadership. Even Commander Gordon Koang Chol, whom they had incorporated into their treacherous coup, was not offered a portfolio in the INEC. The full INEC of the Nasir faction was not formed until after the failure of the peace talks in February 1992. The explanation given for this delay was that many of the supporters of the coup were still in Garang's camp and for their own security and safety their names could not be announced. In reality, there were no supporters of the coup still in Garang camp, especially after the genocide in Bor and Kongor in 1991. Even those who had initially supported the coup; for instance, Dengtiel Ayuen Kur and Telar Deng, defected from the faction immediately when they returned from the trip to Europe in February 1992[1]. The only person who could have been counted to be still in Garang's camp, and who later joined the Nasir faction was Cdr William Nyuon Bany who, until 27 September, 1992, was the SPLA Chief of Staff.

But William Nyuon Bany's defection was under a completely different circumstance. It is fallacious to allege that he defected out of conviction to support the Nasir coup. His anger with the SPLA which provoked his rebellion was out of his inability to assert his authority in the SPLA as its Chief of Staff, something that put him at loggerheads with many of his recalcitrant subordinates in the Movement.

The manner in which Riek Machar managed the affairs of the Nasir faction between August 1991 and March 1993 did not show any departure from the old methods of the SPLM/A leadership against which he staged the coup. For somebody to criticise an organisation to the point of committing such horrendous crimes and yet gravitate to the same methods is unforgivable. Riek Machar instituted two structures called Interim National Executive Committee and Interim National Liberation Council which meant nothing in practice. The Interim National Executive Committee became functional only in 1993 after the formation of the SPLM/A-United. The Interim National Liberation Council never met until he dissolved it in 1994 just before his bogus convention in Akobo. Riek Machar and Lam Akol faired no better than the original SPLM/A High Command for which they had high contempt. This, in fact, explains why many people were so reserved about supporting to the coup. The people were not convinced about the slogans raised by Riek Machar and Lam Akol regarding the issues of democracy because they themselves were not democrats.

The Nasir faction started off with the worst human rights abuses which made their criticism of John Garang and the SPLA a mockery. People did not understand the intentions of Riek Machar from the beginning. He appeared a very kind person, ready to meet and talk with anybody, but behind this façade of a smiling and seemingly benevolent Riek Machar, there was another Riek Machar who was ruthlessly ordering the cold-blooded murder of SPLA Dinka officers in Nasir. Riek Machar pretended he was innocent of all these crimes, but we have not heard of anybody being tried for the murders that continued to take place under his nose in Nasir.

Dr Garang exhibited strong autocratic tendencies in his leadership methods and one can vouch for that up to the time of the SPLM first National Convention in 1994. In a situation where there are no institutions, regulations and rules, the exercise of personal rule, ruthless as it may have been, became the norm not the exception in the SPLM/A. However, whoever came up against such a system should have presented a better and more advanced model, otherwise the criticism and coup became unwarranted, especially in face of loss of life and the humanitarian disruption it caused. Riek Machar instituted structures like the INEC and appointed secretaries but would not allow those secretaries to function and formulate their policies. He also appointed the officials to head the INEC departments, as well as the junior officials to these departments, creating confusion among these junior staff who paid their allegiance more to Riek Machar rather than to their immediate bosses.

There was an example in the Department of Humanitarian Affairs which, in addition to External Affairs and Peace, was the only functional department in the whole INEC of Nasir faction. Under the Department of Humanitarian Affairs was the Relief Association for South Sudan - RASS. Riek Machar appointed one person the director of RASS who was widely known to be corrupt. The director of RASS did not cooperate with Secretary for Humanitarian Affairs, and that made the humanitarian and relief work very difficult. In a meeting of the INEC in December 1992 in Waat, Riek Machar insisted, against the opinion of the members of INEC, that the office of RASS director should be transferred from the field to Nairobi, even at a time the director was conducting himself in a way that should have warranted disciplinary action.

In another incident, the members of INEC in Nairobi had voted to suspend a colleague who had for no obvious reasons withheld their monthly stipend. Although initially Riek Machar, who was then in Kampala, endorsed the decision, the following day he changed his mind and informed the members of INEC about this change through his bodyguard. The drama that ensued the following day forced some of us to resign from the leadership. It was really unacceptable that junior officers should dare to insult members of INEC accusing them of plotting a coup against Riek Machar.

In the subsequent developments and contradictions, which evolved in the faction, it was the same RASS director who defected to the SPLM/A mainstream in protest against his transfer to another department. Also it was the same Secretary for Humanitarian Affairs who accused Riek Machar of tribalism. This man defected to the NIF government when he was transferred from humanitarian affairs to be the spokesman of and Secretary for Information and Culture in the South Sudan Independence Movement.

By his style, Riek did not provide a credible alternative leadership to warrant the fuss he and Lam Akol made in Nasir against the SPLM/A and the leadership of Dr John Garang de Mabior. Riek Machar's pretence to the leadership of the South Sudan did not impress many Nuers. In fact, they saw him as a weakling who had no consistent policy line. It was precisely because of this that his colleagues in the INEC tried to undermine his authority and his commanders in the field openly defied his instructions and orders. Can such a leader, like Riek Machar with his unpredictable character, lead a national liberation movement? A relief worker who visited his headquarters in Nasir in 1992, came back with the impression that '... there is a little boy in Riek Machar that keeps coming out every time we sit discussing serious matters'[2]. He was probably right. Only very junior relief workers, who came to Nasir, liked Riek Machar because he constantly gave audience to them even for very trivial matters

Riek Machar is such a consummate liar, though many people before did not know this. Apart from the lies about his military engagement with the enemy, Riek Machar did things or ordered things done which would be attributed to other people when those things went wrong. In this way, many people, especially among the international community believed Riek Machar was such a nice, open and liberal person, when he was the very opposite. In fact, many of his friends and acquaintances could not believe it was Riek Machar they knew, especially his rhetoric about the South Sudan and its freedom when he went to sign the 'Political Charter' with the NIF regime in Khartoum. When it was proved it was he, they then said he was forced to do that because the Ethiopians, Eritreans or American were against him and did not extend military assistance to his faction. This is simply because Riek Machar had cultivated such a 'likeable' image with the members of the humanitarian and relief workers that won him a British army general's uniform from a UN/OLS security adviser in Lokichoggio.

Dr Riek Machar was at times over courteous. He would interrupt an important INEC meeting to receive and only shake hands with even the most junior of the relief workers, especially if he happened to be a European or American; he would take his time introducing his colleagues to that relief worker. This had a big impact on many of those relief worker. They were elated by this touch of Riek Machar's simplicity, deliberately overplayed. We did not feel the weight of such courtesy and its impact on the relief workers, some of them working for the Operation Lifeline Sudan, except after the split within SSIM/A in 1995, when the areas under the control of the new SSIM/A leadership were virtually blockaded by the humanitarian agencies including the UN/OLS itself. The personal relations with Riek Machar compromised the efforts and translated into to political support, even by people and agencies that were supposed to deliver humanitarian assistance in the most neutral and transparent manner. Indeed, there were times when Riek Machar was seen giving orders to relief workers as if they were his officials.

The most unfortunate thing in all this was that some of these NGOs staff and relief workers failed to discover the true character of Riek Machar and many who left South Sudan earlier, including perhaps his late British wife, did not get the opportunity to discover him. They believed that Riek Machar would not engage in dubious practices. This is not true and it can be proved that Riek Machar is two characters in one person. In January 1993, Nasir forces in Ganyliel western Upper Nile abducted a world Food Programme river barge convoy travelling between Malakal and Juba. I had just then been appointed Director General for the Department of Humanitarian Affairs and on 19 January 1993, had travelled to Nasir to attend to a problem involving looting of food and stealing of personal property of one UN worker when the news of the incident in Ganyliel came in.

Mr Jean Luc Siblot, the WFP programme officer, who accompanied me to Nasir, was ordered by Nairobi to demand an explanation from Riek Machar. So on our way back to Lokichoggio we made a stop over in Waat, where Riek Machar had arrived half an hour earlier from a mobilisation mission in the Sobat basin area. At the beginning, Riek Machar did not seem to want to talk but, after my insistence, he came out to the shade of the 'laloab' tree where Mr Siblot was seated. Riek Machar first feigned ignorance when he was informed of the incident in Ganyliel by Mr Siblot before turning angry. He even ordered his radio operator to look for the commander of Ganyliel, ostensibly to show Mr Siblot that he (Riek Machar) was not pleased with the incident. The operator came and murmured something in Nuer which I could not understand. Anyway, Riek Machar assured the WFP official that nothing would happen, the food would be allowed to continue its journey to Juba. We went back to the plane happy that the situation had been effectively handled.

Four days latter, the barge was still docked in Ganyliel in spite of the fact that a food monitor had been flown there to oversee the leaving of the barge. Jean Luc Siblot and myself had to undertake another journey to Ganyliel. We spent three hours discussing the incident. Cdr Simon Maguek, the commander of Ganyliel, was a soft-spoken person who took much time trying to prove a simple point. I knew there was something dubious in his answers because every time I invoked the name of Riek Machar, the chairman and Commander in Chief, Maguek remained unimpressed, a very unusual behaviour by an SPLA officer. I called off the meeting and gave orders that he (Maguek) should accompany the two WFP officials to the barges in the morning to see the amount of food left and allow the barges to leave for the rest of their journey.

In a closed meeting with the commander and after rebuking him about how his actions have shamed the leadership of the Nasir faction, he showed me a radio message from Riek Machar.

> From: Sennar (Riek Machar)
> To: Radar (Simon Maguek)   FLASH   18/1/1993
>
> 134/01/93. The UN barges will reach your end by tomorrow. They should be stopped by all means. Unload all the food and let the people take as much as they can. The rest should be stored for the army. I want a feed back immediately.

I was dumbfounded and could not say anything. I had to put up an honourable face with Jean Luc Siblot and Simon Wilson, drumming up some false defence for the unfortunate incident. To placate the WFP and the OLS, we surrendered to them the video camera confiscated by the soldiers from one of the relief workers. As a result of our manoeuvres, the WFP, UNDP, and the government of Sudan immediately reversed the decision not to supply the area with food on the grounds that a repeat of the same incident could not be ruled out.

Riek Machar fed his supporters with lies as a strategy to maintain their allegiance. In one of my visits to Leer in 1994, the area commander informed me Riek Machar had sent a message to all units informing them that he had received armament from the Israelis, Eritreans and Ugandans and that he was then trying to find means of flying these arms into the country. This surprised me a great deal because I had just come from and left Riek Machar in Nairobi. As a member of INEC, I should have been more informed of such important policy matters than the area commander. I told him that was very good and kept quiet, hoping to raise the issue as soon as I met Riek Machar in Nairobi. The radio message that Riek Machar had sent was very long, but the relevant part read as follows:

> From: Sennar (Dr. Riek Machar)
> To: All Units.
>
> 116/2/94
>
> 1. Dr. Lam Akol is claiming that I dismissed him because I failed to secure supplies for our troops and that I want to hand over the SPLM/A United to Garang. These are false. First, I have secured supplies from the Americans and Israelis that shall be supplied through the Kenyans, Ugandans and Ethiopians. The Eritreans on their own have given us supplies. I am now organising how these supplies can reach our areas.

The whole thing turned out to be a bluff, and one wondered why a leader of Riek Machar's calibre would undertake such an exercise which would not give him or his faction any dividends. Since then I have not taken whatever Riek Machar said for granted.

Whether or not Riek Machar himself was serious about his claims is something still baffling me. A leader has no reason whatsoever to create the impression among his followers and supporters that he was capable of disinformation because that could be disastrous for the people's confidence in him and the morale of his army. One pertinent example is what the commanders in Lou area did when they realised that Riek Machar would neither deliver any military supplies nor stop the war between the Lou and Jikany sections of eastern Nuer which had lasted over a year[3].

This war had not been resolved and was likely to recur during the dry season of 1994 when the Lou went to the Sobat river basin for grazing, water and fishing. In anticipation of trouble, the Lou commanders, therefore, sent a delegation to Malakal to secure ammunition from the NIF government. This was because the Jikany, through their men in the system in Malakal, were being supplied ammunition by the government and that could tilt the balance in their favour. Commander Simon Gatwich Dual had this to say when I met him in Akobo in September 1994.

> ... I went to Malakal and met Zubier Mohammed Salih, the vice President. He asked me whether I wanted money. I told him; no I did not want money. What I wanted was ammunition because we were expecting a serious military offensive from the SPLA through Bor, and so me must defend ourselves. Zubier was very happy and he ordered that we should be given thirty boxes of AKM ammunition. This is what we used in the war against the Jikany...

Commander Simon Gatwich and others were arrested and detained on the orders of Riek Machar for not having established independent contacts with the enemy but for having involved themselves in the war between the civilian populations. In the Akobo conference for peace and reconciliation between the Lou and the Jikany, Riek Machar would not mention anything about the collaboration with the enemy as a factor in the escalation of that conflict. Nor would he point an accusing finger against all those who took independent decisions to establish contacts with the enemy, including the deputy chairman Cdr Kerubino Kuanyin and Cdr William Nyuon Bany, the Chief of Staff.

The extent of the SPLM/A United's collaboration with the enemy would have remained an unresolved mystery in my mind had I not had the opportunity to attend the Akobo conference of reconciliation and peace between the Lou and the Jikany which Riek Machar immediately transformed into a Convention of SSIM/A. I was able to meet face to face with some of the officers and men, people like Yusif Kunda, Ben Obur, Cdr Jeremiah Afrika and others, who were in Juba or had gone to Khartoum and other enemy garrisons; I learned from them first hand what they did in the enemy's areas with the knowledge of Nasir leadership. It was a very pathetic situation. All along, we had been defending Riek Machar's nationalism and patriotism when, in fact, he was dealing with the enemy.

Riek Machar has a very strange way of interpreting his collaboration with the NIF regime. He believed that unless the SPLA and Dr John Garang were defeated there could never be peace in South Sudan. According to him, therefore, it was justified to use any means, including collaboration with the NIF regime, to achieve that objective. Once Garang and his army were out of the way, Riek Machar would resume the task of liberating South Sudan. This obtuse logic could not be taken seriously. We told Riek Machar and his colleagues that self-determination for the people of South Sudan cannot be won by one faction. We argued that unity among all the leaders as well as concerted military action against the common enemy were indispensable preconditions for success of the struggle for self-determination and, hence, independence of South Sudan.

The defections from the Nasir faction.

Since the August Declaration which resulted in the formation of the Nasir faction, the subsequent establishment of the SPLM/A - United and the change of name to South Sudan Independence Movement/ Army - SSIM/A, the leadership of Riek Machar has suffered serious internal contradictions and infighting among it commanders and cadres. Many of these contradictions developed as a result of the policy of collaboration with the NIF enemy; yet Riek Machar himself through his inability to make quick decisions or, as a result of his inconsistency, generated others. Though the existence of contradictions is a normal development in any organisation, the question is: why is it that Riek Machar has managed to survive up to this moment as leader of the faction despite all his weaknesses? This can be answered in terms of the tribal schisms that accompanied the Nasir Declaration in 1991.

It will be recalled that the SPLA war with Anya-nya was fought on the Dinka - Nuer lines as if the SPLA were a Dinka organisation. Many Nuers, even those who latter joined the SPLA after the peace and reunification agreement of 1988, have not fully recovered from the moral and psychological delirium arising out of the false guilt that the Nuers have failed to take the leadership of the South from the Dinka. Thus, when an opportunity like the Nasir coup availed itself, to challenge this perceived 'Dinka hegemony', many Nuers found themselves automatically supporting Riek Machar and the Nasir faction. In 1992 and 1993, many Nuer officers and men, who were found by the coup in Equatoria deserted and fled to Upper Nile, not because they understood and supported the ideals of the Nasir Declaration but simply because they were Nuers[4].

Ironically, the political and military survival of Riek Machar and the Nasir faction could be reasonably linked to this lack of political objectivity of many of his supporters, who took solace in preserving and protecting the Nuer tribal prestige, dignity and honour. This is unfortunate because it completely negated the objective for which the people of South Sudan, including the Nuers themselves who have paid dearly for this cause, have always taken up arms. Riek Machar has exploited these tribal sentiments and concerns in a very dishonest manner and now he is torn up in a moral and psychological dilemma between the shame of betraying the trust and confidence the people of South Sudan have put in him and the guilt of genocide which he unleashed on the people of Bor and other areas South Sudan.

There are times when Riek Machar has behaved more of a Nuer chauvinist than a South Sudanese nationalist something he had toyed with since his school days. He believed in the fighting strength of the Nuer people that he got tempted to stake his bid for leadership of South Sudan on the assumption that the Nuer people would place him on the throne by force. Some patriotic Nuers, who chose to differ with him over some of these tragic policies, have been portrayed as traitors of the Nuer people. For instance, Commander William Nyuon Bany was assassinated in cold blood on Riek Machar's orders because he chose to disengage himself from collaboration with the NIF and to work for reconciliation and reunification with SPLM/A. Commander John Luk was also vilified and attempts made on his life because he supported William Nyuon and took over the task of pursuing the process of reconciliation, reunification and integration with the SPLM/A.

From what has been unfolding in the Nasir faction, the SPLM/A-United and latter in SSIM/A, Riek Machar, in his subconscious being, is re-enacting the more or less mythical scenes fashioned by infantile imagination and fairy tales. As already mentioned, according to some legends in the Nuer land, Riek Machar had been destined to be the liberator of the Nuer nation[5]. Perhaps it is this legend, which Riek Machar, in spite of the objective reasons of his leadership shortcomings, has used to insist on becoming the leader of the reunified Movement. Otherwise, Riek Machar assertion that 'Garang gets it over my dead body' is hard to explain.

From its inception the Nasir faction never enjoyed stability, at least at the level of its leadership. The failure of Riek Machar to constitute the INEC was a source of dissatisfaction for some of the commanders in Nasir who had pinned their hopes to being appointed in it. This was the source of friction between Cdr Stephen Duol Chol and Cdr Gordon Koang Chol which landed the former in Riek Machar's detention camps.

The cold blooded murder of the Dinka officers was another dimension which widened the rift between the Nasir leaders and some of the commanders who did not entertain the policy of ethnic lynching. This catalysed and accelerated the defection of Dengtiel and Telar Deng referred to above. In the course of time and because of the policies adopted by Riek Machar, the Nasir faction became identified as a Nuer faction, something that pushed people, like James Othow Along, the zonal commander of the Shilluk mid west, into independent collaboration with the NIF government in Malakal.

In Nairobi, the Nasir faction was highly fragmented. The merger with the so-called Imatong Liberation Front helped the sharp polarization of the group due to the inclusion of people, well known for his connections with the Sudan Embassy intelligence service[6]. The fragmentation of the patriotic elements within the Nasir faction strengthened the collaborationist trend led by Dr Lam Akol. Each one took independent decision and action that allowed and enabled Lam Akol and his group to steer the faction in the direction they wanted[7]. Had all those who were opposed to collaboration with the NIF acted in concert, things would have been different in the Nasir faction. The belated decision taken by Commanders William Nyuon, John Luk and others in August 1995 to oust Riek Machar from the leadership of SSIM/A was a more appropriate approach.

The establishment of the SPLM/A-United

The birth of the Nasir faction was like a miscarriage. It needed an incubator for its leadership to evolve into a credible alternative. But why is it that the Nasir faction was born without a full fledged leadership and why did it take long to establish? One possible explanation was lack of cadres to constitute the INEC. But the real reason is that the coup was declared without enough political and military preparations. Lam Akol and Riek Machar acted in a hurry out of fear that Dr John Garang would apprehend them. This is because most of their plans had been discovered. Thus, in order to pre-empt Garang's counter-moves, the coup had to be announced without adequate groundwork.

To attain stability and credibility in the eyes of the people of South Sudan and the world at large, Dr Lam Akol set out to forge alliances. The SPLM/A -United was born out of advanced opportunism to ensure political survival of the entire group that comprised it. The internal contradictions within the Nasir faction made it desperate for allies including the NIF regime. The establishment of the SPLM/A-United was also a convenient venue for the political and military come back for some of the ex-political detainees.

In 1992, certain unfolding political and military developments unfolded in South Sudan left significant marks on the political landscape, some of which contributed to the formation of the SPLM/A-United. These included - the collapse of the Nairobi peace talks between the two factions of the SPLM/A brokered by the People for Peace in Africa and the New Sudan Council of Churches; the temporary merger of the SPLM/A delegation to the Abuja peace talks in Nigeria in face of arrogance of the NIF delegation; the departure of Commander William Nyuon Bany from the SPLM/A and the formation of the SPLM/A Forces of Unity and Democracy which allied itself to the Nasir faction; and the escape from the SPLA detention camp in South Sudan of Kerubino Kuanyin Bol, Arok Thon Arok and Faustino Atem Gualdit and their flight to Uganda.

Of all these developments, many of them engineered by the SPLM/A Nasir faction in Nairobi and in the field, the most interesting was the timing of William Nyuon Bany's rebellion and the arrival in eastern Equatoria in June 1992 of the 'Block Busters'. It was widely believed that the arrival of the 'Block Buster I' in Equatoria, coinciding with the defection of Cdr William Nyuon Bany from the SPLM/A was planned to re-enforce him. On 27 September 1992, the day William Nyuon Bany staged his 'withdrawal' from Pageri, Dr Lam Akol was in London following his visit to Libya with Tiny Rowlands. The press statement announcing the rebellion did not originate William Nyuon Bany's supporters in Nairobi but from Lam Akol in London. It was faxed to the representative of Nasir faction in Nairobi with the clear instructions to make it look as if it was released in Nairobi. This gives credence to the version of events that the meeting in Abuja between Lam Akol and William Nyuon Bany prepared for this eventuality.

The defection of Cdr William Nyuon Bany and the events that ensued exposed the opportunistic character of some of the ex-political detainees released from the SPLM/A detention through the effort of the Nasir faction. Upon their release and on their arrival in Nairobi, none of these detainees joined the Nasir faction. They maintained a separate organisational entity – ex-political detainees, on the ground that they wanted to reconcile the two factions of the SPLM/A. But, most importantly, most of them hated Dr Lam Akol and did not want to identify with his organisation.

But, as soon as the news of William Nyuon Bany's defection reached Nairobi, the members of this group joined him and became his spokesman. Many of them had expressed reservations about Lam Akol and were opposed to his collaboration with the enemy.

Within the Nasir faction in Nairobi a crisis over the position of Commander William Nyuon Bany was exaggerated to the point that it almost caused a split in the faction[8]. Dr Lam Akol, John Luk and Taban Deng Gai were accused of plotting to substitute Cdr William Nyuon Bany for Dr Riek Machar as leader of the Nasir faction. Some of these stories reached Riek Machar and, as a result, he became so hostile to Lam Akol, Luk and Taban that he ordered them to travel to Waat for a briefing[9]. It was clear then that Commander William Nyuon Bany had not joined the Nasir faction. He only wanted support which Lam Akol, Luk and Taban had assured him earlier while still in Nairobi. But why Riek Machar assumed that that William Nyuon Bany was joining the Nasir faction is hard to tell.

Mr Joseph Oduho was flown to Nairobi from an airstrip in northern Uganda sometime in late February 1993. At that time, Cdr Kerubino Kuanyin, Arok Thon Arok and Faustino Atem Gualdit were in Kampala waiting to go to Kenya. Tiny Rowlands played a big role in establishing the contacts between the Kerubino's group in Kampala and the Nasir faction in Nairobi until a conference to unite the three groups into one faction. The NIF government financed this conference, which lasted two weeks, with funds channelled through Lonrho. The three groups were the SPLM/A Nasir faction, SPLM/A Forces of Unity and Democracy (William Nyuon Bany's group) and the Kerubino Kuanyin's group.

The conference did not actually commence on 12 March as was planned. A serious disagreement ensued in the preparatory stage regarding the chairmanship of the meetings. Both Kerubino and Arok invoked their former seniority in the SPLM/A High Command and, therefore, insisted Kerubino should chair the conference. The Nasir faction could not accept that argument on account of it being the real force on the ground. Some of us thought the chairmanship of the conference should go to Mr Joseph Oduho because of his age and experience in the political struggle in South Sudan. We even suggested that if the leadership of the SPLM/A-United were given to Oduho, it would help to improve the image of the Nasir faction and, perhaps, it would pave the way for reunification of the whole Movement. It was agreed in the end that the leaders of the three delegations should constitute the collective chairmanship of the conference.

The formation of the SPLM/A-united ended in a fiasco marked by the murder of Joseph Oduho and many other senior officers of the faction in Kongor on March 26, 1993[10]. The circumstances of his death created strong feelings among the Equatorians who believed it was a deliberate act to eliminate him from the contest for the leadership of the Movement. This, in addition to their disillusionment with the distribution of the portfolios of INEC, provoked the desertion *en masse* of Equatorians from the SPLM/A-United, and the subsequent formation of the Patriotic Resistance Movement of South Sudan (PRM) under the leadership of Alfred Lado-Gore.

The exit of Lado-Gore, Barri Wanji and others marked the disintegration of the SPLM/A-United almost along the lines it was formed and through the same forces. Its formation was not intended really to promote the liberation struggle but rather to create a political space for economic accumulation by those who had access to the NIF resources. In fact the SPLM/A-United was a NIF regime's Trojan horse in the Sudanese liberation movement, with a definite and concrete programme of fighting to defeat and destroy the SPLM/A. To many of its leaders, its formation was intended to revenge the excesses of the SPLM/A and Dr John Garang. Therefore, it was not a part of the national liberation process. In this vein, it was morally correct for those who worked inside it to undermine its treacherous policies. That is where the difference occurred between us and those who deserted to form the PRM. We decided to remain in the SPLM/A-United with the hope of struggling to change it from inside. How would the crimes of the leaders of the SPLM/A-United be known if there were no people there to witness and record them?

Barri A Wanji and Alfred Lado-Gore, who led the walk out of the SPLM/A-United, were right in their analysis of the treacherous nature of the SPLM/A-united leadership for two reasons. First, the faction was tied to the NIF regime and was isolated from the masses of South Sudanese people and their friends in the international community. Secondly, the NIF regime was channelling funds to the SPLM/A-United leadership in order to destroy the SPLM/A. However, we disagreed with them because splits, separation and independent action were not the best methods of struggling to defeat the treacherous trend in the SPLM/A-United.

No social and political organisation is immune to the kind of contradictions as those which accompanied the formation of the SPLM/A-United. Contradictions in an organisation are inevitable but they cannot be resolved by escapism and fragmentation. By deserting the SPLM/A-United and setting up a separate political structure, the PRM leaders unwittingly strengthened the treacherous elements in the SPLM/A-United through the natural process of concentration. Their numerical strength in the factional leadership gave them political clout. They, therefore, controlled the faction and had a free hand to carry out whatever the NIF government wanted them to do. It would definitely have been different if there had been a strong opposition within the SPLM/A-united to restrain and check the flirtation with the enemy.

To narrow the contradictions within the SPLM/A-united to merely a question of positions in the INEC was really taking the issue out of its ideological and political context and relevance. Worse still, to have articulated the problem in terms of the marginalisation of the Equatorian with regard to the sharing of leadership positions in INEC was completely off the mark. This simply implied that if these commanders had been offered what they perceived as powerful positions in the INEC, they would not have objected to the collaboration with the NIF regime. Accordingly, collaboration was the pretext rather than the main reason for quitting.

The position adopted by these comrades not only weakened the case for the anti-collaboration elements in the SPLM/A-United, but it also was a major set back for the reconciliation and the reunification of the SPLM/A which, in turn, would have accelerated the process of liberation in the Sudan.

The desertion of the 'Equatorians' did not mark the end of division and split in the SPLM/A-United. At least there are two power centres: one around Dr Lam Akol, Kerubino and Arok Thon, who controlled the resources of the faction; and the other around Dhol Acuil, Amon Wantok, Chol Deng Alaak - the so-called Bahr el Ghazal group. Although the main contention and contradiction remained the question of collaboration with the NIF regime, the struggle for ascendancy in the SPLM/A-United took the centre stage. It become intense, reaching its peak in late 1993 to early 1994, and culminated in the removal of Dr Lam Akol from the powerful position of Secretary for Foreign Relations and Peace in INEC.

For a short time after that, the power struggle among these two centres shifted to the replacement of Lam Akol. In pursuit of power and personal interests, the factional leaders ignored the central issue of liberation which, in all practicality, can only be achieved through a concerted political and military action. This definitely required reconciliation and reunification of the fighting forces. The intense hatred of the leadership of Dr Garang, especially among the ex-detainees, which bordered on paranoia, became a big problem in the SPLM/A-United as it paralysed any efforts at reconciliation and reunification. It also made very difficult meaningful collective political work in the faction. Thus, under the pressure of these contradictions and other personal clashes, the SPLM/A-United, within a year from the date of its formation in March 1993, disintegrated. This resulted in the formation of tribal and regional splinter groups.

The disintegration of the SPLM/A-United

Where political and ideological bonds are weak or non-existent, and the coherence and solidity of an organisation is based on feelings and emotions, any slight internal crisis engender and strengthen centrifugal forces. The Nasir coup and the split within the SPLM/A it engendered were to lead to further splits within the SPLM/A-United and the fragmentation of SSIM/A. This was because the contradictions were personalised and former comrades in arms became incompatible to the extent that splinter groups proliferated.

The contradictions in SPLM/A-United were congenital; the sharp personal differences that ensued were accentuated by the behaviour of Cdr Kerubino who exasperated people like Alfred Lado-Gore and Prof. Barri Wanji, rekindling their old fears and strong hatred for him before he was arrested and detained in 1987. Although, Prof. Barri Wanji had originally supported Kerubino's candidature for the chairmanship of the conference, he was appalled by Kerubino's subsequent behaviour and decided to quit the SPLM/A-United and to join hands with Lado Gore to form the Patriotic Resistance Movement (PRM).

The primary contradiction in the SPLM/A-United leadership centered on the question of collaboration with the enemy which emphasised the escalation of the conflict with SPLM/A. This itself intensified the internal split among those who were benefiting from the financial handouts of the NIF and those who did not. The prospects for economical accumulation made reconciliation among these leaders, in a city like Nairobi, very impossible. Kerubino and his group did not care to build a strong opposition force both to Garang and to the NIF. Their opposition to Garang's leadership and the SPLM/A propelled them to cultivate an alliance with the NIF government that was inimical to the interests of the people of South Sudan. The main task of the patriots was to organise opposition to collaborators without undermining the unity of the SPLM/A-United

The formation of the PRM as a separate movement from the SPLM/A-United in 1993 was another split within the anti-Garang camp which led to the emergence of tribally based splinter groups. The PRM itself smacks of Bari tribalism because, with the exception of Prof. Barri A Wanji (Golo) and Mr Deng-tiel Ayuen Kur (Dinka-Bor), the rest of the members of PRM hailed from the Bari tribe, mostly intellectuals working in Nairobi or Kampala. The PRM had no military presence on the ground in South Sudan. Nevertheless, abroad they maintained a political space in the national liberation struggle with a superb theoretical articulation of their position.

The second split within the leadership of SPLM/A-United occurred in February 1994 with the disgrace and dismissal of Dr. Lam Akol from the powerful position of Secretary for External Affairs and Peace in INEC[11]. Pretending to have acquiesced to Riek's orders[12], Lam Akol sneaked into Tonga where he appealed to the Shilluk tribal sentiments and took over the command of the Shilluk midwest. Back in South Sudan, Dr Lam Akol started issuing radio messages declaring himself the leader of SPLM/A-United. When Riek Machar changed the name of SPLM/A-United to the SSIM in September 1994, Lam Akol immediately declared himself the bona fide leader of SPLM/A-United operating only in the Shilluk Midwest. The presence of Mr Peter Abdalla Sule as Lam Akol's deputy in SPLM/A-United was just a ploy to give his faction a South Sudan national face. Lam Akol had initially tried to forge an alliance with Nuer commanders from the Lau and Laak/Gawaar areas and with the NIF government militia commander Gabriel Tang-ginya but this alliance broke up in April 1995 for reasons worth mentioning.

Following his arrival in the Shilluk Midwest, Lam Akol embarked on a programme of destroying Riek Machar politically and militarily. He allied with Tang-ginya to rout Riek's SSIM/A forces from the Zeraf Valley. The Shilluk forces were at first reluctant to cross the Nile to fight in Zeraf Valley. But after the NIF government promised the provision of ammunition they accepted to cross to fight SSIM/A. It is worth mentioning that with the promise of more military logistics, the Shilluks were ready to fight against the SPLA in Atar area.

The ferocity with which the Shilluk soldiers fought against the forces of Riek Machar in Fangak and Manajang areas was exceptional. They did not take prisoners but instead finished off any Nuer wounded in action. This triggered off a conflict with their allies who rightly accused them of unnecessary brutality and escalating the conflict by inflicting many casualties on the Nuers, and leading to an early break with Tang-ginya in June 1995 when Lam Akol started crying foul stating that he was expecting an attack from the Nuers.

Although it has been inundated by internal contradictions, resulting from Lam Akol's mal-administration and absence of a clear agenda coupled with personality clash between him and his deputy Peter Sule on the one hand, and between him and James Othow on the other, a large part of this army went over to the enemy with the zonal commander James Othow Along who was subsequently appointed the commissioner of Tonga province by the NIF government after precipitating a split with Lam Akol; the SPLM/A-United remains essentially a Shilluk army.

Within the SPLM/A-United, the dismissal of Lam Akol and the way it was effected by Riek Machar was not taken lightly by his protégés in the INEC. In fact, although many of his colleagues wanted his wings clipped by removing him from the powerful position of Secretary for External Affairs and Peace, they did not want him dropped from the INEC. This created tension within INEC between them and Riek Machar but they failed to win the battle for Lam Akol's reinstatement. This group was thrown in disarray when Commander John Kulang escaped to Khartoum, and Commander John Luk was arrested and detained in Waat; meanwhile Arok Thon Arok resigned and Peter Abdalla Sule disappeared into Kibera without trace only to appear in Tonga with Lam Akol five months later.

Soon after all this, Arok Thon Arok resigned from the SPLM/A-United. This was accelerated by two factors: The weakening of his position in the leadership of SPLM/A-United which was heightened by the failure of its forces to gain a foot hold in Kongor, Arok's home area, after being routed by SPLA in March 1993. Arok's claim to leadership position in the SPLM/A-United on account of his presumed control of Kongor was irreparably damaged. After the dismissal of Lam Akol, Riek Machar appeared as if he had turned his back on the collaboration with the NIF government and it looked as if he was set to purge all those who were involved in this collaboration with the enemy. Arok Thon, therefore, resigned in order to pre-empt his disgraceful purge from the SPLM/A-United. However, without openly forming another faction, Arok Thon quietly organised his Bor supporters whom he knew had been infuriated by the murder of judge Martin Majier Gai.

The departure of Lam Akol and his group from Riek Machar's faction boosted the influence of the Bahr el Ghazal group in INEC. They now became the confidants of Riek Machar. Their ascendancy was temporary because they soon suffered the humiliation similar to that of Lam Akol and his group. Riek Machar refused to investigate allegations of financial irregularities and misappropriation of the faction's funds and protected those responsible, in defiance of the wishes of his colleagues in the INEC.

Riek Machar's lack of transparency and accountability annoyed the Bahr el Ghazal group which began to distance itself from the SPLM/A-United. Riek Machar had banked on the possibility of these leaders going to their respective homes in order to assist in discrediting the SPLA politically and its eventual military removal from the area. This meant that they were to travel to Mankein to join Kerubino[13] or travel to Ganyliel where they would be given Nuer troops to take them to their home areas[14]. Although this was theoretically feasible and desirable, but in practice it was like a foreign invasion and was therefore rejected partly because these commanders did not enjoy local support.

The final break with the Bahr el Ghazal group came in September 1994 when they refused to travel to attend the conference of Peace and reconciliation between the Jikany and Lou which was held in Akobo. And like what Arok Thon did, this group had to resign en masse to preempt their dismissal by Riek Machar. Thereafter, they formed what became known as the Independent Group'. Since they had no new members to join them, they remained an intellectual association of disgruntled officers whose main reason for not rejoining the SPLA, after extricating themselves from SPLM/A-United, was personal hatred for Dr John Garang de Mabior. In fact, some of them have become so paranoid about it that they supported Riek Machar in the 'Political Charter' with the NIF regime[15]. Those who persisted in their opposition allied themselves to another USAP renegade who made a living in Nairobi by capitalising on a dubious project he called the 'Unity of armed and unarmed Southern groups and Movement,'. Without military support on the ground, the Bahr el Ghazal group remained ineffectual and, in fact, by so doing, has disarmed and deprived itself of active participation South Sudanese affairs.

Another splinter group that was mid-wived by the NIF government in Nairobi was the so-called South Sudan Freedom Front - SSFF, formed by Dr

Richard K Mulla which South Sudanese in Nairobi mockingly called South Sudan Food First. After his dismissal by Riek Machar from the position of Secretary General of SSIM/A, Richard Mulla formed a loose alliance of Equatorians opposed to the policies of SSIM/A in eastern Equatoria, along the line chartered by some of the Equatorian commanders[16] in SSIM/A who had earlier rebelled against Cdr William Nyuon Bany. This group joined hands with the Ugandan rebel forces of Joseph Konyi's Lord's Resistance Army under the tutelage of the NIF government. Their common function was to fight against the SPLA along side the government forces while at the same time fighting the SSIM/A forces in east bank Equatoria. In an effort to win over other Equatorians in and out of the SPLM/A, this group called itself 'Equatoria Defence Forces' which later signed Riek's 'Political Charter' with the NIF government. In fact, these so-called Equatoria Defence Forces are Joseph Lagu's Trojan horse for making a come back into the political scene of South Sudan.

The divisions within the SPLM/A-United and later SSIM/A, motivated by scramble for power and leadership, continued unabated until the original face of the Nasir faction and its objectives were completely obliterated. This fragmentation and differentiation of the Nasir group was a reflection of the progressive tribalisation of the splinter grouplets. This was made possible by the political and social environment in Nairobi where most of these splinter groups were born. The humanitarian agencies operating in South Sudan made their resources available for these grouplets to come to life and to survive in Kenya. Relief and humanitarian assistance, therefore, became an important factor in the politics and economy of splits and divisions among South Sudanese both inside the country and abroad. The possibility of enjoying easy life and politicking in Nairobi with the assistance of the international humanitarian agencies encouraged South Sudanese leaders to break ranks, making their unity for the purpose of liberation, impossible. This can be explained in terms of the emergence of an entrepreneur class that recognised the economic significance of war and which sought to benefit from the proliferation of the indigenous NGOs for the first time in South Sudan[17].

On another level, some international humanitarian agencies and their personnel encouraged the fragmentation and proliferation of the so-called political movements in the name of democracy and political pluralism in a future South Sudan. These movements were nothing more than self-serving economic organisations whose aims were to reap benefits from the relief business. They reasoned that splits would definitely lead to the escalation of the conflict and intensify humanitarian disruption which in turn would create employment and business opportunities for the NGOs engaged in humanitarian work in South Sudan.

For example, Dr Lam Akol was able to maintain himself in Tonga by making relief intervention a top priority in his political agenda at a time when there was really no need for relief in the Shilluk area. The landing of light relief aircraft from Lokichoggio in Kenya, carrying very little relief items with minimal impact in the area[18]. The reappearance of white faces, in the form of relief workers in Tonga, was something that boosted the image of Dr Lam Akol among the Shilluk people. His abduction of an armed UN World Food Programme relief barge and Romi Delos Santos, the Filipino relief worker in May 1995 while allowing a military convoy of the NIF government to pass freely on the Nile near Tonga, enabled him to extract recognition from the UN Operation Lifeline Sudan. The UN/OLS had to pay twice for the release of the Filipino and to meet the expenses of Peter Sule's journey including his subsistence in an expensive Nairobi hotel while he was engaged in political and diplomatic work on Lam Akol's behalf. Though this enhanced the authority of Lam Akol in the Shilluk area, it created a relief dependency among the people who had hitherto been self-reliant.

Two hitherto unknown relief agencies namely *Commitato Collaborazio Medico-* CCM (Italian) and MedAir (Swiss) were the international friends that kept Lam Akol afloat in the Shilluk Midwest. Even after being dislodged from Tonga and Orinyo by his deputy, Cdr James Othow, these agencies continued to fly him into some isolated location north of Kodok. In which case, relief became just a means of maintaining a small group of his followers. In fact, there was virtually no civilian population in that place which meant that CCM and MedAir were not acting in response to a humanitarian situation but in support of Lam Akol's faction to ensure his survival in the political theatre. This was an obvious misuse of taxpayers' money.

The splits, divisions and fractionalisation of the SPLM/A-United with the subsequent formation of tribal or regional-based splinter groups can be attributed to the inadequacy of the Nasir faction as an alternative leadership in the national liberation struggle and a logical consequence of the policy of collaboration with the NIF enemy from the beginning. The result has been what the NIF government had set out to achieve by that collaboration: dividing the liberation movement, defeating and destroying the SPLM/A and, finally, imposing its 'peace from within strategy'.

The rationalisation of the failure of the coup

It is rare that a national liberation movement takes off and achieves its objective or comes to power without having passed through the tunnel of contradictions, in-fighting and perhaps splits. It is equally rare that in a single country two or more armed political factions came to power at the same time without having reunited themselves organisationally in the form of a front or otherwise. Many liberation movements which have split have always resolved their contradictions through elimination of one faction by the other either physically through military prowess e.g., the struggle between the EPLF and ELF in Eritrea or, after many years of fighting resulting in many deaths and displacements, a compromise is struck by the warring parties in which they agree to share power e.g., MPLA and UNITA in Angola, ANC and the National Party in South Africa, FRELIMO and RENAMO in Mozambique; or one of the parties (the weaker one) dissolves itself into the powerful one as in the case of SPLM/A and SSLF in 1983 or Anya-nya 2 in 1988. The formation of a political front, EPRDF, enabled the rebel groups in Ethiopia to achieve victory in 1991.

The initial objective of the Nasir coup was not just the removal of Dr John Garang de Mabior from the leadership of the SPLM/A per se but to undertake a process of the democratisation and the institutionalisation of the rule of law and respect for human rights in the SPLM/A. Although these ideas were expressed in national terms (South Sudan), the real motives were, as was later to be proved by the actions of the Nasir leaders, parochial and tribal. These objectives were centred around the establishment of a 'Nuer patria'.

To prove this point, let us look at the behaviour of Mr David Reath Malual, the Commander of William Nyuon Bany's headquarters in Ayod. On hearing the announcement of the coup, David Reath Malual radioed William Nyuon Bany to say that if he (William) did not support this Nuer bid for leadership of the South, then he should give up the struggle and go to stay with his family in Nairobi. True to his ethnic loyalty, Reath Malual was later to be the staunchest supporter of Riek Machar against Cdr William Nyuon Bany and Cdr John Luk in Lau area following the split within SSIM/A in August 1995. The same could be said of other commanders, especially of the Anya-nya 2 whose enthusiasm for the coup could not be measured.

Since they were from a pastoral background, they were inspired by clan or tribal concerns and interests rather than national ideals. But this is a serious flaw because the Nuers as a people have always exhibited high tendency towards Southern patriotism. The behaviour of the intellectuals had profound influence on their definition the enemy. This explains the unprincipled alliances they easily made with the enemy. Their allegiance shifted from being part of the South Sudanese nationalist movement to that of buttressing an oppressive regime in Khartoum even for very small gains.

Many tribes in South Sudan, because of their experience with foreign oppressors and their inter-tribal conflicts, have become conscious of the tribal and ethnic identities and petty differences that, out of frustration, they easily push these feelings to ridiculous and dangerous dimensions that make them forget or overlook the atrophying effects of the oppression and the dangers of complete loss of resilience and national objective. The Nasir coup and its Nuer agenda catalysed the Nuer xenophobia against and their contempt of the Dinka people. The lines were drawn on false premises that since the SPLM/A, which because of Garang's leadership was taken to be a Dinka movement, received support from the Ethiopians, Uganda etc., then the only option left to the Nuer was to join hands with the NIF government.

Their hatred of, reinforced by the contempt for the Dinka eclipsed the dangers posed by the NIF fundamentalist brand of Islam which aims to obliterate both the Dinka and the Nuer, inter alia, as ethnic and cultural entities in the Sudan. Since the Dinka would not yield leadership to the Nuer, as if that leadership was something to be shared in the fashion of sharing a traditional tobacco pipe practiced by our people in the villages, then the project - the national liberation struggle - should be spoiled. So flowed the reasoning of these unenlightened commanders. But since they could not succeed in the ruining the project - national liberation struggle - which in itself is not a Dinka project, but that of the entire people of South Sudan and since Garang, according to Riek Machar, could only get the leadership of a reunified movement over his [Riek Machar] dead body, then the way out of this artificial impasse must be separate and parallel existence of the two movements - SPLM/A and SSIM/A.

However, Dr Riek Machar introduced the concept of parallel and separate existence of two movements as early as 1992 when he toyed with the idea of changing the name of the Nasir faction as a way of stopping the fighting with the mainstream SPLA. This was discussed in a meeting in Waat in December 1992 by the five members of INEC who formed the core of the Nasir faction. At that time, Riek Machar seemed to suffer from intense guilt of having started a devastating fratricidal war among the South Sudanese which had claimed thousands of innocent lives. According to Riek Machar then, if the Nasir faction adopted a separate and different name the inter-SPLA fighting would cease. The only way to stop inter-SPLA factional fighting was for the Nasir faction to relinquish its claim to SPLM/A and, hence, abandon efforts to overthrow Dr John Garang de Mabior - which was the raison d'être for the coup.

But stopping the fratricidal war in the South would also have put the Nasir leaders into difficulty with the NIF government. Military and financial support of the regime to the Nasir faction depended on how much the Nasir leaders implemented the Frankfurt agreement. Apart from stopping the military logistical support, there was a possibility of the NIF government's offensive against the Nasir faction, especially after the adventure of Riek Machar in Malakal in October 1992. So the idea of changing the name was frozen until the faction was able to achieve victory over the SPLA in Equatoria. The mobilisation of human resources for the Equatoria expedition was made the priority and Riek Machar was given full authority to lead the force himself through Kongor and Pibor areas, making peace with the Bor and Murle people. This project fell into trouble in Kongor in March 1993 until it was completely abandoned.

Tragedies in South Sudan come in series that follow each other in very close succession. The military devastation of Bor and Kongor districts at the hands of the Nasir faction and the Anya-nya 2 in 1991 was followed by famine and disease in 1992. The looting of the cattle destroyed the economic base of the Bor people whose lives are built on rearing large herds. Because of the war, the people were unable to cultivate and, hence, the looting of the cattle exacerbated the famine resulting in their migration to Waat, the nearest relief centre, in search of food.

The gruesome pictures of human corpses - victims of hunger, not fighting - left to the vultures to devour, cast the spotlight of international humanitarian attention on Waat in October - November 1992. The population of Waat had just exploded as a result of the influx of the Dinka. Although the international humanitarian intervention brought the situation under control by the end of November, yet another problem of water shortage arose; the wells in Waat and its environs would not suffice. A radical solution, therefore, needed to be devised and quickly.

In a meeting between the UNICEF chief of operations and coordinator of UNOLS, Mr Philip D O'Brien, it was agreed that the only optimal solution to the humanitarian situation in Bor and Kongor was to have Panyagor opened as a relief centre. This would now allow the Dinka people, trapped by hunger in Nuerland, to go back to their homes from where the international community would serve them.

What appeared on the surface like a genuine humanitarian concern was in effect a political- military stratagem. Kongor and Panyagor became the epicentre of a vicious military conflict between the Nasir faction and the SPLA mainstream between March and April 1993 which claimed many lives including that of Mr. Joseph H Oduho, the veteran Southern politician and statesman, who was killed on 26 March 1993. The area of Kongor Waat, Ayod and Yuai became known among the NGO community as the 'Starvation Triangle where people perished in their hundreds as a result of war, hunger and disease[19]. As a consequence of this fighting, the SPLA gained complete control of Kongor area and, therefore, all routes from Upper Nile to Equatoria, frustrating the southward movement of Riek Machar and his troops once and for all.

Two years on, Riek Machar together with some of his cohorts attempted again to change the name, not of the Nasir faction, but of the SPLM/A-United into South Sudan Independence Movement/Army. This was, nevertheless, contested by many in the faction's leadership who still favoured the idea of reconciliation and reunification of the liberation struggle. There was no point in changing the name if there was still room for reunification. Moreover, the name 'SPLM/A' had become a historical icon that only those who were not part of the SPLM/A subculture did not see any myths about it and wanted to do away with it. Dr Riek Machar could not entertain any opposition to whatever he had set his mind on. The change of the name had to be done come what may, to the extent that he rejected the Lafon Declaration which everybody else saw as an opportunity for the Nasir faction to disengage from collaboration with the enemy. The underlying reasons was to crown his theory of parallel existence.

According to his logic, the parallel and separate existence of SPLM/A and SSIM/A was feasible and could even allow for military collaboration, including sharing of logistics in the struggle against Khartoum. For example, Riek Mhar expected the SPLA to allow SSIA forces to pass through its territory on their way to the international borders with Kenya and Uganda. This perhaps is the height of childishness and obscurantism. This can only be occasioned by fudging under the shallow and simplified notions of parallel existence very serious political and military issues of reunification and reconciliation between the two armies which have spent more than three years fighting each other. This kind of thinking exists not in the realm of practical politics but in hallucinations and day dreaming.

Sharing military logistics between SPLA and SSIA and allowing a peaceful movement of SSIA forces through SPLA controlled territory could have occurred provided that:

- either the two armies had ceased fighting each other and agreed jointly to engage in combat activities either jointly or separately against the NIF army and its militia. This would have meant that the strategic alliance between SSIM and the NIF government had been revoked and a SSIM Declaration to that effect is publicised. In such a situation, SPLA and SSIA will have imperceptibly merged, albeit, through their joint action against a common enemy;

- or the two armies had adopted the same or identical political objective and programme which could either be the secession of South Sudan as proposed by SSIM or the liberation of the New Sudan (South Sudan, Nuba Mountains and the Ingessina Hills) as proposed by the SPLM and is acceptable to the separatists in SSIM.

These are two optimal conditions under which Riek Machar's logic for practical cooperation between the two armies could operate. But then the question is: Why, in all honesty, did the two armies remain separate if they had one common enemy to fight, had an identical political programme, they operated from the same territory and, in fact, hailed from the same nationalities, these armies which had originally, and not long ago, been part of the SPLA ? What prevented these armies from uniting into one powerful army ? In such a situation the two movements and armies should have been able to thresh out the question of leadership of the reunified movement which remained the contentious issue, especially after all the issues raised in the Nasir Declaration have been or were being addressed by the SPLM. The best thing would had been immediate reunification.

This was the line of reasoning of the officers and members of the SSIM National Executive Council which Riek Machar haughtily eschewed without considering the possible implication. It was reasoned that the best resolution of the leadership problem was for Dr Riek Machar to become the deputy of Dr John Garang in the reunified SPLM/A. This was a correct and honest appraisal of the position of SSIM/A and of Riek Machar himself. But he reasoned that John Luk, George Maker and others, who pushed for that solution, were now colluding with Garang to deny him (Riek Machar) the leadership of the reunified movement and, by extension, the South Sudan. He was so incensed by this that he declared: 'Garang will get the leadership of the reunified SPLM/A upon by dead body'. He, therefore, proceeded to shuffle out of the NEC John Luk, George Maker Benjamin and Daniel Koat Mathews. This was a bureaucratic rather than political act that accelerated the split within SSIM/A.

In his philistine obtuse temperament and in order to appease his self ego, Riek Machar destroyed what would have been a single act of patriotic solidarity among the people of South Sudan, and their good nature of self forgiveness. The reason he gave was that if he were to come under Dr Garang again, the whole of Nuer community feeling betrayed would join the NIF government. In other words, the Nuer people would rather prefer to be dominated by northern Sudanese than accept to be led by a fellow South Sudanese. But the real irrationality of this situation was that Dr Riek Machar himself wanted to become the leader of an independent South Sudan; the question which begs itself then is: would that independent South Sudan exclude the Dinka ? And if not, what would happen then if the Dinka choose to face Dr Riek Machar with his own ethno-centric logic[20]? Or, alternatively, should the cause of the people of South Sudan just be lost because the Nuer and Dinka are fighting over the leadership? An intellectual like Riek Machar should tell the people of South Sudan something more than this.

Another argument which Riek Machar puts forward to rationalise the parallel existence of more than one liberation movement was that, since many people died as a result of the split, unity was not the acceptable proposition because it was difficult to justify the losses. He feared that if he accepted unity under John Garang, the people would condemn him for starting the split only to rejoin the Movement after causing destruction to the people and weakening the Movement. Other tribal chauvinists around Dr Machar quickly compounded his dilemma by telling him that if he accepted reunification of the Movement as Anya-nya 2 did with SPLM/SPLA in 1988, this would damage the reputation of the Nuer people as a whole for lack of perseverance and consistency.

Dr Machar's moral dilemma is his own creation. In South Sudan, fighting between tribes, clans, sections etc., is not a new phenomenon. There are countless examples of wars fought between and among the various tribes, clans, and tribal sections of the South. The latest example of these type of conflicts happened recently in the SSIM/A controlled areas between two primary sections of the Nuer people, namely Lau and Jikany. One thousand eight hundred persons lost their lives in this conflict and hundreds of thousands head of cattle were looted from both sides. But, in spite of the heavy losses of lives and property on both sides, the conflict was resolved in Akobo by Nuer chiefs and elders from the different Nuer areas using traditional methods of conflict resolution. The two sides forgave each other for the lives and property lost. It was possible to arrive at this settlement because both sides to the conflict recognised the need to restore harmony, peace and security to their communities. None of the two sections demanded compensation for the destruction it had suffered from the acts of the other. Both sides mutually agreed that maintaining the status quo was the best way to resolve the conflict[21].

In view of the above, Riek Machar's line of thinking was fallacious and had no basis either in the traditional customs or in modern diplomacy and political interactions. Reconciliation and reunification with the SPLM/A was a less expensive option of resolving the conflict, he himself precipitated, than the unconditional surrender or capitulation to the Islamic fundamentalist regime. Dr Riek Machar should stop pretending that he is fairing well in that situation. The NIF government is operating on a political - ideological strategy which sees Riek Machar and other renegades as tools for implementing its programme. The NIF regime will not allow him to wield the kind of power and authority he was used to in the SPLM/A before and after the split. It will not take long before he storms out or break himself free of the virtual detention he is under in Khartoum. Dr Riek Machar should have carefully analysed the implication of signing the 'Political Charter' as an equal to Kerubino Kuanyin Bol, his deputy in the SPLM/A-United and in SSIM/A.

The NIF government is not interested in doing political business in Khartoum with South Sudanese intellectuals who have taken up arms the like of Riek Machar. It prefers to deal with them abroad, like Dr Lam Akol, to cover the eyes of the international community. Inside the country, the NIF government, like any other oppressive northern regime prefers to deal with the like of Kerubino, Paulino Matip Nhial, Gabriel Tang-ginya, James Othow Along and others. The fact that Gabriel Tang-ginya attacked Riek Machar forces in Fangak area and Lam Akol was dislodged by his deputy in Tonga, Orinyo and other places in the Shilluk Midwest with the military assistance from the NIF government, is a testimony to the NIF's penchant for instigating disharmony and conflict among the South Sudanese.

Dr Riek Machar will live to regret and curse the day he rejected and mindlessly threw away the Lafon process. He will live perpetually to suffer remorse for assassinating in cold blood Commanders William Nyuon, Peter Manyiel Kueth, Gordon Koang Banyping and many others who laid down their lives to reconcile the people of South Sudan and reunite under their historic movement - SPLM/A.

The 'Political Charter' which Riek signed with the NIF government on 10 April 1996 is the logical consequence of the parallel existence of more than one liberation movement that he obstinately insisted on against the well-meaning advice of many people. The split within SSIM/A, the refusal of the Ethiopians to render support and give him sanctuary in the border areas, the successes of William and John Luk in Lou area, have all compounded the crisis of Riek Machar, rekindling the fears in 1992 which pushed him into a firm alliance with the NIF government. However, the 'Political Charter' does not bail him out because it makes him part and parcel of the NIF government machinery in which he will never dream of being the deputy of Omer el Beshir. Had Riek been meticulous, and had he possessed the clear political vision why he wanted power, he should have accepted being deputy to Dr Garang in a reunified and rejuvenated SPLM/A.

By August 1994, when the Akobo conference for the reconciliations and peace between the Lou and Jikany was convened, the contradictions within the SPLM/A-United had reached their peak point. Cdr Arok Thon had resigned, Cdr John Kulang had escaped to Khartoum and Cdr John Luk and others had been arrested and detained in Waat. Riek Machar's detention centres were now teaming with senior officers and commanders who have been arrested in connection with the Lou - Jikany conflict and the burning of Nasir town. With the Bahr el Ghazal group having resigned en masse, the social base of the SPLM/A-United had shrunk and Riek Machar's genuine supporter were reduced to a few new comers into the liberation struggle.

His former colleagues in the Nasir faction had all deserted in disgust with his inconsistency. Riek Machar, therefore, remained at the head of an empty structure surrounded by sycophants of the like of David de Chand, Joseph Nyok Abiel and others. His policies had alienated nearly everybody he started off with in 1991; it did not seem to bother him or disturb his conscience that his former friends and colleagues had turned against him - a very rare show of self-confidence, reflective of his philistine exhibitionism which borders on idiocy and naïvety.

The Akobo conference for reconciliation and peace among the Lou and the Jikany was preceded by spectacular political events in the South Sudan theatre. While the SPLM/A-United leaders were involved in political squabbles and settling personal vendetta, the SPLM/A was working to convene its first national convention. Riek Machar woke up very late to the reality that democratisation and the creation of structures in the Movement etc. for which he had justified the coup in Nasir in August 1991, were being put into practice by the SPLM/A.

In May-June 1994, the SPLM convened its first national convention, which was a resounding success, given the conditions at the time. Delegates came from many locations in the New Sudan (South Sudan, Nuba Mountains and Ingessina Hills) and from northern Sudan. It was the first major structural and political reform in the SPLM since its inception in 1983. The convention elected the National Liberation Council and the National Executive Council, with Dr John Garang de Mabior and Commander Salva Kiir Mayardit elected chairman and deputy chairman respectively.

Riek Machar was then in Nairobi preparing for the conference of peace and reconciliation among the Lau and the Jikany, scheduled to take place in August in Akobo, and was now mobilising material support from the international community which responded benevolently and generously.

A few days before the peace conference closed Riek Machar called for an INEC meeting whose agenda was not disclosed, and for which we had not prepared ourselves. During that meeting Riek Machar announced his intentions of turning the peace conference into the SPLM/A-United convention whose deliberations would commence immediately after the closing session of that conference. No counter arguments against this turn of events were accepted no matter how convincing. Riek Machar had made up his mind and there was no way of postponing his convention because, according to him, 'there will never be an opportunity again to bring together that number of people'.[22] He insisted that the new name for the SPLM/A-United - South Sudan Independence Movement and South Sudan Independence – Army - SSIM/A must be introduced without delay because the people were ready for the change. I was appointed the chairman of the preparatory committee which I thought was meant to silence my criticism.

Since the objective of the exercise was to adopt the new name - SSIM/A, something for which the minds of the commanders, officers and men of the SPLM/A-United, and even the Nuer civilian population had been prepared, any resistance was meaningless because it would have achieved nothing and, further, it would have soured the already fragile relations with Riek Machar. So we decided to make the best of a bad situation. The preparation for the convention started in earnest.

The first thing we discussed in the committee, which Riek Machar himself insisted he must attend, was the question of what to call the convention. Eventually, it was agreed that the meeting should be called the 'Founding convention of South Sudan Independence Movement/Army (SSIM/A)'. This was based on the practices of founding conferences of political parties which are conducted by their founding members, no matter how small the number. Since the interim period of eighteen months agreed upon in Kongor on 26 March 1993 had already expired, it was agreed that the INLC and INEC should be dissolved and permanent structures put in place.

Riek Machar can be a very difficult person when he decides not to accept an idea no matter how correct and logical. Sometimes, without convincing reasons, he will close his mind to any further suggestion, betraying his claims to be a genuine democrat. This is partly because of his shallow experience in political organisation and action. As the chairman of the preparatory committee, I had to spend much time consulting with him and most of this time disagreeing on almost every minute detail of the convention work. In order to commence the deliberations of the convention, there were certain procedural matters to be cleared. One was the dissolution of the standing bodies: INLC and INEC to give way for the formation of permanent structures. By way of example, I pointed out that it was imperative to dissolve the INLC and INEC to form the National Liberation Council and the National Executive Committee. It took me time to convince Riek Machar that during the first SPLM national convention the High Command was dissolved and Garang himself had had to resign in order to be re-elected. Riek Machar could not countenance the idea of resigning as chairman, even as a temporary formality.

The dissolution of the two bodies had to be done after their respective terminal meetings. It would be out of the reports of the secretaries in the INEC. He was also expected to draw his report to the convention from the terminal deliberations of the INLC. Riek Machar had no time for all these formalities. He felt strongly that it was a waste of time to do so.

The first session of the founding convention of SSIM did not end in a good manner. Riek Machar had smuggled into the convention ex-SSU activitists and had wanted to turn the exercise into a replica of SSU meetings. A motion to adopt the speech of the chairman and commander in chief to the convention before being discussed was narrowly defeated. It had to be discussed in full. Riek Machar drew daggers with those who criticised the practices of the faction since 1983; more specifically when the delegates bitterly criticised the collaboration with the NIF regime and the break down of law and order in areas under his control and the failure to bring an early end to the Lou - Jikany conflict. Many of the speakers stressed the need for reconciliation and reunification with SPLM/A. The conference specifically demanded from Riek

Machar to order Cdr William Nyuon Bany, then said to be in Juba, and Commander Kerubino Kuanyin Bol, then in Abeyei, to report to the convention, and that the Nuer troops in eastern Equatoria be withdrawn back to Upper Nile.

There was a discrepancy between strong speeches delivered by some members of the convention and their subsequent actions. On the basis of the strong statements for reconciliation and reunification with the SPLM/A, Riek Machar's submission for the change of the name to South Sudan Independence Movement (SSIM/A) should have been rejected. The acceptance of Riek Machar's scheme automatically negated the notion of unity with the SPLM/A and of the liberation struggle. But, of course, it was difficult to expect any major departure because most of the intellectuals present, many of them from abroad, had not been part of the SPLM/A before the split or were those who have joined the SPLM/A-United out of narrow solidarity with Riek Machar. In fact, the convention had been dominated by people like Dr Michael Wal Duany, Dr David de Chand and other Nuer zealots who turned it into an exercise at the formalisation of the 'Nuer patria' concept.

The convention went into committee work. I was made to head the economic committee although I thought my major contribution would be in the political committee I did not know that Riek Machar, with the assistance of Dr Michael Wal Duany, had wanted to use the political committee to bulldoze some of his myopic political vision for the Nuer patria. This was the central point around which the deliberations of the convention revolved. The first issue which caused a lot of heat was whether South Sudan would remain in three or be divided into more regions or states as Riek Machar insisted those regions should be called. There was a strong presentation that, since the South was still at war, then there should only be three regions. This was turned down and the discussion on this topic was stifled by the chairman of the convention, Mr Joseph Nyok Abiel. South Sudan was divided into seventeen so-called states not very different from the NIF states which were meant to divide the people more rather than to unite them. The upshot of this exercise was that in the end Riek Machar's Nuer patria was sanctioned with four states namely: Bieh (Akobo and Waat), Phow (Fangak and Ayod), Latjor (Nasir and Maiwut) and Liech (Bentiu).

Although the concept of forming states on ethnic lines was criticised, in practice, given the geographical disposition of SSIM/A, it was the Nuer states that, were going to be functional; it must have been understood in the light that except for Bentiu town, the Nuer Patria was already 'liberated'. This created tension in the convention with representatives of other areas in Upper Nile. Equatoria delegates were satisfied with only three states in Equatoria. The delegates from Bahr el Ghazal (only two) suggested that they would only go for three states.

The problem now was in Upper Nile, which exceptionally looked as if it was going to have ten states including the four Nuer district-states. To resolve this, Riek Machar decided that there would be only five states with the creation of Northern Upper Nile (Kodok, Malakal, Renk and Bailiet), Bieh (now include Pibor and Pochalla), Phow (encompassing Bor and Kongor) sates. That formula was still contested but, as the chairman of the convention, he vetoed any further discussion on the subject and those who were not satisfied had to give in to Riek Machar's wishes. What some of us knew was that it was just a face saving formula which would not survive.

Then it came to the election of the two councils, the National Liberation Council and the National Executive Council of SSIM/A. Riek Machar had collected all the information on the way the SPLM first national convention was held and how the members of the two councils were elected. He had wanted to copy the recent SPLM procedures during its convention. The exercise was that the delegates from a particular county, in the case of the SPLM, would sit and elect their representatives in the National Liberation Council (NLC) who would in turn recommend somebody to the Chairman those to be appointed to the National Executive Council (NEC). Riek Machar wanted exactly the same thing done and he got in trouble with the Northern Upper Nile state, whereby the Shilluk, the Dinka and the Maban people were lumped together against their will. It was here that I decided to call it quits with Riek Machar.

He, and not our delegates, had chosen three of us: Commander Daniel Deng Alony (then in the government garrison of Melut), Mr Elijah Awan and myself to be the members of NLC representing Northern Upper Nile state. Riek Machar coerced Elijah Awan into announcing my name so that I could take my position among the other members. I refused and stayed put, waiting to see what Riek Machar was going to do after such defiance that sent silence through the house. I was to see the consequences of my action three days later when I was blocked boarding the plane back to Nairobi. In fact, Riek Machar must have suffered the fact that he could not arrest and detain me as that would expose him in a negative light.

The founding convention of SSIM did not achieve what the SPLM first National Convention had achieved by way of uniting the rank and file of the Movement. The Akobo convention ended up in sharp divisions among the leaders, cadres and the people. Immediately after this meeting, there was an attempt on the life of Riek Machar. Its main objective of this convention, unfortunately, was to bless the separate and parallel existence of the SSIM/A and SPLM/A.

That Riek Machar would brave anything in order to maintain parallel and separate existence of SSIM/A and SPLM/A is just because he does not want to deflate his ego. He refused to accept the reality of the situation that the coup of 1991 had utterly failed to achieve its objective. Riek Machar is like somebody acting out of guilt for what he has done and feels ashamed to admit it. In fact, he does not belong to the generation of astute politicians. He operates in the realm of dreams and political obscurantism. A politician must assess the political situation and calculate his options based on reality and not on wishes or whims. A politician must know when to go on the offensive and when to retreat or be on the defensive.

The option of separate and parallel existence was not Riek's original idea. This was drilled into him by his close associates who exploited the situation for their own parochial interests. This is precisely because, had Riek Machar and Lam Akol wanted separate existence from the very beginning, they would not have staged what they called the creeping revolution. They would have gone about their business forming their Movement without having to cause the death of so many people through a futile attempt to oust Garang from the SPLM/A leadership.

The separate and parallel existence of SSIM/A was something on which Riek Machar could hinge his political options after the failure of the coup and the collapse of his dreams following the disintegration of the SPLM/A-United. In that case, he had no reason even to quarrel with people like John Luk and George Maker who wanted him to adopt a political position which would have cost him lest in terms of personal dignity, respectability and acceptability in the eyes of the vast majority of South Sudanese. Had he opened his eyes and mind wide enough, Riek Machar would have discovered that his real enemies in SSIM/A were not those he shuffled out of National Executive Council at the height of his emotional stress but those who ensnared him and filled his mind with nonsense about being the 'Moses of South Sudan' or the prophesied 'liberator' of the Nuer people.

Riek Machar should have drawn valuable lessons from the failure of the Nasir coup to garner the required support for his ousting of Dr John Garang. The mood of the people in the SPLM/A and their priority was not in favour of factionalism. Many SPLA officers and men believed the differences arising from and revolving around personalities, John Garang included, could be resolved only after the immediate conflict with the enemy has been completed. This explains why many of the leaders: Joseph Oduho, Martin Majier, Victor Bol Ayualnhom, Kawach Makuei, Kerubino, Arok Thon and many others remained in the SPLA detention without anybody, whether their relatives or political friends, raising a protest about their detention.

Even people like Cdr Arok Thon, who often boasted of having the support of more than forty five percent of the SPLA officers corps, spent nearly six years under detention and had to escape from the detention camp without any of these officers coming to his rescue. This proves that what mattered in the SPLM/A and in South Sudan for that matter, was not the personality of the individual but the cause for which the people have taken up arms and have sacrificed much. This perhaps is the most positive thing that enabled the SPLM/A to survive since 1983 in spite of the difficulties and serious internal contradictions it has encountered. Those who did not agree deserted individually and quietly with or without much ado[23].

So Riek Machar's insistence on parallel and separate existence of his movement is yet another error of political judgement after the Nasir coup that made him miss a golden opportunity for 'retreating in order to advance', an opportunity for growing politically and militarily in shadow of Dr John Garang, leader of the SPLM/A. As deputy in a reunified and rejuvenated SPLM/A, Riek Machar would have had the opportunity to avoid punishment for the crimes he committed against the people of South Sudan and other marginalised areas not least, among these, the unleashing of terror and genocide against the people of Bor and fomenting the Lou-Jikany conflict.

On the other hand, had he accepted the Lafon Declaration and the process of reconciliation and reunification he would have provided a strong basis for reforms and building of democratic institutions in the SPLM/A. This is because after the SPLM/A first national convention 1994, no one was interested in reverting to the old methods. Even John Garang himself had renounced his dictatorial and autocratic leadership methods in the new political environment. Thus, in the final analysis, had Riek Machar carefully taken stock of the political developments he would have achieved with the Lafon process in 1995 what he failed to achieve with the Nasir coup in 1991, at least in terms of personal power and the transformation of the Movement.

Even assuming that Riek Machar did not want the reunification of the Movement, he could have pushed for his separate existence in a manner that would have reaped him political capital. The gesture for reunification and reconciliation was initiated by SSIM/A patriotic commanders after taking action against the NIF forces in Lafon. In fact, Riek Machar's chief of staff, Commander William Nyuon Bany, was in Juba when his officers and men took action. The NIF government rushed him to Lafon to release the government soldiers and possibly reverse the situation. Commander William Nyuon Bany found it difficult and had to acquiesce to the dictates of his officers and men and immediately established links with the SPLA. Had he concentrated his energy on reconciliation and reunification and not on the position he would occupy in a reunified Movement, perhaps Riek Machar would have won sympathy for his parallel and separate existence if Garang and the SPLM/A had rejected him. This would have put Garang on the defensive; Riek Machar would have carried the support of many people in South Sudan and would have exposed Garang and the hawks in the SPLA as the obstacles to unity.

But Riek Machar concentrated on what position he would occupy that he became almost paranoid about it. Yet Garang was willing to accommodate Riek Machar in the high interest of reconciliation and reunification of the liberation movement. In his letter of 5 June 1995, Garang assured Riek Machar that:

> ... Finally, one of the recurring issues that has been raised to me by some of our people and by friends in the international community is your role in a reunified Movement. I take this opportunity to assure you personally that this should not constitute a problem. In its last meeting, the SPLM National Executive Council (NEC) resolved that the leadership of the Movement will be restructured in such a way as to adequately accommodate those who broke away from the Movement in 1991, so that they play their appropriate roles in the reunified Movement...

Garang's letter destablised the SSIM/A and sent Riek Machar on the rampage against his own officers, accusing them of having defected to Garang. Instead of responding positively to Garang's reconciliatory gesture, Riek Machar scattered his forces to the point of exposing not only his front but also his rear and flanks. Besides a tragic fratricidal war ensued in central Upper Nile leading to a major humanitarian disruption and the assassination of Cdr William Nyuon Bany.

The question of Riek Machar being accommodated in the second position in a reunified Movement was already causing problems with the SPLM/A ranks. That position was not vacant; it was occupied by Cdr Salva Kiir Mayardit, who was much senior to Riek Machar in the hierarchy of the SPLM/A before the split. Talk was doing the rounds within the SPLM/A circles that if offering Riek Machar that position was going to heal the split, then Salva had to be persuaded to accept whatever compromise in the higher interest of the people of South Sudan. In any case, it would have been difficult to convince the SPLA officers and men to accept Riek Machar as the second in command at the expense of those who had remained loyal to the Movement in the wake of the Nasir coup. In fact, Riek Machar, by his refusal to accept the Lafon Declaration, made things easy for the SPLM and has saved it another contradiction and a possible split within its ranks.

Dr Garang's letter should have been studied objectively and this is what John Luk and George Maker wanted. But Riek Machar placed his emotions and the question of leadership before reason relying on those who placated and elated his ego through flattery; to reward those sycophants he began dispensing bogus political and military positions. For instance, he appointed an officer at his headquarters 'acting governor' of Latjor state. Without analysing what that meant in practice, the young man became so obsessed with Riek Machar's leadership that he alienated himself from his family and relatives under whose care he grew up. Between October 1994 and June 1995, the SSIM/A witnessed an upsurge in the promotion of officers to the rank of commander which Riek Machar dangled in the face of his officers and men to buy their support and loyalty[24].

It was highly irresponsible and unpatriotic of Riek Machar to have treated with contempt his officers who precipitated the Lafon events. Many of these patriotic officers and men felt betrayed by his actions and out of frustration, with lack of progress in the process they had initiated, precipitated another split in the ranks of SSIM/A. The announcement of 14 August 1996 was an attempt to save the Lafon Declaration from disappearing in the hot air of tribalism and from eventual collapse when Riek Machar turned the declaration into a political tool for stirring tribal hatred and animosities.

Notes

[1] Dengtiel and Telar attended the Frankfurt talks between the NIF delegation and the Nasir delegation; they discovered that there was something treacherous in the meetings between Lam and Ali el Hag and they, therefore, decided to resign from the faction.

[2] The former Director of IRRES, Mr Svein-Tore Christeffersen.

[3] The Lou - Jikany conflict was discussed in a meeting between Riek Machar and the Chiefs of Lou in December 1992 and the culprits who were going to cause the war to break out were named, some of them very senior officers of the Nasir faction. Riek failed to take any measures and in April 1993 the Lou and Jikany war broke out in the 'Toich'.

[4] Of course there were isolated incidences in which some Nuer officers and men in the SPLM/A mainstream were summarily executed on accounted of their ethnicity. This heightened fear among the Nuers and found it more expedient to desert and run to Upper Nile.

[5] The Nuers have never had a unified or centralised authority in their history. In Ngundeng's songs, there will emerge a leader who will unite the Nuers in the west and east of the Nile. The east of the Nile includes, of course, Ethiopia and Riek Machar has painstakingly been working hard to bring Ethiopian Nuers to his support. The attacks on Gambella he ordered before was in preparation for return of that region to the control of Sudan government.

[6] In 1982, Ernest Kenyi and others acting for the Sudan Embassy Intelligence service in Nairobi, drugged late David Dak and his colleagues, placed them in coffins for dead, and flew to Khartoum. It was only due to providence that they stayed alive and were rescued from Nimeri jails by the April Uprising in 1985 when they were finally set free.

[7] Mayom Kuoch, instead of standing in solidarity with us, decided to steal Taban Deng Gai's brief case loaded with foreign currency brought from the NIF delegation to Frankfurt and disappeared. He has appeared long since in Khartoum. Dengtiel and Telar took similar independent decision to resign from the faction. Professor Barri Wanji in his usual disruptive behaviour stormed out of the faction in a frenzy that could not be controlled after a quarrel with Lam Akol over his camera. Dr Achol Marial, who at the beginning played it coolly as long as he had access and controlled to the purse of the faction, departed from the faction because he was promoted or rather appointed as secretary for Health and social services in the INEC, which removed him from the control of the faction's money. All these defections, although they were manifestations of the political contradictions in the faction, took personal trends, thus preventing collective action to correct the situation. This was to continue later in the SPLM/A - United, whereby comrades put high stakes on their personal dignity than on the national issues.

8   In fact, a split was simmering in the faction and such names like the 'Nairobi faction' of the Nasir faction started to be heard in the office of RASS.
9   JOHN LUK refused to execute Riek's orders but Lam Akol travelled to Nasir instead and from there to Abuong to meet the forces returning from the attack on Malakal. However, in December, the INEC meeting was called in Waat and there was a show down over William's refusal to join Nasir faction.
10 Although Kongor was the site of bitter in fighting between the SPLA mainstream and the forces of Nasir, Riek Machar, refusing to heed advise about a imminent SPLA attack, convened the leadership meeting of the SPLM/A-United in Kongor. He, his late wife Emma, Lam Akol, Kerubino and Arok Thon narrowly survived the attack. A German TV team that went to visit Riek in Yuai, not very far from Kongor, after the incident also missed being captured by SPLA, shattering once and for all Riek's baseless confidence in his military prowess.
11 This action proves the futility of dismissing from, shuffling out of a position in the INEC or staging a coup against a guerrilla leader because, unless there was success in apprehending him, it is utterly impossible to be effective.
12 Immediately after his dismissal, Lam Akol made on 12 February 1994 a press statement that he had accepted to climb down as that was a normal practice in any organisation.
13 Cdr Chol Deng hails from Abeyei and to go there he had to pass through Gogrial area and that meant being together with Kerubino.
14 Cdr Dhol Acuil (Tonj), Cdr Amon Wantok (Rumbek) and Prof. Isaac Cuir Riak (Yirol).
15 Cdr Arok Thon Arok and Cdr Chol Deng Alaak.
16 Cdr. Martin Kenyi, Emanuel Ocholimoi and later Dr Theopolus Ochang Lotti, Riek Machar's Secretary for Humanitarian Affairs.
17 Every splinter group that broke loose, kicked off with the formation of its humanitarian and relief wing, became the conduit for funds from the international community.
18 The freight of these planes did not exceed nine hundred kilograms because much of the space is taken by fuel for return flight. It was the most expensive way of delivering relief.
19 The humanitarian agencies wishing to take relief to the area were denied access by the warring parties which exacerbated the situation.
20 William Nyuon Bany et al (1995) 'Riek Machar is the obstacle to the unity'. A document published just before the announcement of the ouster of Riek Machar from the leadership of SSIM/A on August 14th.
21 Ibid.
22 The delegates, especially those from western Upper Nile, Equatoria and Nairobi were transported by the NGOs; the food for the conference was provided by the WFP, LWF, SCF and others.
23 There were cases of SPLA officers and men deserting to the enemy, e.g., Francis Jago Nyibong, who captured Pochalla in April 1986, deserted the SPLA and went to Khartoum in 1989.
24 Some of Riek's positions were really bogus and had no meaning. For instance, the position of 'acting governor' would arise if there were no deputy governor since his deputy would carry out the functions of the governor in his absence. But the hopes are raised in those appointed and gave them the illusion that there was an opportunity for being a governor. This policy paid back in that many of those who stuck to Riek were those occupying some of these positions.

5

The Political Charter: No act of Chivalry

... But man, proud man.
Dressed in a little brief authority.
Most ignorant of what he's assured.
His glassy essence, like an angry ape,
plays such fantastic tricks before high heavens as to make the angels weep...

Measure for Measure
William Shakespeare

Politics is the art of the possible, so they say. In a power contest among many political parties and groups in a liberal democratic setting, like that which exists in some western countries, each politician works to further the partisan interest of the party, along side the national interest. Thus, politicking becomes the art of the possible within the context of an array of alternative means and methods of arriving at the helm of state power. This should be different from the exercise in revolutionary politics or the politics in a national liberation movement, where what is at stake is not the interest of the individual or that of a particular political or ideological group but the liberation process itself, which must be nursed and nurtured in a manner that each and every group must subordinate their individual and partisan interest to that of the general and public interest. The tribal or regional interest, in this respect, should be subordinated to the national interest. It will be completely out of line with the logic of revolutionary nationalism, if one were to project the interests of one's tribe or region over and above those of the nation, particularly when it is still in a state of nucleation.

The contradictions in a national liberation movement, therefore, should not be heightened to the extent of threatening its very existence and the process it undertakes to achieve. In such a situation such as that which obtained in the SPLM/A before the Nasir Declaration in 1991, those in positions of the leadership who wanted reforms effected could have implemented some of these democratic actions in their areas of deployment while at the same time agitating for changes that would eventually encompass the whole SPLM/A. Since the carriers of the reform message were not democrats in themselves, their methods were definitely bound to be *putschist*.

If, instead of staging the Nasir coup, Riek Machar and Lam Akol had entertained the idea of working quietly for reforms within the SPLM/A, implementing them at the same time, they would have served two significant ends: First, it would have delayed indefinitely, if not postponed, the military confrontation between them and the SPLM/A leadership until they were able to dictated the terms. Secondly, it would have allowed time for better organisation and mobilisation of public opinion inside and outside the SPLM/A for the changes. After the disappearance of the Ethiopian factor[1] in the resolution of the SPLM/A internal contradictions, the leadership definitely would have been forced to resolve the internal contradictions through dialogue and building of a genuine consensus. Thus, it was imperative and significant that Riek Machar and Lam Akol attended the meeting of the High Command scheduled for July that year.

The third purpose this tactic would have served is that it would have allowed time for many of those who wanted reforms in the Movement to reach their positions and commands, boosting the response and support for the process of democratisation within the SPLM/A. By staging their coup prematurely, Nasir leaders, both Riek Machar and Lam Akol played into the hands of the NIF government and became puppets in the hands of Omer el Beshir. First, the NIF dangled the possibility of secession of South Sudan as a means to peace in the country. They both took the NIF seriously and worked to get something out of it.

In fact, as Dr Lam Akol declared on his arrival in Nairobi in September 1991, that the war is not winnable. The defeatism drew sharp criticism from many South Sudanese circles in Nairobi, who started asking whether Dr Lam Akol arrived at this conclusion that the war is not winnable only after the Nasir coup. And how could the war not be won when the SPLA was on the offensive and had the balance of forces in the South tilted in its favour? Lam Akol even claimed that the NIF government was genuine in its efforts to reach a negotiated settlement to the conflict in South Sudan. That is why he put all his trust in the NIF regime. According to him, what the South needed was an honourable peace deal with Khartoum concluded by shrewd negotiators like himself.

But for all the talk about peace, the NIF exploited the political windfall brought about by the demise of Mengistu regime and caused by the sudden withdrawal of the SPLA from Ethiopia. It bombed the returnees camps, especially in the Sobat river basin. Because of this bombing, together with lack of food in the area, forced a lot of people, including some SPLA officers and men, to proceed to Malakal and surrendered to the enemy. As a result, many civilians in areas under the control of the Nasir faction felt they had no choice but to accept the NIF government 'peace from within' programme.

The fact that Riek Machar surrendered unconditionally and went to Khartoum to 'look for peace' and that Lam Akol refused to support a declaration made by Dr Hassan el Turabi, the leader of the National Islamic Front, on 23 March 1996²², can be interpreted in many ways: Either Lam Akol realised that the whole programme of 'peace from within' was going to fail and, therefore, jumped out of it in time or that he did not forgive Riek Machar and, hence, did not to associate with him. It is also possible that he wanted to embark on his own independent project with the NIF government.

The other scenario could be that since Lam Akol posed no military threat to the regime, it was more convenient for Dr Turabi to keep Lam Akol temporarily out of the programme of 'peace from within' in order to confuse the international community, especially the governments in Akol Horn of Africa³. Lam Akol's visit Addis Ababa to look for military logistics from the Ethiopian governments was probably encouraged by the NIF regime to rationalise its accusation that the rebels were receiving military assistance from neighbouring states. Ethiopia was a convenient target because its government had accused Khartoum of sponsoring terrorism following the attempted assassination of Egyptian President Hosni Mubarak in 1995. Accordingly, Lam Akol's presence in Addis Ababa and his request for military support, coming especially at the time of the signing of the *Political Charter* in Khartoum, were designed to project him in a false image of still being in the liberation struggle. Had he received military logistics it would have been used by the NIF to blackmail the Ethiopian government.

Lam Akol's political games were very transparent; his visit to Ethiopia ostensibly to look for relief access to Shilluk midwest area cannot be taken at face value. His political existence in that area was not based on fighting the NIF government but on collaborating with it to defeat the SPLA and destroy the liberation process. He has been hiding behind the façade of relief just to enable him maintain a political and diplomatic space in Nairobi. The link had been provided by some of his close associates in African Rights Watch. The idea was to establish a relief consortium called Sudanese Humanitarian Initiative Liaison Unit (SHILU). The declared objective of this agency was to solicit funds for relief and humanitarian assistance into the Nuba mountains, the southern Blue Nile and the Shilluk midwest. The plan was to isolate, the two governors of southern Kordofan and southern Blue Nile from the SPLM/A headquarters. Those concerned with the initiative did not want to have the SPLM leadership involved. That is why the SPLM/A became suspicious and subsequently rejected the so-called humanitarian assistance initiative which presumably was part of the political games of the NIF government.

The plan was feasible and, therefore, would have made relief and humanitarian assistance to these areas cost-e ffective. Initially, since Lam Akol had rejected the idea of going to Khartoum, it gave the Ethiopians the impression that there was some form of cooperation between Lam's SPLM/A-United, and the SPLM/A. This that was never the case as the

Ethiopians were to realise much later and they agreed with the SPLM to stop the initiative. After the initial contacts for humanitarian assistance were finished, Lam remained in the Ethiopia to conduct political work among the Nuer and Shilluk refugees in Addis Ababa. He travelled to Gambella to visit the refugee camps in Itang and Piny-udo; tried to discredit both the SPLM/A and Riek Machar, while projecting himself as the authentic leader of South Sudan.

By signing the *Political Charter* with the NIF government, Riek Machar sealed his capitulation and unconditional surrender. Though Lam Akol's refusal to sign the political charter, he continued to undermine and discredit the SPLM/A and its leaders. Accordingly, both men were living embodiments of the NIF programme for 'peace from within', which is a logical consequence of the Nasir coup. Their move was never political chivalry in the least because they have not had the courage to swallow their pride and bow to the demand of the people. Instead of reconciling with the SPLM/A, both Riek Machar and Lam Akol have, in their separate ways, chosen to fraternise with the enemy.

Lam Akol could have joined without much ado the reunification and reconciliation process started by Commanders William Nyuon Bany and John Luk. But he would not commit himself because, like Riek Machar, he suffers from a lot of guilt apart from the importance he attaches to the position he would occupy in the reunified Movement. In fact, Lam Akol is very bitter with what William Nyuon Bany and John Luk but did not dare to condemn them for fear of exposing his motives. The fact that Commander John Luk did not insist on certain positions as a condition for rejoining the SPLM/A mainstream has kept Lam Akol and other splinter leaders lingering outside the liberation process and this makes their motives questionable. Indeed, their equivocal behaviour can easily be interpreted as serving the strategic purpose of the NIF regime.

The NIF 'peace from within' programme

In essence, the NIF government's 'peace from within' programme must be synonymous with capitulation and unconditional surrender. It is, in fact, an affront to just and democratic peace settlement. The NIF ascension to power in a military coup in June 1989, just four days before the launching the Sudanese peace initiative between the political parties with the SPLM/A, was a rude negation of the peace process. But since then, and because of the dictates of the global and regional circumstances, the regime was forced to engage in peace talks with the SPLM/A. Instead of addressing issues which would resolve the conflict, the NIF has been buying time to prepare itself for a decisive defeat of the SPLA.

That is why the talks in Addis Ababa (September 1989), Nairobi (December 1989) under the auspices of the US former President Jimmy Carter, the Abuja

I (1992) and Abuja II (1993) peace talks under the auspices of the Nigerian President Ibrahim Babangida and lastly, the IGADD peace talks (March - September 1994) under aegis of the IGADD heads of state committee for the Sudanese conflict, chaired by President Daniel arap Moi, failed to make any head way. The IGADD sponsored peace talks reached and got stalled at a more advanced phase. It had formulated the Declaration of Principles (DOPs) as the most viable option for a peaceful resolution of the conflict in the Sudan. The NIF rejected the 'Declaration of Principles' and the peace process was frozen for nearly five years between September 1994 and July 1997.

The NIF's strategy for achieving this 'peace from within' continues to promote splits and divisions within the liberation movement to prevent their reunification through bribery with bogus appoints like that dished to Riek Machar (assistant president) or Paulino Matip Nhial (major general in an army he does not command). No one should be surprised by these tactics of the NIF government. This underpins the formation of ten states, which are not economically viable, is part of the grand strategy to weaken the South through balkanisation.

The 'peace from within' was the basis for which the Nasir faction, SPLM/A-United and later SSIM/A received military and financial support from the NIF regime and Lam Akol was the focal point of these treacherous transactions. As such he should not pretend have dissociated himself from the regime's programme. He was the main architect for its formulation and went far enough in implementing it. In August 1993, under the cover of the occasion of the installation of the Shilluk Reth, Lam Akol met a delegation of the government in Fashoda to discuss the 'peace from within' strategy. Reth Kwongo Dak Padiet was apprehensive, knowing that such a partial peace plan would not bring about an end to the war. He, therefore, advised both Lam Akol and the government delegation that if they wanted his mediation, they should be frank and honest. However, it was in the Fashoda meeting that they agreed to take the matter to Riek Machar for finalisation. In fact, the light aircraft that exploded in mid air in Bentiu area in September 1993 was carrying the government delegation to Riek Machar's headquarters in Mankien[4].

The NIF regime wanted to be seen talking peace with the SPLM/A-united for its strategic calculations not only internationally but also in Upper Nile. Internally, since the 'peace from within' was designed to be a piecemeal approach, the idea then was to link Riek Machar and Lam Akol to the internal forces and with the NIF functionaries, people like Mungo Ajak, then the deputy Governor of Upper Nile, Ustaz Ahmed el Radhi Gaaber, Abu Gassessa and others, some of whom perished in the plane. The NIF targeted Lam Akol whom they knew enjoyed the lime light as Secretary for External relations and Peace. Having worked out all the details with Lam Akol in Fashoda, the NIF delegation now proceeded to submit the draft to Riek Machar for endorsement.

It is possible that Riek Machar and Lam Akol did not want to be part of the implementation of 'peace from within'. It is possible that they hoped collaboration with the NIF would enable them maintain a political and military presence in South Sudan. But the NIF government is not run by naïve and mediocre people. The NIF politicians planned to extract maximum political capital out of the collaboration with this faction of the rebel movement. The NIF theoreticians knew well that the real power in the South remained in the hands SPLA, not Riek Machar or Lam Akol. However, the significance of these two ambitious and power hungry men to the NIF government lies in their willingness to execute the NIF plans that aimed at breaking its isolation at national and international levels. And every consignment of arms they received tied them firmly to the NIF programme, widening the gap between them and the SPLM/A and the rest of the South.

In this they have proved loyal dogs to the NIF, contrary to their proclamations - Riek Machar has finally travelled to Khartoum, while Lam Akol remains outside trying his best to draw away commanders of the SPLM/A, like Commander Yousif Kowa and others, to edge them out of the liberation struggle. While the interest of Riek Machar and Lam Akol in collaborating with the NIF regime brought just parochial gains, the NIF hoped to reconquer territories lost earlier to the SPLA, but now were under the control of these engineers.

Riek Machar had been receiving military logistics without himself being involved physically with the NIF leaders, either inside or outside the Sudan. He failed to reconquer eastern Equatoria on behalf of the NI. At the same time, he lost to the SPLA most of the military logistics supplied through his chief of staff. The NIF had become a bit capricious and rather suspicious of Riek Machar whether or not he remained steadfast to the 'peace from within' programme negotiated by people other than himself. To push him further to the wall, knowing that he would not defend Nasir not even for five minutes, the NIF dispatched in March 1995 a force of *mujahideen* and regular army to recapture Nasir as a means of calibrating Riek Machar's reaction against this action to his collaboration and commitment to peace from within programme. The NIF entered Nasir peacefully contrary to his hullabaloo in Nairobi that he had fought the invading force killing fictitious numbers. Nasir was the first garrison Riek Machar handed over to the NIF government in exchange for collaboration. His next gifts to the NIF regime may be Akobo, Ayod, Leer and many others which he pretends to control.

The Political Charter

It goes without saying that a comprehensive peace to the Sudan can only come about when all the parties to the conflict are involved in the peace process.

There is no way that any two parties can conclude a deal, like the one concluded by Riek Machar and Zubier Mohammed Salih, and expect it to bind on all the others. Examples of such political deals abound in recent Sudanese history. For instance, when General Nimeri signed the Addis Ababa agreement with the Southern Sudan Liberation Movement in 1972, it was rejected by nearly all the northern political forces. Nimeri had come to power in a military coup, overthrowing a democratically elected government of Mohammed Ahmed Mahgoub, just like the present NIF regime. Therefore, he did not have the mandate of each and every Sudanese to conclude this Addis Ababa agreement with all its constitutional implications. Thus, for eleven years it remained a deal between southerners and Nimeri while the rest of the North stood against it, working to undermine it[5]. In order to please these northerners, Nimeri himself abrogated the agreement unilaterally, plunging the South and the country into chaos and confusion in 1983.

In another development, SPLM/A signed the Koka Dam agreement in March 1986 with the National Alliance for National Salvation (a consortium of political parties and trade unions that spearheaded the popular uprising that brought down the Nimeri regime in April 1985). The Koka Dam conference was boycotted, and the agreement thereof, dubbed as the Koka Dam Declaration between the SPLM and the National Alliance for National Salvation, was rejected by the DUP and the NIF. This forced Sadiq el Mahdi to renege on implementing the provisions of the Koka Dam agreement when he became prime minister immediately after the general elections on the ground that the DUP, the junior partner in the coalition government he headed[6], was not a signatory, and that the SPLM/A should seek a separate agreement with DUP first so as to enable him implement the Koka Dam agreement. In November 1988, the DUP negotiated and agreed with the SPLM on the modalities of resolving the Sudanese conflict. Sadiq's reaction to this Sudan peace initiative was to throw the DUP out of their coalition government and replace it with the National Islamic Front.

This shows how agreements which do not have the support of all the parties can ran into difficulties when it came to implementation or when the political situation changes. Politics is not dictated by the 'good will,' but by the political, economic and social interests of the contending parties. The NIF, like the Umma and/or DUP, is playing the same game. When it was in the context of sectarian politics, the NIF rejected the concept of negotiating with the SPLM/A. But when it usurped state power, the circumstances forced it to talk to the SPLM/A, having regard to the relative strength of that Movement and balance of forces. Its present intransigence stems from the consideration that SPLM/A has been sufficiently weakened by splits and in-fighting so it can afford to be evasive using the 'peace from within' programme.

Viewed against the above exposition, the *Political Charter* has the same characteristics as the Addis Ababa agreement in that it was between two parties to a conflict that involves more than fifty other parties, including the trade unions and other popular organisations which make up Sudanese civil society. It will definitely not bind these parties when the regime is overthrown and they take over the power.

The *Political Charter* is being given political projection as a basis for peace negotiations between the parties that signed it. Whether there are peace mediators that can pick it up and use it as ground for starting another peace process besides the stalled IGADD initiative, remains to be seen. However, the most significant fact that must be borne in mind is that the forces that can disturb the peace arrangement that accrues from the charter, namely the SPLM/A, the NDA and others, are opposed to this charter. The regime needs the charter not as a peace instrument but only to solve some of its acute logistical problems in the war front by pitting the South against itself. For the NIF regime, it is even more urgent, given the growing strength of the SPLA, reflected by the recent offensive, to regain the initiative military and tilting the balance of forces in its favour.

The NIF regime, therefore, by signing the *Political Charter* is trying to achieve what the people call killing two birds with one stone. Through this charter it hopes to use Riek Machar (a Nuer) and Kerubino Kuanyin Bol (a Dinka) to divide and engage the South Sudanese in fratricidal war. At the same time, it is designed to kill the IGADD peace process by promoting its bogus 'peace from within' strategy.

It did not take Riek Machar and his supporters long to discover that they have committed a grievous mistake by acting out of emotions. He had not made the necessary preparations for the *Political Charter* and for travelling to Khartoum. He had not sufficiently gauged the feelings of South Sudanese who are getting the brunt of the NIF policies inside the government-held towns, including Malakal, Juba and Wau. He had assumed, just like what he did in 1991 when he announced the coup that, because of the war, the people in the government-held towns were fed up and wanted immediate peace, and would, therefore, embrace him with his *Political Charter*. To his astonishment, the people in the NIF held towns rejected that charter as a sell-out.

The *Political Charter* contains fourteen points which are vague and subject to multiple interpretations, making it unsatisfactory and, therefore, unacceptable to all parties to the conflict. This is because the NIF regime does not want to commit itself to a definite political formula. The weakness of the past agreements between the South Sudanese and the northern political establishment has always been existence of duplicity in the interpretation of the contents of those agreements.

The Khartoum regimes have never shown good faith in their dealings with the South. For example, in December 1955, the southern members of parliament voted for the independence of the country on a promise that the North would in turn support the Southern demand for Federation. The northern politicians vaguely promised that the 'federation will be given full consideration', but no sooner had independence been granted than they turned around and claimed that the 'federation had been given full consideration and was found not working'.

The above examples clearly show that the northern politicians have always unashamedly made promises which they did not intend to honour. Recently, the NIF government has resorted to vague statements during the IGAD peace process[7]. This deliberate vagueness has derailed the IGAD peace process. Even the proposed set-up of a Southern Coordination Council in article 11 of the Charter is nothing new. Sadiq el mahdi and his government (1986 - 1989) created it as a means of engaging the South Sudanese politicians in divisive politics.

Unlike the IGADD Declaration of Principles 1994, the *Political Charter* cannot be the basis for negotiating a just, democratic and lasting peace in the Sudan. In fact, it is the very negation of the IGADD peace process. It does not make reference to what Riek Machar always was his pet project - self-determination of the people of South Sudan. The IGADD Declaration of Principles gives the people of South Sudan, the Nuba Mountains and the Ingessina Hills the right to exercise 'self-determination' in an internationally supervised referendum while the Political Charter speaks only of a 'referendum' without clear reference to self - determination for which it was meant to be a mechanism.

It has been mentioned in a rather cynical manner that Riek Machar's political charter with the NIF is an equivalent to the Asmara Declaration, which puts the SPLM/A in the same mould with the northern opposition parties - Umma, DUP among others and that Riek Machar was pushed to that position because his application to join the NDA was rejected. The Asmara Declaration can not in any way be compared to the *Political Charter* for many reasons. First, although most of the northern political parties in the NDA are equally guilty of war crimes and atrocities committed against the people of South Sudan since independence and, although it is true that the present NIF regime grew out of the womb of sectarianism, these parties are now in opposition to the regime. And by the logic of politics an alliance with them against the NIF regime serves the cause of the South. The only optimal political condition under which South Sudanese and other marginalised people in the Sudan can achieve their aspirations through force of arms, as it is going to be, is to have these parties divided and at each other's neck.

Moreover, for the first time, the Umma Party and the DUP have come to recognise the right of the people of South Sudan to self determination. The National Democratic Alliance, therefore, is a positive democratic process. This is a major departure from the northern establishment's southern policy that has been in force since 1953.

The Asmara Declaration speaks of a transitional period in which all the oppressive laws which restrict the rights of the people, shall be repealed and their excesses addressed. In contrast, the *Political Charter* still adds fuel to the conflagration by emphasising that 'Sharia and the customs shall be the sources of legislation'[8]. The Asmara Declaration is a document signed by parties which consider themselves equal in the struggle for the democratic transformation of the country and has the support of the region while the *Political Charter* is, at best, a formalisation of a collaboration started in 1991 which, in the final analysis, are terms for capitulation by Riek Machar to the NIF regime. He found out rather belatedly that he enjoyed no support regionally and even among the Nuer people. The *Political Charter* is, in the words of President Omer el Beshir, 'a return to the fold of the homeland of those who have carried the gun against the state'[9].

The euphoria that accompanied *Political Charter* is already fizzling out. Even its protagonists have come to recognise that talking about it lays bare many inconsistencies inherent in it. It shows that there was no basis for the charter in the first place. The NIF regime is definitely not interested in a peaceful resolution of the conflict, for if it did the North would end its domination and hegemony over the South and which freezes its programme of Islamisation and Arabisation in east, central and southern Africa.

The *Political Charter* does not change the balance of forces on the military front. This is because, since the Nasir Declaration in 1991, Riek Machar has been in alliance with the NIF regime and, in fact, has been fighting the SPLA with all that he had in terms of man-power. He failed to dislodge the SPLA from eastern Equatoria in order to reach the international borders with Kenya and Uganda. Although the NIF managed to take over towns like Torit, Kapoeta, etc., the SPLA remained resilient and, after effecting internal restructuring in 1994 - 1995, was able to go on the offensive. On the other hand the SSIM/A split into two, with William Nyuon Bany and John Luk controlling large areas of Fangak and Lau, thus considerably reducing the effectiveness of Riek Machar. The *Political Charter* has not brought in any new forces that would augment the military position of Riek Machar.

Instead it has created sharp divisions between him and those of Gabrie Tang-ginya. Besides, Riek Machar's insistence on maintaining some form c independence from the NIF regime is causing much friction with thos commanders in Fangak and Bentiu[10] who have been paid militia of the regim This opposition leaves Riek Machar with a small margin of forces he ca commit entirely to the enemy's side if he chooses. That will not affect the balance of forces much because since 1991 he has been doing nothing but fighting the SPLA along side the NIF government.

The impact of the charter on the quest for peace

There have been serious attempts in the past for a just and lasting peace in the Sudan, but these attempts have come to nought simply because the northern political establishment has always sabotaged them. For instance, in 1965, the resolutions of the Round Table conference on the problem of Southern Sudan could not be implemented, and the deliberations of the Twelve-men committee (formed by the conference) could not proceed successfully because of the hurdles placed in their way by the northern political parties. The same parties worked hard to undermine the Addis Ababa agreement until it was finally abrogated by Nimeri in 1983.

The peace initiatives to bring an end to the on-going war have also been many but they stalled because the northern political establishment's agenda of Arabisation, Islamisation and oppression of the South Sudanese and other marginalised people, militates against the conclusion of a just, democratic and lasting peace in the Sudan.

The Nigerian peace initiative came after the split of the SPLM/A and after the regime has made in-roads into the liberation movement by entering into a strategic political and military alliance with the Nasir faction. The Abuja peace talks between the NIF regime and the SPLM/A (1992, 1993), and the subsequent Nairobi peace talks (1993) between that regime and the Nasir faction (then SPLM/A-united) were just an exercise in public relations.

The IGAD peace initiative (1994) on the conflict in the Sudan came at the suggestion of the Sudan government at a time the SPLA had its back to the wall in Nimule. The NIF government assured of militarily defeating the SPLA wanted now to isolate it diplomatically, especially in the region. The NIF government jumped out of this peace process when the IGAD countries formulated the 'Declaration on Principles' as the democratic basis for resolving the conflict. The regime exploited the deterioration of diplomatic relations between the Sudan and its neighbours - Uganda, Eritrea and Ethiopia – precipitated by the regime's penchant for exporting its brand of Islamic fundamentalism through acts of terrorism and undermining the national security of these countries, to reject the Declaration of Principles and thus kill the IGAD peace initiative. In fact, the NIF strategists had believed that the IGAD countries, because of their internal political difficulties, could not take a firm stand on the peace talks. For the NIF regime, the purpose of these talks was to isolate the SPLM/A diplomatically while preparing the ground to destroy it militarily.

In order to deal a last death blow to the IGAD peace initiative, the NIF government has been shopping for new mediators and new fora for Peace talks between it and the SPLM/A, while at the same time manoeuvring to sabotage the efforts at reconciliation and reunification of the SPLM/A[11]. The regime has been conducting separate talks with individual commanders of SPLM/A-United and SSIM/A in the field[12] in its drive to make reunification among the Southerners and the liberation movement impossible and to create easy conditions for those who want to make separate peace deals. Apart from Political Charter with Rieck Machar, the NIF government has recently signed what it called a 'Declaration of Principle' with Mohammed Haroun Kafi, the renegade SPLA officer from the Nuba Mountains. This means that the regime does not seriously take any external mediation. It prefers to deal directly with the likes Riek Machar, Kerubino Kuanyin, Lam Akol and Martin Kenyi.

In another desperate move to undermine the IGAD process, the NIF regime has picked on the Barcelona Symposium (1995) and the atmosphere it created, as an alternative forum, not really to engage the SPLM in meaningful peace negotiations, but only to break itself out of isolation, especially in the wake of the imposition of the UN Security Council sanctions on the Sudan. The UNESCO-sponsored symposium and the two days workshop that preceded it, in Noordwijk, the Netherlands, in May 1996 almost afforded the NIF government an opportunity to involve the SPLM in its scheme of destroying the IGAD peace process[13].

The significance of the involvement of Sudan's neighbours in resolving its internal conflict can not be overemphasised. It is the first time the countriesß neighbouring the Sudan have come out in support of a process which could lay down the basis for a genuine, just and democratic resolution of the conflict in the Sudan. The war in the Sudan has serious consequences on its neighbours and, therefore, cannot be treated as an internal problem - a grave mistake that African leaders have made in the past. This in itself was bound to influence the decisions and its external ideological commitments of the NIF regime.

A resolution of the conflict in the Sudan, whether peaceful through a negotiated settlement or by force of arms with the SPLA shooting itself into the major towns of South Sudan, can be achieved when parity in power has been established. The IGAD's DOPs, now reinforced by the apparent state of hostility between the Sudan and her neighbours, may play a positive role in the quest for peace. The various regimes that had power in Khartoum have prosecuted the war in the South on the basis of an Arab and Islamic cause and have consequently received political, economic and moral support from the Arab world. In contrast, the South resisted the systematic process of Arabisation and Islamisation with meagre material support from its friends but without any kind of commitment from the African countries. The NIF regime will take seriously the peace process, whether by IGAD or any other mediators, when it knows that SPLA has support or is likely to be given support to continue the armed struggle. The SPLM, therefore, as a major force in the conflict must stick to the IGAD's DOPs and its mediation effort as the only guarantee for the resolution of the conflict.

In view of the above considerations, Riek Machar - NIF's Political Charter has done much harm to the cause of the people of South Sudan and other marginalised areas and to the peace process itself. Armed with this bogus political gimmick, the NIF government projects the façade of a peace lover, when, in fact, it is prosecuting war. The declaration of jihad made three years ago has not been revoked and Omer el Beshir is busy raising his one million mujahideen for the war.

The *Political Charter* accentuates the divisions among South Sudanese and, hence, makes the attainment of peace among them impossible. This has already been proved by the NIF government projecting both Riek Machar and his deputy Kerubino Kuanyin as two separate and distinct entities when they signed the charter. A peaceful resolution of the conflict in the Sudan or between North and South, as it appears, is predicated on the prior resolution of the South - South conflict represented by the SPLM/A and SSIM/A and any other splinter groups. The *Political Charter* has blocked any further efforts at reconciliation and reunification of the South Sudanese groups because Riek Machar and the rest have wilfully incorporated themselves into the NIF regime's war machine against the oppressed people of the Sudan.

The *Political Charter* raises the spectre of bloody tribal wars along the Dinka - Nuer border in Bahr el Ghazal and Upper Nile. It has turned back the wheel of the peace process, transforming it into a vicious circle, whereby every new mediation starts from the scratch. With this tactic, the NIF government hopes to gain time during which, it hopes, the SPLM/A will have withered away or through the acts of genocide and aerial bombing of the civilian targets, the South would have disappeared as a result of massive depopulation.

Therefore, by engaging in side talks with disgruntled and former SPLA officers or by its so-called 'peace from within' programme, the regime is sabotaging any genuine peace initiative which would address the fundamental issues of the conflict. The peace negotiations favoured by the NIF are those which will go on until it gains the upper hand on the military front. As Prof. Fishers puts it in another context:

> ... The difficulty ... lies not in the lack of potential substantive options, but in the failure to design, negotiate and pursue a process that moves us forward from where we are now to where we would like to be..."[14]

The Political Charter: No act of Chivalry 165

The regimes in the Khartoum have been picking and dropping mediators to the conflict in the Sudan since 1986 and have made the peace process a farce, representing a failure to pursue a process that moves the negotiations forward. In all the negotiating sessions, the Sudan government delegations have been pursuing one single agenda of a united Sudan, which is Islamic and Arab in cultural orientation. This is a political agenda that denies the people of South Sudan and other marginalised areas their inalienable right to self determination and, at the same time, stroves to maintain racial and cultural superiority of the Arabs. This was arrogantly put by Dr Ghazi Salauddin el Atabani, then leader of the Sudan government delegation to the fourth and last session of the IGAD peace talks in Nairobi on 22 September 1994, which statement, because of its significance and bearing on the interpretation of the *Political Charter* and its implication on the peace process, must be quoted in full:

> ... 'Self-determination'. The fate of Sudan has been determined way back in 1956, when Sudan attained independence. The Southern part of the country, which had deliberately been underdeveloped and culturally isolated by the British, has never been dealt with as a political entity by any regional or international authority.
> Whereas the claim to an independent Southern Sudan was adopted very briefly by the Anya-nya rebellion, which has been staged by the British just prior to independence, it has never been an original claim of the present SPLA rebellion. On the contrary the SPLA rebel movement has been renounced for its unionist claims. Its shift to separatist positions can only be seen as a negotiating tactic.
> Self-determination, alas, separation, of Southern Sudan is bound to elicit a chain-reaction afflicting the rest of Africa. This is an eventuality which the founding fathers of the Organisation of Africa Unity (OAU) have consciously tried to avoid when they stressed the inviolability of the colonial borders in the OAU charter, to which Sudan is signatory.
> The Sudanese government is therefore committed to handing over the "same Sudan" to future generations. Self determination or any other term that might cloak separatism is a non-issue and the government is not ready to dwell upon it. It would be more appropriate instead to address the substantive issues that constitute the true basis of the problem and to work out the guarantees required to safeguard the final agreement...

These are the words of the representative regime that has already made up its mind about destroying the peace process. Given the manner in which the Muslim Brothers operate politically and their single-minded determination to impose their will, Riek Machar, or any other South Sudanese leader who might be tempted to follow Riek Machar's pig-headedness, will have no room for political manoeuvre. He will have to adopt to what the NIF government has laid down for him.

The *Political Charter* has been emphasised as the only option for peace in the country when clearly it is not and will not be the basis for a lasting peace in the country. The difficulty with negotiating peace or constitutional arrangements of the Sudan that accommodates all Sudanese ever since the Juba Conference 1947, through the Round Table Conference on the Southern Problem in 1965, and many other fora, has been that the peaceful resolution of conflict in South Sudan, must conform to the strategy to perpetuate Arab political, racial, religious and cultural dominance in the Sudan and Africa at large. To the northern political establishment, the peace process to resolve the conflict in the South must be reinforced with strong racial prejudices and territorial conquest implemented with ruthless massive displacement of the Africans from their homes. What is happening in South Sudan, Nuba Mountains and Ingessina today is tantamount to ethnic cleansing to dispossess the Africans and to make land available to the Arab tribes. This is similar to the conflict in Dar Fur[15], which the authorities in Khartoum have all along preferred to call 'armed robbery'.

There has been a persistent conspiracy by the Arab dominated regimes in Khartoum to sabotage peace efforts which they fear would circumvent their long term strategy of an Arab Sudan. In that respect, these regimes had to adopt the policy of internalising the conflict among the South Sudanese. What Omer el Beshir has done by signing the *Political Charter* with Riek Machar is not new. It is an equivalent of Sadiq el Mahdi's so-called 'Internal Settlement Plan' of 1966/7 whose strategy was to divide and rule the people of South Sudan[16].

The 'Internal Settlement' scheme collapsed and so will the 'peace from within' because both don't address the fundamental issues of the conflict. They deny or rather ignore the genuine concerns and aspirations of the people of South Sudan and other marginalised areas in the North. At present Sadiq el Mahdi finds himself paradoxically in alliance with the South Sudanese simply because of the wrong policies his regime adopted towards the South. Unless the will and aspirations of the oppressed people of South Sudan, Nuba Mountains and other parts of North Sudan are satisfied, there will be no lasting peace in the country and Omer el Beshir, like Sadiq el Mahdi, may one day find himself in alliance - not with Riek Machar, but with the forces he is trying very hard to sideline within the liberation movement.

Although the Riek Machar- NIF *Political Charter* has halted the peace process brokered by IGAD countries, it is just transient. The peace process has stalled because of the apparent weakness in the Movement caused by the splits and in-fighting. This is bound to change sooner or later. The NIF divisive tactics may delay the pace of the liberation struggle but it will not prevent the ultimate victory of all the oppressed people of the Sudan. The renewed SPLA offensive which has gained an irreversible momentum based on the solidarity of the people of South Sudan will soon spread to the Red Sea hills, Dar Fur, the Butana, Gezira and Khartoum itself. By the time the NIF begins to take the peace talks seriously, it may be too late to hand over the 'same Sudan' to future generations.

Notes

1. As mentioned earlier the support of the Mengistu regime to the SPLM/A included provision of logistical support for quelling or arresting dissidents: armed guards, transport facilities etc.
2. Dr Hassan Abdalla el Turabi declared that Dr. Lam Akol had accept the Political Charter and was expected in Khartoum in two days for the signing ceremony set for April 21st. el Hayat Newspaper No. 12082 of Monday March 25th, 1996.
3. Dr Lam Akol went to Ethiopia twice in three months between April and July 1996 and has been telling the Ethiopian authorities that it was Garang rejecting the reunification and, hence, should be supported with military logistics. The Ethiopian were able to prove the falsity of this when they brought him and Commander Salva together in a meeting and he was asked to quit Ethiopia.
4. The Shilluks up to this moment believe that the Government delegation was not serious about the peace they were talking about, hence the wrath of the Gods came down on them before they could reach Riek Machar.
5. The Port Sudan agreement (February 1977) between Nimeri and the leadership of the National Front clearly stipulated, a condition for their participation in the May system, that Nimeri had to abrogate the Addis Ababa Agreement and return the political and administrative situation in the Southern Region to what it was before May 1969.
6. This has been the usual games played by the Umma and DUP. In March 1965, following the ascension of Luigi Adwok Bong, Representative of Southern Front to the Supreme Council of the State, to the presidency of the Council and, hence, as a Southerner, became the Head of State for one month, the Umma Party and the National Unionist Party (DUP before merger with People democratic Party in 1967) entered into a secret deal which amounted to an unholy alliance that put a brake to the rotation of the presidency of the Supreme Council, making Ismael el Azahri (NUP) the permanent President of the Supreme Council and the Umma Party to become the Prime Minister in any coalition government they entered into, thus ensuring their permanent hold onto the power of the Sudanese state. The Umma and DUP have since played a political game that made each appear as in agreement while the other would be dissenting but in the end of the day they are in complete agreement that a particular issue should be resolved in the way that favours their mutual interest. Hence, in Koka Dam, the DUP boycotted while the Umma attended.
7. The Sudan Government's Response to the Draft Declaration of Principles on July 22nd 1994.
8. Article 6 of the Political Charter.
9. Excerpts from the speech of the President of the Republic Omer el Beshir. Republic of Sudan Radio Omdurman in Arabic 0430 GMT 02 March 1996.
10. Those of Tang-ginya want Riek Machar to commit himself wholly to the NIF side, there is no point for him to behave half-heartedly: signing the political charter with the government, receive arms and financial support and yet wants to be a rebel, maintaining a separate and independent force. He either goes in with the government completely or he should be fought and defeated. They have already started operating against what Riek Machar calls his forces in Fangak. Paulino Matip Nhial is another character who does not like Riek Machar. In fact Paulino goes to Khartoum and meets Omer el Beshir without Riek.
11. It is reconciliation and reunification of the SPLM/A because, in fact, all the officers who formed the splinter groups: SPLM/A-united, SSIM/A, PRM, SSFF, etc., were all members of

the SPLM/A. If the cause of the split were removed, then there were no other reasons why the Movement couldn't reunite.

12 Dr Lam Akol (SPLM/A-united) met Major General Zubier Mohammed. Salih, the Vice President of the Sudan, in Atar on March 20th. 1994, again in 1996 in Lul, this was after meeting with Police General George Kongor Arop, the second Vice President in Fashodo in March 1995. Zubier met with Commander Simon Gatwich Dual (SSIM/A) in Malakal in April 1994, Commander Gordon Koang Bany Piny and Commander Nyang Chol in 1995 after their rebellion against Riek Machar.

13 The UNESCO Director General had invited Dr. John Garang, the SPLM Chairman, to attend the opening session of the symposium. This would have been an opportunity to show Garang shaking hands with the NIF Foreign Minister, Ali Osman Mohammed Taha, a thing that would confirm the NIF propaganda that they were going to the Netherlands to negotiate peace with the SPLM/A, a bluff to the IGADD countries, the SPLM can not afford.

14 Roger Fisher et al (1994) Beyond Machiavellian: Tools for coping with conflict. Harvard University Press (1994) pp. 6. Fisher and his colleagues were talking about the difficulty of negotiating the problems of the ethnic minorities in Bosnia and former Soviet Union.

15 Harir Sharif (1991) 'Arab belt' versus 'African belt': Regionalisation of ethnic conflict and restoration of peace in Dar Fur, western Sudan.' A paper presented to the workshop on 'Short cut to decay: The case of Sudan, Bergen February 20 - 23 1992.

16 Mansour Khalid (1990) *The Government They Deserve: The Role of the Elite in the Political Evolution of the Sudan*. K.P. International London. pp 233.

6

Lessons from the Nasir Debacle

... We trained hard, but it seemed that every time we were beginning to form into teams, we would be reorganised. I was to learn later in life that we tend to meet any new situation by reorganising and a wonderful method it can be for creating the illusion of progress while producing confusion, inefficiency and demoralisation...

Caius Petronius (AD 66)

The Nasir coup of August 1991 was, no doubt, a big political, diplomatic and military setback for the SPLM/A. It disrupted and spoiled the SPLM/A withdrawal from the bases in Ethiopia, following the demise of Mengistu regime. The coup stemmed from the failure of the Movement to institute democratic structures which could have been avenues for resolving its internal contradictions. In a sense, the coup was probably a blessing in disguise' in that it has helped to bring about the qualitative transformation on the SPLM/A. In the words of Louis Aragon:

> ... There is more strength to be drawn for the future from defeats than from many a victory, most of them amount to nothing more than empty publicity. It is out of the misery that mankind's future will grow rich, not out of blazing self satisfaction and gratification (my addition) that continually assail our ears...[1]

The Nasir coup, ironically, stimulated the renewal of the SPLM through the first national convention in 1994, the SPLA senior officers conference October 1995, the conference on Humanitarian issues between the SPLM, the United Nations Operations Lifeline Sudan and the humanitarian agencies operating in the war torn South Sudan, November 1995, the SPLM conference on civil society and civil authority in the New Sudan in May 1996. It can be said, after all this, that the emergence of the SPLM/A-United (March 1993), and later SSIM/A (October 1994), following the Nasir coup, helped cleanse the SPLM/A of opportunism and irresponsible ambition. The subsequent disintegration and capitulation of the Nasir leaders to the NIF government have proved useful lessons for the national liberation process and the entire people of South Sudan.

The Nasir coup triggered off a chain of events resulting in the lost of thousands of lives through the fratricidal war that undermined the unity and solidarity of the people of South Sudan and the advantage it handed to the NIF regime on a silver plate. Hopefully, the lessons drawn from these tragic events will give birth to the 'New Sudan' that really answers and satisfies the aspirations of the people, marking the end of the ills of oppression, social injustice, religious intolerance and discrimination, tribalism, sectionalism, nepotism, corruption and greed for power, and accumulation of wealth at the expense of the vast majority of the oppressed people.

The SPLM is not a political party *sensu stricto*; it is an amalgam of political and ideological trends united by a common objective of national liberation. The political and ideological line of this Movement should of necessity reflect the aspirations, interests and concerns of these component groups. It was the apparent disregard, slighting and marginalisation of other political opinions that precipitated the contradictions resulting in armed confrontation within the SPLM/A in the early days of its life. As mentioned earlier, it is the establishment of genuine internal dialogue and political debates, reinforced by internal and external ideological struggle, that guarantees the unity, solidity, coherence and healthy development of the Movement.

The experience following the Nasir coup and the process it triggered off, including its own demise, form a basis for critical reflections and political evaluation of the SPLM. In this respect, it is absolutely necessary to highlight the political changes that accompanied the SPLM first national convention 1994 as an eye opener for many people in the South Sudan. The resolutions of the Convention have been published[2]. The deliberations were conducted as if SPLM, far from being a political movement, had acquired the status of a state. Thus, we hear that the 'separation of powers' of the three organs of the state- the Judiciary, the Legislature and the Executive having been adopted and the appointments have been made in accordance with that principle. But, judging from its composition, the Convention appears to have been a bureaucratic exercise rather than a democratic reorganisation of the Movement[115].

We pride ourselves in the achievements of the convention. However, the appointment of the Chief Justice to represent the legal arm and the formation of the National Liberation Council as the legislative body of the New Sudan, the National Executive Council, as its government, have made a mockery of ourselves, masquerading as a state. We are informed that the powers which hitherto used to be exercised by the High Command of the SPLM/A have now been devolved to and vested in these organs. This a caricature of a Westminster type state structure which is hardly suitable for a national liberation movement like the SPLM. It was a political compromise that not necessarily facilitates the development of democracy in the Movement. As Dr. John Garang must have summed it up honestly, " you need to make dummy appointments"[4] in order to satisfy the wishes of some people who, coming late to the SPLM, wanted a replica of the regional government in Juba before the war. But the question then is: why make dummy appointments when the opportunity for making correct decisions still exists. In any case, the separation of powers has not been enforced. John Garang remains the chairman of NEC as well as the NLC.

One of the demands of the Nasir coup was the establishment of structures and institutions in the Movement. But, what sort of institutions? Were they meant to be state institutions or the Movement's institutions designed to give the liberation struggle a national content and political ideology? Drawing from what happened in the Nasir faction and its other variants: SPLM/A - United or SSIM/A, this demand was just a smoke screen for snatching the leadership of the Movement. However, it appears that the 1994 SPLM first national convention missed an opportunity to build solid democratic foundations for the Movement based on the realities of South Sudan.

The recommendations of the various conferences and workshops which the SPLM conducted from April 1994 to May 1996, except for those of the SPLA senior officers conference in October 1995, have not been implemented. Even those resolutions concerning social and economic development in the liberated areas have not translated into policies and actions. It looks as if people are keen to make resolutions but don't care about their implementation. Though the National Executive Council have deliberated on some of them, they have not yet been ratified by the National Liberation Council because it has not met since its formation in 1994. Then why was it necessary to make appointments which are not functional? This question should be addressed by the SPLM/A leadership to avoid the repeat of past contradictions which inflicted so much harm on the Movement and the people of South Sudan.

In retrospect, therefore, the SPLM first national convention has not built a strong foundation for the New Sudan. The changes in the SPLM and SPLA appear to have been inspired by external factors rather than the dynamics of the internal situation, which would reflect the relief internalisation of the lessons learnt from past mistakes. The interaction with the NGOs community in operation, demanded a certain degree of openness and transparency on the part of SPLM and its official in the SRRA. This was helped by the sessions of conferences, workshops, seminars etc., for capacity and institution building, which exposed many of SPLM officers to external influences, provoking further changes in the way SPLM operated.

The SPLA senior officers' conference came at a time when the SPLA was under pressure from the NIF government the Nimule front and when the operations for the recapture of Kapoeta had stalled. But there was an environment of relaxed optimism. There existed a climate of ease in which people talked openly about what they liked or didn't. This spirit of dialogue was carried to the conference and that assisted in defusing the anger bottled up over the years. It was that kind of conference which could have forestalled the Nasir coup and the subsequent split that has cost the people of South Sudan many lives.

The impact of open and frank talk on the conference has been the revitalisation of the SPLA as a military machine. Indeed, soon after the conference, the SPLA regained the upper hand in the Nimule front (October 1995), recaptured Pochalla (March 1996), and Khor Yabus in southern Blue Nile (April 1996). Many SPLA officers and men who had deserted their positions voluntarily returned in a wave of excitement following these victories. For the first time in four years, since the Nasir coup, the SPLA was able to regain the initiative on the military front. One can talk of the process of rejuvenation having taken roots and the SPLA having emerged in a new form, new personality, and new discipline. As a result, the SPLA officers', and men's respect for human values and dignity of the people of South Sudan and other marginalised areas was enhanced. Its capacity for sustaining the war of liberation was enforced by engagement in productive activities, reducing its dependence on external resources.

The SPLA is only a means to an end - liberation. It is not the motive force. It is the Movement, the ideas, and the organisation we call the SPLM which is the dynamo of the process It is this dynamo; how it functions that will determine the course of events in the New Sudan. The on-going process of liberalisation and openness in the SPLM and among the people of the New Sudan, if not reversed by some spectacular mischief, is what will put the SPLM in its right perspective as the driving force of the whole process liberation, including the war. In talking about lessons from the Nasir débâcle, the SPLM and its organs should first of all be the object as well as the subject of these reflections. The SPLM/A should learn from its past mistakes in order to push the liberation process forward.

There are lingering ideas that SPLA is different from the SPLM. At this stage of the national liberation struggle they are not different from each other. They are two sides of the same coin - national liberation. To dissociate political (SPLM) and military (SPLM) functions, that is to say that the SPLA prosecutes the war without its officers and men undergoing political training is actually to mutilate both the political and military components of the Movement. The essence of the problem at present is to discover precisely how to make the SPLM and its organs and the SPLA dovetail and work to each other's advantage and to that of the people all over the liberated areas. This is what must be understood by everybody, including those in the international community who have been calling for a divorce between the SPLM and the SPLA.

According to western perceptions, the growth and progress of a viable civil society in the New Sudan hinges on the process of the liberalisation and democratisation of the SPLM. The strength of this process in the SPLM, reflected in the awareness of the people and their conscious participation in their affairs, is the only way to measure its success. It will have to proceed in the manner people understand and internalise it for their own benefit.

The SPLM is the political Movement while the SPLA is one of its several organs of struggle. The idea of the army, which is a people's army, being separated from the people came in the context of distribution of relief supplies, donated by the international community. And to make that relief neutral, it was felt that it must be targeted to civilians who have nothing to do with war. This approach is based on the false premise that SPLA is different from the people. This no longer holds, as emergency relief has given way to rehabilitation and developmental endeavours. The attitude of the NGOs and the international community should change so that the process of development becomes participatory, with the SPLA included.

One of the lessons to be learnt from the experience of the last five years following the Nasir coup is that without developing the SPLM, as the main driving force in the war of liberation, it would be a waste of resources and time to continue the struggle. The thrust in the wake the conclusion of the reunification and reconciliation process triggered off by the Lafon Declaration 1995 is to build the SPLM and SPLA into genuine organs of the people power. In fact, this should give a fresh impetus to the revolutionary armed struggle to progress to its crest. It really matters little if we are brought back to our starting point as long as the conditions for winning the real victories can be seen and the militants whose participation rested on impatient illusions have either to give up or find more profound motives for their continuation in the struggle.

The reconstruction and development of the SPLM is an enormous task which requires perseverance, courage and total commitment in order to consummate the struggle for the creation of the New Sudan. The New Sudan will, of necessity, be built on the backs of the people; it is utterly impossible to motivate and mobilise the people, including even the army - SPLA, without a clear cut political programme to carry out the armed struggle to defeat the enemy and, thereafter, to commence the task of rehabilitation and reconstruction of the physical and social infrastructure which war has destroyed.

In this process of rebuilding itself, the SPLM needs more advanced organisational and ideological tools to accomplish the task. We are struggling against a well organised enemy in control of vast resources of the Sudanese state as well as those it can easily garner from the Arab and Islamic countries. In order to defeat or to make the enemy acquiesce to the demands and aspirations of the people, we have to be better organised with the meagre resources at our disposal. What all this requires is relentlessness and total commitment to the cause of the people on the part of the revolutionary nationalist and intellectuals.

Going by the objective situation and the recent political history of South Sudan, the SPLM is the only force that is capable of galvanising the majority of the people in South Sudan and to transform their reality. The SPLM has the potential for transforming itself into a mass Movement capable of changing the armed rebellion into a people's mass action to take the state power from the minority clique. There is no other political force in South Sudan with such a potential. In this respect, SPLM must reorganise itself and embark on the task ahead.

The ideological struggle within the SPLM

The SPLM is, or should be, viewed as ideas, policies, programmes articulated to mobilise the people for their own liberation. Ideas and concepts undergo fundamental changes as a result of their development and as a result of the changing political, economic and social environment under which they were formulated. As an organisation of the oppressed people of the Sudan, the SPLM is, therefore, also a platform for the transformation of these ideas into actions and policies, through debate and dialogue between the combatants themselves and between them and their leaders. The necessity of dialogue, debate and other forms of communication were stressed in another context by Paulo Ferreri in the following words :

> ... In the dialogical theory of action, the organisation of the people represents the antagonistic opposite of manipulation. Organisation is not only directly linked to unity but it is a natural development of that unity. Accordingly the leaders' pursuit of unity is necessarily also an attempt to organise the people requiring witness to the fact that the struggle for liberation is a common task... The correct method in revolutionary action lies in having complete and genuine dialogue with the masses. The conviction of the oppressed that they must fight for liberation is not a gift bestowed by the revolutionary leadership but as a result of their own conscientisation...[5]

The SPLM/A should internalise these words in order to build a solid foundation for the liberation and reconstruction of the New Sudan.

The evolution of correct ideas in the SPLM will not be spontaneous nor will they be supplied from somewhere readymade. They must evolve in the course of the political debate and ideological struggle to be carried out inside as well as outside and at all levels of the Movement. It is necessary outside, among the masses of the people, in order to distinguish between the real and false friends and to disseminate our correct and true ideas and to win over more people. It is a big mistake to assume that all the oppressed, whether in South Sudan, Nuba Mountains, Ingessina and even the North itself, will automatically support the liberation struggle. The oppressors are, in fact, using the oppressed to fight the liberation movement. So we need to intensify the battle of ideas to expose the propaganda of the oppressors and to convince the people that the SPLM/A is the embodiment of their interests and aspirations. Inside the SPLM and its institutions and structures, ideological struggle is an imperative for reinforcing the unity and effectiveness of the SPLM by identifying its weak points and purging its rank and file.

The word 'ideology' has always scared many people and it has been identified with Marxism. The oppressors have use it to invoke the memory of communism and totalitarianism have used it. But in the context of this book it is used to urge that the SPLM/A policies, decisions and programmes should be consistent with and be a result of genuine political ideas generated by the debate among the combatants. The ideas are articulated in a scientific manner as to make them and their applicability sustainable. Those concerned must build consensus only after a thorough discussion. Ideological struggle or the battle of ideas should be used to combat the culture of silence and gossip among the officers and men of the SPLA. It also sharpens the people's understanding of their problems and enables them to analyse and draw correct conclusions.

It is through dialogue and debates that the people are able to communicate with their leaders. And these debates and dialogue should not be just a monopoly of the intellectuals or of the military elite, but should be open to all. This is exactly what it means when we talk of building of a strong civil society in the New Sudan. The New Sudan society should be made of conscious and fearless citizens who are ready to sacrifice much for their freedom and social justice. The concepts of civil society developed in the conference hall in New Kush - Heiman, should not be allowed to fizzle away; they should be transformed into actions to meet the material needs of the people. To quote the words of Ferreri again:

> ... If true commitment to the people, involving the transformation of the reality by which they are oppressed requires a theory of transforming action, this theory cannot fail to assign to the people a fundamental role in the transformation process. The leader can not treat the oppressed as mere activists to be denied the opportunity of reflection and allowed merely the illusion of acting whereas in fact they would continue to be manipulated...[6]

Participation in political debates and discussions at any level is a right and a duty for the members of the SPLM and vital for the individual's intellectual development and also for the organisation. It clarifies some of the vague ideas in circulation, through criticism and counter criticism. However, political debate should not be undertaken for its own sake nor should it be carried to the extremes of igniting a fist fight between comrades. Carried to such extremity it can become inhibitive. Political discussions and debate should not be on sterile and matters unconnected with the liberation process. Carried to the abstraction, it could be a debilitating phenomenon in the political process and it is not desirable that political discussion of comrades involved in a noble task should degenerate into abuse and illogical utterances which fuel passions. Therefore, people who cannot tolerate arguments and other opinions should not trouble themselves involving others in debates and discussions that can easily lead to quarrels and fights.

Political or democratic pluralism?

Political pluralism is a western concept of political organisation and action in the state, sometimes called multi-party democracy. Each and every party organises itself to win the minds and hearts of the people, in fact the party represents the interest of a particular group of people - class or otherwise. In US, the dominant parties are the Republicans and the Democratic Party. In Britain, there are the Conservatives, the Labourites and the Liberal Democrats. They compete for parliamentary seats in elections and the power of each party in the House of Commons is reflected by the number of parliamentary seats it is able to win. The party with the highest number of seats forms the government. This is a version of multi - party democracy in western cabinet systems.

A national liberation movement, like the SPLM/A, is not a state and, hence, can not exercise this kind of democracy. By its nature and component forces, a national liberation movement or front comprises many small political and ideological groups united by the objective of liberation either from a colonial power, internal oppression or for secession. There have been many liberation movements, some of which have achieved their objectives while some have fizzled away. The Palestinian Liberation Organisation (PLO) African National Congress (ANC), FRELIMO, MPLA, EPLF to mention a few, are examples of liberation movements which fought wars for specific and respective objectives.

In South Africa, the ANC emerged as a party of the anti-apartheid encompassing peoples of all colours. The Communist Party of South Africa joined the ANC while still maintaining its independent forum, without compromising neither the ANC nor its principles. So we had leaders of the CPSA as also leaders of the ANC without any contradiction. People like Joe Slovo, Chris Hani were well known as members of the ANC as well as of CPSA. The political exercise in the ANC can not be described as multi-party-ism or political pluralism just like the one described above in Britain or USA. It is democratic pluralism being exercised here within one and the same organisation. This is also practiced in the other liberation movements.

The PLO emerged in 1967 after the Six Days War between the Arab and the state of Israel. It in fact replaced the 'Storm' of Ahmed Shukary. It comprised the various political and ideological trends current in the Arab world then. All these trends are represented and participate in all the organs of the PLO in a democratic manner prescribed by their charter.

The National Democratic Alliance (NDA) is an alliance of the northern political parties, the SPLM, the trade unions and important national personalities (independents) in the Sudanese political spectrum opposed to the National Islamic Front regime, presently in power in Khartoum. The base line of this alliance is to overthrow of the regime but not necessarily the social transformation of the Sudan. Thus, the alliance can and will eventually break up after or even before the overthrow of the NIF regime. The underlying principle in the NDA is political pluralism. The same thing can not be said of the SPLM.

A fundamental defect afflicts South Sudanese in their political action. This has prevented the emergence of a political ideology and a culture of political action. This has manifested itself in the SPLM and in other political structures that were formed in the South. The South Sudanese don't give themselves time to analyse and evaluate issues; hence, sometimes important matters are taken for granted and or are done on interim bases to suit the exigencies of the time. The fact that some of us are still grappling with what we are up to at this time is a clear indication of that affliction. We don't, or are often too timid to, ask our leaders what they mean if we don't agree with them. Put in another way the leaders are not reproached, criticised or opposed in public and few leaders accept private or individual criticism and/or advise. A pretender goes away satisfied that his views have been accepted. It is always assumed that particular leaders will disappear and, therefore, a new person with new ideas will come. It is this that has reinforced the lack of political leadership and consistency in our political struggle over the years. It is, therefore, quite important that we understand what we are embarking upon such that we are able to develop according to our terms.

The SPLM comprises rudiments of many small political and ideological groups representing real or assumed interests. It is only accidental that they have not crystallised; otherwise it would have complicated the situation further. They will evolve into full fledged political groups in future, depending on the dynamics of the internal situation in the SPLM. There are many liberation movements which split into many parties on or before achieving their objective and this inevitably results in the escalation of the war. It happened in Angola on the eve of independence when UNITA was ushered into the front with the assistance of the Portuguese and Apartheid South Africa. The same thing happened in Mozambique following the victory of FRELIMO in the war of liberation; RENAMO was manufactured to destroy the gains of the people. In

Uganda, the National Resistance Movement (NRM) has gone a long way to resuscitate and revitalise Uganda after years of destruction. Nevertheless, the Lord's Resistance Army and the West Nile Bank Front rebel groups, who were part of the repressive regimes overthrown by the NRM, are now wrecking havoc on the innocent civilians in north and north-west Uganda.

Unless the political growth and development of the SPLM is steered in such a manner as to avoid all the pitfalls of these national liberation movements, we might be in for more troubles. That is why it is necessary that things are thoroughly explained, understood and accepted by everybody or at least the majority of the people. The split with Anya-nya 2 in 1983 and the split in 1991 after the Nasir coup are important lessons that we must draw upon when rebuilding the SPLM as a genuine national liberation movement. The danger looms that internal contradictions within the SPLM could be exploited by our political adversaries in the north for the policy of divide and rule and, precisely because of that, patience and consistency in ideas must be exercised.

In a fragile environment of tribal chauvinism and irresponsible opportunism exercised by the elite, political and military alike, democratic pluralism in the SPLM must be approached cautiously. There is a strong obsession with uniformity among the various South Sudanese nationalities and ethnic groups; that explains why it has been easy to militarise because any dissension or divergent opinion is viewed suspiciously. The desire to subordinate the individual to the general is very strong and that is possibly why it might be difficult for democratic pluralism to take root in the thinking and practice of our people. But that does not mean we must abandon the struggle for tolerance of differing views. On the contrary, we should intensify the propagation of awareness and knowledge of correct ideas in our midst.

It has always been the case that the elite desire freedom for themselves but they deny it to others; this is not far-fetched. We have just mentioned how the SPLM/A, a national liberation movement, shouting the slogans of freedom, equality and justice, turned itself at some stage into an oppressive machine. The culture of political tolerance must be inculcated such that our yearning for freedom and justice, is not bridled. The suppression of lone voices breeds timidity and the display of an appearance of smooth untroubled face, which masks large crevasses and cleavages, tear the organisation apart.

Differences of opinion are natural and, in fact, necessary for the development of the organisation. As members of the SPLM, we are expected to agree with the broader issues of principles and objectives or with broader issues of the strategy of the Movement as spelt out in its basic documents. But differences of opinion can and will arise over the minute details of the major issues and that must be taken for granted. These difference are reconciled through dialogue and debate and criticism of one position or ideas should not be construed to reflect hostility. It is this dialogue and debating issues that rid us of the filth in our midst; it is the tool against tribalism, nepotism, corruption and other social ills. It is the multiplicity of political opinions in the SPLMs and their streamlining to be consistent with the objectives and aspirations of the people, that will make it strong and endure in the face of future challenges.

With the correct approach to democratic pluralism, the SPLM with its present social composition can, like other liberation movements that have attained power through the struggle of the people, endure and transform itself into a political party *sensu stricto* representing the interests of the vast majority of the South Sudanese people after the attainment of power. If that has to happen, then the SPLM has to open up to the genuine democratic changes within; that must be now than later. These changes cannot or must not be allowed to wait until after the war with the enemy is won because by then, it may be too late to retain the support of the people. By democratising as early as possible, the SPLM will put itself in a strong and vantage position to rectify many of the mistakes that have been committed against the people. Moreover, the SPLM, now enjoying the monopoly of organisation and mobilisation, will have an enhanced capacity to strengthen itself in order to implement its political programme.

As a political party, as well as a national liberation movement spear-heading a national revolutionary armed struggle at present, the nurturing of the concept of democratic pluralism by the SPLM is a healthy intermediate strategy to prepare itself for future tasks. In this connection, the SPLM leadership needs to seriously consider some of the following as practical steps in the development of the SPLM as a democratic pluralist institution.

- The most urgent and significant task, beside the military confrontation with the enemy, which the SPLM leadership must address itself at present is to commission the drawing up and publication of the SPLM Constitution and its internal regulations. There has been deliberate attempts to obscure and confuse the SPLM constitution with the Constitution of the New Sudan. These are two separate entities. The SPLM constitution defines and outlines the objectives and methods of the struggle being waged by the SPLM, it goes on to define the membership and the code of its leadership. SPLM can win the minds and hearts of the people only on the basis of knowledge of what it is, stands for, and the relationship between its members. In this respect the slogan of " a wic ku, angic ku[7] is an obscurantist slogan that discourages the acquisition of truth and must be discouraged.
- The other equally important step the SPLM leadership needs to undertake is the publication of the SPLM political programme. This important document contains elaborate action plans encompassing almost the daily activities of the entire SPLM membership, and the masses of the people of New Sudan in the political, economic, social services and the diplomatic fronts. Its reflect the sum total of their rights and duties in the struggle for freedom and liberation.

With these two instruments, the SPLM can be assured of unity, coherence and solidarity among its members, and of the support of the masses of people of South Sudan and other marginalised areas. With functional institutions, the SPLM can sustain itself without having to depend on the popularity and charisma of its leaders. Identifying the survival of the Movement with and staking its existence on certain individuals can be disastrous; it reflects the absence of rigorous organisation and ideological clarity.

The National Democratic Alliance

Much of the Sudan's political evolution since independence in 1956 has been influenced by the events in South Sudan. This has, inter alia, been the catalyst for change of governments, either through peaceful transfers or through military coups. And in all this, the South Sudanese paid maximum price for minimum returns. In terms of socio-economic parameters, we see that central Sudan has undergone some measure of development and the physical infrastructure is far more advanced than that in the south, west, east and far north. The situation in the south is made more dismal by war which has destroyed almost everything which existed before 1983.

As a concomitant process to political turmoil in the country has been the gradual radicalisation of Islam and its transformation into a political force in the body politics of the Sudan. The Muslim Brotherhood which started as a small group of intellectuals has grown into a major political actor that was able to usurp state power in a military coup in 1989. The National Islamic Front grew out of the bosom of the sectarian parties and to their chagrin. It is the NIF's usurpation of power that ironically has brought the other parties in the political spectrum very close to the SPLM/A.

The National Democratic Alliance established in 1990 is the natural extension, spatially and temporally, of the National Alliance for National Salvation formed in the wake of the March - April 1985 popular uprising which toppled the Nimeri regime. The irony of history of contemporary Sudan is that the northern political parties don't seem to learn from their experience. Between 1983 and March 1985, the major parties in the north: Umma, DUP and even the Communists were allies (at least morally) of the SPLM/A. In 1985/6, following the demise of the May regime, they started condemning or vilifying the SPLM/A and Dr John Garang for refusing to join the government. Between 1986 and 1989 they actually fought to defeat and destroy the SPLM/A. But the greatest irony lies in the fact that those northern leaders who oppressed the south, murdered its best sons and daughters, stand to be the beneficiaries of the sacrifices made by these South Sudanese whom they had only despised yesterday.

The NDA and its establishment only proves how unreliable these northern political parties. Once in power, for which they are presently striving, they may forget and ignore the fundamental issues of the country and go about their political game about how to maintain themselves in office. Not only that, they take for granted the commitments they make while still out of power as mere political stratagem.

When the NIF staged their coup in June 1989, no one even remembered that there was the 'Charter for the Defense of Democracy', signed by all the parties, to stage civil disobedience immediately against any future coup makers. The political games played by the Umma Party and Democratic Unionist Party in their traditional coalitions, form weak, corrupt and sectarian governments, leaving the country so sick that people were forced to yearn for some form of military way out. Indeed, somebody aptly put it in 1985 that the traditional and sectarian parties prepare the country for military dictatorships while the masses of the people destroy the military dictatorships for these sectarian parties to come back to power.

Thus, the NIF coup, a farcical replica of the 25 May 1969 coup, came ironically as a relief to the ordinary Sudanese against the evils of sectarianism. It looks as if this vicious circle may not be broken. There has not been any fundamental transformation in the philosophy and policies of these major political actors, namely the Umma Party and the Democratic Unionist Party, even when they have now opted for alliance with the SPLM/A and others in the National Democratic alliance.

It is the right and duty of every member of SPLM to appreciate the nature of the alliance with these northern political parties. I am not trying to discourage any alliance. But what we have to be conscious about that alliance: What it is, why it is necessary, its strengths and weaknesses, and how it will possibly come to an end, whether after or before achieving the national objective. The secession of South Sudan may be the only way out of the present political abyss in the Sudan. But I also cherish the unity between the peoples of the South, the Nuba Mountains and the Ingessina Hills who because of their cultural affinity as African peoples suffered from Arab oppression, domination, exploitation and arabo-islamic acculturation. I am not impressed by the theory of Africans taking over state power in the Sudan as a way of eradicating the injustices. It will be like substituting African for Arab domination. To break this cycle of oppression and domination, the South and its allies in the Nuba and Ingessina must opt out of this Sudan.

From this perspective, I look at the NDA not as a bridge to the formation of one secular democratic Sudan, but as a convenient forum for a peaceful dismemberment of the Sudan, and the formation of two separate, independent and sovereign entities, just in the same way the Czechs and the Slovak republics were formed from the former Czechoslovakia, following the collapse of the totalitarian state. The baseline for the NDA is the overthrow of the NIF regime. Are the people of the Sudan to re-enact the experiences that have escalated the conflict between the Arab-dominated North and the South for more than four decades? To do that would be as futile as the war the Serbs fought in Slovenia, Croatia and in Bosnia - Herzegovina. The alliance of the SPLM with these northern parties should, therefore, be based on clear objectives acceptable to the people of South Sudan.

A prominent leader of the NDA in Nairobi stated that 'the Sudan needs a reinforced uprising' similar to that of April 1985 or October 1964, but like an architectural structure, it must be reinforced with iron rods. In practice, it means that the NIF regime will be brought down by a popular uprising supported by 'armed' groups inside Khartoum. What then will be the role of the SPLA? It seems it is not counted among these 'armed' groups. This speaks volumes because the SPLA is in fact the prominent armed component of the NDA and yet the northern politician and theoreticians don't count it. It really sums up what remains 'unsaid' in the relations within the NDA. And here I beg to disagree with Prof. Francis Mading Deng[8]. What remains unsaid in the NDA, and must unite Sudanese both from north and south, is that since we are two different separate people, who have been fighting the wars just because of that fact, let us solve the question of war by simple division of the country.

There are many advantages to be drawn from secession of South Sudan by both the two halves of the Sudan. The fact that it can bring about peace is one most significant advantage. Let us draw an example from the Horn of Africa. The Eritreans fought the war of their independence for thirty years. It was equally destructive as the war in South Sudan today. The same forces of national oppression held power in Addis Ababa as the Jelaba is doing in Khartoum. It took Ethiopia years of criminal terror and millions of lives lost to produce the democratic forces that rid it of the Dergue. The slogan the EPRDF raised in June 1991 was 'Peace is better than Unity'. This is quite true as it is pertinent to the situation in the Sudan. What the Sudanese need most now is not 'unity' which has engendered war and destruction but 'peace' for them to rebuild their lives.

What propels me more into this secessionist mood is the consideration that the wheels of history will never be reversed. Sudan will never be returned to what it was in the fifties when the awareness of the people was still low. We are in the last four years of the twentieth century in which national self identity is a strong force all over the world and I don't think South Sudanese, the Nuba and the Ingessina or the Fur or the Beja are an exception. They, like the rest of humanity, love themselves and would want to assert their existence as a people with their languages, culture, religions etc.. Nor, on the other hand, will the 'Jelaba' relinquish and eschew their greed for wealth in this stage of primitive capital accumulation in the Sudan out of good will. This brings me to the question of the military component of the NDA. Since 1990, the task of taking the NIF by the horns has been left to the SPLA, which many northern intellectuals treat just like a political hunting dog; how can the Umma Party which boasts of a large armed following - the Ansars - speak of overthrowing the regime in power without committing its followers into combat against the NIF forces and its *mujahideen*?

In January 1996, the Umma Party and the Democratic Unionist Party, along side other political forces in the opposition against the NIF regime, have finally recognised and accepted that the people of South Sudan, the Nuba Mountains and the Ingessina Hills shall exercise the right to self-determination in an internationally supervised referendum after an interim period of four years following the demise of the NIF government. This is one positive thing ever done by the sectarian parties since independence in 1956. However, we should not be complacent as to lose sight of the circumstances that brought this alliance about. It is possible that these parties can renege on this important document, especially if they arrive to power in Khartoum as a result of a situation other than that mapped out in the Asmara Declaration.

I don't want to jump events nor do I want to play the prophet of doom, but I wish to express genuine fears and concern about the commitment of some of the northern compatriots (up to this moment) to the exercise of the right of self-determination by the people of the New Sudan. As I alluded above, the political events in the Sudan will not exactly follow the plan of NDA. There are likely to be variations, even serious ones, which might reverse the whole thing.

The NIF is not a static force. It moves and responds with the movement of events, nationally, regionally, internationally, and makes its own political calculations for survival. The NIF is not a monolithic monster. It has started to reveal fissures and cleavages within its ranks which will make its core act with political caution in the interest of Arabism and Islamism in the Sudan. Which makes it possible that the NIF core can acquiesce to the terms of the Umma and DUP for sharing political power to the exclusion of the SPLM.

This springs from the fact that the NIF, Umma, and the DUP all represent the political interests of the Jelaba and any delay in the implementation of the Asmara Declaration, which calls on all the parties to commit their forces to military combat against the NIF government, can only be seen in the light that these parties, in their higher interest, may want the SPLM/A sufficiently weakened by the war against the NIF and its southern Sudanese satellites, such that when time comes for the sharing of power, they will be the dominant and powerful forces.

Therefore, the Asmara Declaration and the recognition of the right of self-determination must be viewed in this perspective. There should not be much euphoria about it nor must we be complacent that the Jelaba will willingly let the people of South Sudan go. It will be only when they have realised that they cannot keep the South any longer without losing power in the rest of the North, i.e., only if the Jelaba see the disintegration of the North, with the west and east going their ways. In this case, it comes as a way of preserving the survival of their rule in the North. The SPLM should be ready to fight against its allies in the NDA any time in the future. And, therefore, what needs to be done now is to prepare the minds of the people for that eventuality.

The resolution of the conflict

The present war will definitely come to an end and peace will break out one day. The question is how and, in this connection, there are only two options. Either through military means, by SPLA defeating the government of Sudan in the South and a de facto situation is created which witnesses the birth of an independent state or the NIF government returns to the IGADD brokered peace talks it withdrew from in 1994. Neither of these options is easy and each will much depend on the circumstances and the progress of war.

The military option
Both the NIF government and the SPLA have the military option as their *raison d'être* although they emerged under different circumstances. The SPLA was established to spearhead a revolutionary armed struggle, while the NIF staged the military coup to achieve power and uses the military means to maintain itself in that power. Until recently, the SPLA had not made progress in the war because it had not correctly applied the laws of a people's war. For instance, the SPLA lost many resources, both human and material, in tactical rather than strategic battles, while its strategic battles produced political disasters. The battles for Jekau (1985), Malual Gaoath (1985), Hiyala (1989) and many others smaller garrisons were all tactical battles but the casualties SPLA suffered were far much higher than would have been expected. The fighting in Juba (1992) was a diversionary tactic, at least to save Torit, but ended in disaster because it assumed strategic proportions for which the SPLA was not sufficiently prepared.

By all accounts, the SPLA is still powerful, and it can end the war on its terms, but only if the war is turned into a people's war proper. One of the things SPLA needs to address, if it is to maintain the initiative, is the practice of fighting on only one front which gives the enemy ample time to shift its forces. This is because it can predict with some degree of accuracy which is going to be the next SPLA target. The SPLA has the capacity to strike at the enemy at any place and time in the war zone, even outside the war zone. It needs to turn the war into an all out struggle for very strategic reasons of playing with the enemy's weaknesses and strength. The enemy gains strength when it concentrates troops in certain localities but then it loses much of the ground to the SPLA as it has now.

The enemy is found only in major towns in the war zone and SPLA controls the major land routes and these towns. On the other hand, the enemy is in danger of losing strength if it disperses its forces in response to SPLA attacks and some of these strategic towns and garrisons can fall easily to the SPLA. This is simply how the SPLA can end this war. But this requires some important and fundamental changes in our approach to the people who have grown warfatigue. What has demoralised many of the SPLA officers and men is not the in-fighting against the enemy but the internecine war triggered off by the Nasir coup. Many people got so discouraged that they either went for resettlement abroad or have gone to their villages and cattle camps. As a result the SPLA has been forced to resort to *kasha* (*mobilisation*) usually done with violence, to raise troops for its plans. Nothing can motivate an SPLA solder in Bahr el Ghazal to come and fight in western Equatoria, for instance. In the past, when the revolutionary zeal of the peasants and the cattle herders was at its peak, it was possible to move forces from one sector to the other without much trouble.

Many SPLA soldiers in eastern Equatoria have gone into the mountains and the effort to bring them down has ended in failure. This is partly because of the way they have been suppressed, oppressed or marginalised by their compatriots. New methods of motivating the people should be worked out, and this can be if these soldiers know that they have a stack in and what they are fighting for. In central, western and northern Upper Nile, efforts have to be exerted to win over the Nuers, Dinka, Shilluks and others who have been politicised against the SPLA and, hence, completely neutralised. It is much better for the SPLM to spend time and energy convincing these compatriots to join the liberation struggle for the motherland than to leave them to surrender and for the enemy to utilise them against the liberation.

The SPLA should then open up many fronts against the enemy in Bahr el Ghazal, Lakes, eastern Equatoria, western Upper Nile and Blue Nile, Nuba Mountains and even in Khartoum itself. This is what will weaken the enemy. At this stage, the SPLA can and should engage in strategic battles for the overthrow of the regime by taking the war to the north as quickly as possible to enable it to reconstruct and rebuild its political, social and economic life.

Peaceful option

In the already mentioned words of Dr Ghazi Salahuddin el Atabani, Sudan exercised self-determination in 1956, and, hence, repudiated a similar claim to by South Sudanese. It must be said clearly that Ghazi has erred. It was northern Sudan that exercised that right and, to put it in the right perspective, it was the Jelaba who really exercised the right to self-determination in 1956.

South Sudan was not part of the Cairo meeting of 1953 nor was it part of all the instruments and institutions which paved the way for the transfer of power from the colonial authorities to a national government, except for the vote in parliament on 19 December 1955. But that vote was predicated on the promise by the northern political elite that South Sudan be granted a federal status with the North.

This was because of the consideration that the federal status would reduce the regional disparities and unequal development between the North and the South. The vote in parliament in 1955 was not a blank cheque for enslavement of the southern Sudanese by the Jelaba as many northern intellectuals tend to make believe, to justify their claim that the resistance of South Sudanese to northern domination was inspired by 'imperialism' or the West[8].

The South Sudanese people, the Nuba, the Beja, the Ingessina and other marginalised peoples of the Sudan, were not part of this *uhuru wa arabu* consummated on first of January 1956. Their voices were suppressed when they demanded their share of the power. The Southern Front has articulated the exercise of plebiscite in the southern provinces to determine whether or not they wanted to separate from the North. This was presented in the Round Table conference on the problem of southern Sudan (1965) which, for the first time, was attended by foreign observers.

This angered the Jelaba strongman Mohammed Ahmed Mahgoub who declared war on South Sudan killing innocent citizens, including 76 government officials who were killed at a wedding party in Wau, about 2000 citizens of Juba and 126 men and children in Watajwok village south of Malakal, and in many others towns and villages throughout South Sudan between July and August 1965. These atrocities followed a government ultimatum for the Anya-nya to surrender their weapons. It was two weeks after becoming the prime minister.

Furthermore, Ghazi is completely wrong to deny that self determination has been the demand of the people of South Sudan. The problem in my opinion has really been the lack of consistency on the part of the southern political elite. For instance, those who wielded power of the southern regional government (1972-1983) were the same politicians who articulated the position of the Southern Front in favour of a plebiscite at the Around Table conference in 1965. But when they came power in Juba, they sent the people to sleep with the slogan of 'national unity' of the Sudan. It is this inconsistency that has frustrated many people who have turned their anger against the regime to themselves.

The unity of the Sudan is what the SPLM/A leadership has been preaching since its inception in 1983, contrary to the expressed opinion of vast majority of the people of South Sudan, including those who joined the rank and file of the armed struggle. The point was lost in the dark of mistrust and power struggle that ensued, preventing constructive internal dialogue. Many had joined the struggle in the hope that it was for the independence of the South.

In South Sudan self-determination has become the focal point for the peaceful resolution of the conflict and has been supported regionally and internationally. The fact that the Nuba, the Ingessina, the Beja, the Fur and other oppressed and marginalised peoples have come to demand the exercise of this inalienable right is partly due to their growing awareness and partly due to the oppressive policies of the NIF regime whose ascension to power in a military coup in 1989, representing the radical section of the Jelaba, has exposed the true colours of this predatory class.

The fundamental question which concerns South Sudan and its vanguard the SPLM is not whether or not one section of the Jelaba in power, be it the present NIF or the coalition of the Umma and DUP will permit the exercise of self-determination in South Sudan. The fundamental question is whether or not the SPLM will be consistent and articulate self-determination as the sole demand of the people of South Sudan and not as a fall back position if the quest for a secular democratic united Sudan fails. It should not be construed as if exercise of the right to self-determination depend on the good will of the Jelaba.

The NIF does not have fundamental contradictions with the Umma Party or the DUP, at least at the level of the ideological and political objective of Arabisation and Islamisation of South Sudan. In fact, many people who have enlarged the ranks of the NIF were mainly from these sectarian parties and a few leftists. At the moment, the NIF at present is working to pass the Islamic constitution which was aborted by the Nimeri coup of 1969. The Islamic Charter Front, as it was known then, was a small party with only three members in the Constituent Assembly. The motive force behind the promulgation of the Islamic constitution in 1967/69 were the Umma and the DUP. Much later on Sadiq el Mahdi[10], when he became prime minister (1986 - 1989), was very reluctant to repeal the September laws -Islamic Sharia laws, introduced by Nimeri in 1983, and until he was overthrown he only froze their application and talked about 'alternative laws' which would not have been any different from the September laws.

In fact, the position of the Democratic Unionist Party is clearer and does not waver in the way Sadiq did. In their policy statement on South Sudan (1986), the DUP states this clearly as follows:

> ... Since the dawn of independence, your party the Democratic Unionist Party, under the patronage of Mulana Sayed Ali el Mirghani, has been working for the establishment of an Islamic Republic in fulfilment of the wishes of this Arab Muslim people whose aspiration is to live in accordance with the Holy Book (Quran) and the tradition of the Prophet. This Islamic Republic almost became a

reality in 1968 through the hands of martyrs Ismael el Azhari and Sherief Hussien el Hindi were it not for the atheistic coup d'état of 25 May 1969 which aborted everything. And now in the aftermath of the glorious April uprising the voices of the atheists are being heard calling loudly for secularism of the state, using as a pretext the animism of the people of the South and their sensitivity to the application of God's legislation (Sharia laws)...

The NIF will not be overthrown tomorrow, or even before it passes the Islamic constitution that Hassan el Turabi has jealously set his mind to achieve. This is in the knowledge that no Muslim coming after this will ever repeal this constitution. And, who knows, they may then surrender the government to the coalition - Umma and DUP because, as alluded to above, Sadiq will not repeal the Islamic laws without risking being accused of apostasy. As such, an NDA government in Khartoum following the demise of the NIF, if that ever occurs, will not immediately bring about secularism. The country will have to pass through the same experience as it did after the demise of the Nimeri regime. No political party will have the will to repeal 'Allah's laws'. Hence, the sectarian parties may not accept the complete destruction of the system based on Islam and Arabism in the Sudan.

In view of the above, and given the readiness of self-seeking South Sudanese to serve the new regime, it is very likely that there will be an escalation of the war in the South between the SPLA and people like Riek Machar and Kerubino Kuanyin whom the new regime may inherit as a way of frustrating the process of rehabilitation, resettlement and reconstruction, and would, as a result, interfere with the holding of a referendum and the exercise of the right to self-determination.

It is my contention that the SPLM has to behave single-mindedly and articulate the issues in accordance with the aspirations of its constituents, the people of the New Sudan, whether or not the NIF regime is overthrown. The NIF regime has endured up to this time largely because of the reluctance of the northern political parties, especially the sectarian ones, to commit their forces to the armed struggle against the regime leaving the task to the SPLA. This could even be a tacit endorsement of the system on the part of these sectarian parties. The NIF has committed some of its cadres to the war front because they believe that is the only means of boosting their chances of maintaining and sustaining that power. If the sectarian parties want to remove the NIF from power they should do the same, otherwise how do they justify their claim to power after the demise of the NIF regime by simply engaging in meetings and issuing of leaflets? No. Of course, the NIF is armed, it is ruthless and has looted the wealth of the country, and will not relinquish power except under strong pressure of the gun.

The options open to the SPLM are rather limited. Even the peaceful resolution of the conflict itself is not going to be easy for the Movement. In the exercise of the right to self-determination and the implementation of the referendum will require a high level of organisation on its part. It is true that the people of South Sudan, in a free and fair election, will vote for secession of the South from the North, no doubt about that. But the awareness of the people must be raised to a level that they will not be manipulated by the Jelaba.

The task, therefore, is not only to commit people to war but also to make them know why and for what they are fighting. And this must be built into the fabrics of the SPLM political work to bring about unity among the people, and to rally them behind the programme and leadership of the SPLM. It is only after this that the people will not need to be conscripted into the army; they will volunteer to join the struggle as they did before in the early eighties. This will no doubt raise our ability to sustain the long cruel war.

The quest for peace and, therefore, the exercise of the right of self-determination is tightly linked up with the realisation of the ideals of freedom, equality, social justice and democracy. There is no way the war can be ended without translating these aspirations into tangible programmes in the hands of the people. Any political arrangement that ignores any of these cherished ideals of the people will just mean a break in which to prepare for another round of fighting. The SPLM, its leadership and the entire people of South Sudan and other marginalised areas should prepare themselves for a real protracted struggle if the Jelaba continue to insist on maintaining the status quo.

Concluding remarks

History does not repeat itself. The Nasir episode and its manifestations were farcical replica of the events in South Sudan between 1960 and 1970. That some leaders leave the mainstream liberation struggle to go back to the enemy as allies or otherwise is not something new in South Sudan's in its long history of struggle against the Arabised northern ruling class.

South Sudanese political organisations have always suffered splits and disunity. This has sometimes been attributed to tribalism and tribal loyalties. There are many tribes and tribal groups in South Sudan but I don't think that is where the problem lies. The principal cause of dissent has been the stifling of democracy within the South Sudan Political organisations to preserve an appearance of unity. An obsession with uniformity at all costs leads to fragmentation.

The SPLM/A did not deviate much from other South Sudanese political organisation that preceded it. As a military organisation, it was deprived of political and ideological clarity from its inception. The absence of vents and avenues for releasing the excessive pressure that built up inside the SPLM/A as a result of oppression, social injustice, abuse of human rights and many others evils led to the explosion that almost shattered the Movement as well as the hopes of the people of South Sudan.

The Nasir Declaration was a reflection of the internal contradictions within the SPLM/A, but inadvertently implemented for opportunistic ends by elements that did not really believe in those ideals. However, like any other tragedies, it has some redeeming sides which should be exploited for the purpose of reversing its negative impacts. For instance, the Nasir coup caused serious military setbacks for the SPLM/A and the oppressed people of the Sudan but these have created a basis for the eventual SPLM/A political victory. The Nasir leaders have ready surrendered to the NIF government, paving the way for the unity of the people of South Sudan.

Dr Riek Machar and Dr Lam Akol staged a coup for which they had not prepared enough, leave alone having the material basis for it. And Dr Garang's contempt for that adventure as a 'theoretical coup' which was doomed to fail has been vindicated. Lam's assertion that :

> The struggle for democracy within our Movement has intensifies and we have decided to jettison Garang out of the leadership of our Movement. The necessary steps on the ground have been undertaken and it will not be long before the whole thing gets into the open...

proved to be nothing more than hallucinations generated by blind ambition and greed for power. What he described as the intensification of the struggle was only in his mind; it was not reflected on the ground. This was proved by the fact that the bulk of the SPLA remained loyal to the leadership of Dr. John Garang.

The big lessons to be learnt from the Nasir debacle is that democracy can only be realised within the frame of the organisations. It can not be detached and achieved from outside. In the SPLM/A, democracy has meaning within the context of existing and future structures. And any struggle for the development of the SPLM/A can only take place within the precincts of the Movement. Any struggle outside the context of the Movement only gives opportunity for those who want to destroy the struggle for national liberation.

In this connection, the SPLM, after the series of structural readjustments, should have no interest in stifling democracy. It has much to gain from opening up to criticism and self-criticism as a means of resolving internal contradictions, and that is how it can survive future tests. In this respect, the Nasir Declaration would have inadvertently helped to transform the SPLM into a democratic and dynamic force in the politics of national liberation in South Sudan.

It is politically prudent to promote democratic pluralism now in the Movement when the conflict with the NIF regime and/or the northern political establishment has not been completed. It will be the only way the SPLM can enrich itself both politically and ideologically. The promotion and support to the growth of the civil society in the liberated areas will also enable the liberation of the productive forces that will enrich the SPLM's experience with the masses of the people.

This book is intended to be a dialogue and a political debate, not only outside the SPLM but within it also. This is to help crystallise and sharpen some of the ideas which are vaguely held by many of our people. The people of South Sudan and their compatriots in the marginalised areas of Nuba Mountains and the Ingessina Hills must from now understand the political and military implications of their decisions, especially in the exercise of their right to self-determination, if they are to avoid future wars. The referendum per se will not bring the desired results. It is the knowledge of that exercise that will determine whether or not the people will make the correct decision. It is known, for instance, that the people of South Sudan want secession and the establishment of an independent state. It is not enough to say that there is going to be a referendum. The people need to be sensitised and educated politically in order to enable them make the right choice lest their ignorance becomes a fetter.

The SPLM should organise and strengthen its organs and the civil structures because it is through these structure that meaningful political mobilisation can be achieved. Political discussions and debate of issues should be encouraged to enable people exercise their mental and intellectual talents. There is a trend in political activity which is gaining grounds in the rank and file of the SPLM. The Movement must not reduce its political work and action to mere bureaucratic office routine. This is dangerous and must be combated.

The struggle will not end when the war is over. It will continue against some of the anti-social traits that have taken roots in our communities as a result of war and war-related causes. Tribalism and corruption in political and economic life are two very dangerous viruses which we, as a liberation movement, need to combat. This is because, if allowed to permeate all aspects of our social life, these viruses will negate the very process which has been underway since 1983 and reverse the formation and consolidation of our national unity. The forum for combating these viruses are the SPLM branches, cells, chapters etc., in the meetings, congresses, and in the liberation councils at all levels, through debates, discussions and honest exchange of views and opinions.

The struggle against tribalism and nepotism is important and imperative as the struggle against disease, ignorance, poverty and hunger. This is because they re-enforce each other and are capable of arresting the wheel of our progress. People should not be afraid of raising controversial issues for discussion. This is the only way to sharpen our awareness and ability to cope the challenges that face our Movement, and to prepare for the future.

Notes

1. La Valse des Odeium. quoted from Regis Debray *A critique of Arms. The Revolution on Trial.* Penguin Books 1974.
2. A Major Watershed: SPLM/SPLA First National Convention: Resolutions, Appointments and Protocol. Chukudum, New Sudan. March/April 1994. Published and distributed by the SPLM Secretariat for Information and Culture.
3. It is worthwhile mentioning that calling of an SPLM convention was proposed to the Nairobi Peace Talks (November 1991) by the Nasir group as one way of resolving the split, caused by the Nasir coup, and the SPLM internal contradictions.
4. Speaking in the meeting of the National Executive Council following the conference on Civil Society and Civil Authority in New Hush- Heiman in May 1996.
5. Paulo Ferreri. *'The Pedagogy of the Oppressed',* Penguin Books 1974.
6. Ibid.
7. A Dinka idiom, literally means 'we know what we want'.
8. He is widely quoted to have said that what is unsaid is what divides people.
9. Imperialism, which developed Jelaba's home and left the South backward. What did the British leave in the South as a token of their inclination towards the South and its people. Was it not the same British whom our people put their trust and confidence in, who betrayed them in 1955, following the Torit mutiny, by appealing to the mutineers to put down their arms because the British Crown would protect them. How many of these mutineers survived the Jelaba's swords of vengeance?
10. The Umma Party refused to implement the provisions of the Koka Dam Declaration 1986 although it was a signatory to it and had made preliminary contacts with the SPLM following the elections on the pretext that the DUP, which was its coalition partner in the government, was not a signatory to the Koka Dam Declaration. This forced the SPLM to seek a separate agreement with the DUP to supplement the Koka Dam Declaration which was called the Sudanese Peace Initiative (1988) which was rejected by Sadiq el Mahdi, dissolving their coalition and taking on board the National Islamic Front.

7

Epilogue
What is the SPLM and where is it ?

Providence dictated that the year 1996 would not close on the Sudan without a spectacular political development, something of international dimensions, happening to punctuate the drudgery of the military and political stalemate that has characterised the political atmosphere for nearly a year after the SPLA offensive early in the year which saw the liberation of Pochalla, Khor Yabus and other areas in eastern Upper Nile and southern Blue Nile. The escape of Sadiq el Mahdi to Eritrea in November 1996 was definitely a big morale booster for the NDA and the Umma Party. There were serious predictions in the air that the NIF regime would come crumbling down under pressure from the NDA in a matter of weeks or so now that Sadiq was free.

As if to pre-empt the obvious questions arising from Sadiq el Mahdi's escape, and his entourage of twenty eight supporters including his son and how they avoided detection, and managed to go through the NIF roadblocks along the way from Khartoum to the Eritrean border, the Umma Party went on the political offensive to explain that Sadiq had to leave the country to deny the NIF regime the opportunity of using his presence in Khartoum as a human shield. It is definitely difficult to make sense of this story. The truth is that nobody would wish to remain in the NIF dungeon if that could be avoided. It was necessary for Sadiq el Mahdi to be free and to contribute effectively to the struggle. Many of us took different ways and means to leave the Sudan in order to join the political struggle against the regime. Moreover, the social and economic difficulties in the country should provide any Sudanese with sufficient justification for escape into exile. In all honesty, the opposition brightened up when the news of Sadiq's escape was confirmed. The problem really arises out of something else, and that is whether Sadiq had really escaped or was simply allowed to leave the country by the NIF regime.

I belong to the last school of opinion. Sadiq el Mahdi was allowed to leave the country and given free and safe passage by his brother in laws, Dr Hassan Abdalla el Turabi, the leader of the NIF and virtually the head of state. The NIF party and government have a well organised and politicised security and intelligence network in the country. They have sufficiently terrorised and cowed the opposition inside the country. According to the NIF regime, the danger to its power base and hegemony only comes from the neighbouring countries. It is only Isais Afewerki, Meles Zenawi and Yoweri Museveni who are the problem because they are agents of US imperialism and Zionism against Islam and Arabism. Of course, this accusation against the neighbouring countries is meant to mobilise internal as well as external political, moral and material support, and to divert the attention of the Sudanese people. The truth is that the main threat to the political survival of the NIF regime is the alliance between the SPLA and the northern opposition. The SPLA military victories in the South and southern Blue Nile could easily spark off a political situation in Khartoum that could get out of control for the NIF with its security apparatus.

The NIF leaders are pretty well aware of the implications of the NDA, especially if some of its leaders are inside the country having contacts with their supporters. The NIF regime, therefore, does not want an internal opposition - what they frequently refer to as fifth column - to nucleate around the personality of Sadiq el Mahdi. For the NIF regime, it was more convenient and politically expedient to allow Sadiq el Mahdi leave the country. The exit of Sadiq el Mahdi, which he must have asked for, therefore, comes within the political manoeuvres of the NIF government. There is little sense in the claim that the NIF leaders intended to use Sadiq's presence in the country as a human shield.

It is to be recalled that the northern opposition has been reluctant, since the formation of the NDA in 1990, to engage in the armed struggle against the regime. They have placed all their eggs in the basket of 'political struggle', or the 'popular uprising' or *intifadha*, of the kind that took place in October 1964 which brought about the demise of Ibrahim Abboud or the March - April 1985 which overthrew the regime of Gaafar Mohammed Nimeri, both of which, incidentally, were brought about by the political and military situation in South Sudan. The conditions for the birth of this expected *intifadha* too has been brought about by the SPLA military victories against the NIF regime. The northern opposition have read the signals very late and found out that the SPLA was not their army. So they have started to raise their own armies whose combined numbers have not yet reached half the size of SPLA forces - the New Sudan Brigade - operating in the North.

This is a dilemma for the northern opposition, especially the Umma Party, whose leader still wears the old robes of effortless political supremacy. This may explain why Sadiq has provactively pronounced that the 'NIF regime be toppled with minimum losses' as soon as he was outside the borders of the Sudan. He also made other statements, especially regarding the leadership of the NDA and the constitution of the NDA Joint Military Command, headed by the SPLA commander in chief, Dr John Garang de Mabior, which almost threatened the very existence of the NDA.

It has taken time for Sadiq el Mahdi and the northern opposition to realise and accept the fact that the SPLA is the real power base of the opposition in the struggle against the NIF regime. This has been proved by the SPLM/A - NDA offensive in southern Blue Nile and eastern Sudan in January 1997, culminating in the capture of Kurmuk, Geisan and a string of smaller garrisons. This chain of victories and the prospect of the SPLA capture of Damazin have sent shock waves into the NIF political nervous system. In order to cover its humiliation on the battlefield, the NIF has begun to conjure up the spectre of foreign invasion reminiscent of that made by Sadiq el Mahdi himself in 1987 when the SPLA first captured the same Kurmuk and Geisan; his intention was to draw Egypt and other Arab and Islamic states into the conflict in South Sudan on the side of their Arab and Muslim brothers.

The SPLA stopped short of capturing Damazin in order to avoid a premature collapse of the NIF regime before it had completed preparing itself and compound the already complex political situation in the NDA. The fall of Damazin to the SPLA and the NDA forces would cut off power supply to Khartoum, Medani etc., in the North and this would provoke a premature uprising. Which is exactly what the northern opposition parties would wish to happen in order to give them an opportunity to rush to Khartoum to form a new government, without creating the necessary conditions for peace in the country. Such an eventuality, given the level of mistrust and lack of confidence among the principal players, would mean the continuation of war because the SPLA would be put in a difficult situation by the same northern parties allied to it in the NDA, which by experience would try to isolate the SPLM/A, both internally, internationally and regionally. In such a situation, the northern parties in the NDA would improvise a pretext for not implementing the provisions of the Asmara Declaration, especially the article on self-determination.

The SPLM/A leadership rightly analysed the situation and took the decision never to play the role of political errand boy for the northern opposition. It must fully participate in the political manoeuvres in Khartoum, following the collapse of the NIF regime. The only guarantee for peace is the implementation of the Asmara declaration of 1996. This also depends on the SPLA physically taking over the New Sudan (comprising the South Sudan, southern Kordofan, and southern Blue Nile). The SPLA shifted the active military front to the South. This was to the chagrin of the other forces in the NDA who had expected the SPLA to proceed with the war to Khartoum. The SPLA is now poised to capture Juba after liberating Kaya, Morobo, Yei, Kaji-keji, Lainya, Jambo, Lui, Amadi, Rumbek, Tonj, Warrap, Yirol, Tali and Tindilo. In these battles, the SPLA destroyed bases belonging to the Ugandan rebel groups capturing thousands of the NIF soldiers and Ugandan rebels of the West Nile Bank Front. This time round the SPLA means business and, according to Dr John Garang, 1997 must witness the end of the war and the building of peace.

For the SPLM/A, unlike the other forces of the NDA, the issue is not just overthrowing the NIF regime. The fundamental issue in this conflict is the restructuring the state power in the Sudan which will allow the peoples of South Sudan, the Nuba Mountains, and Ignessina Hills and other marginalised groups in the country to exercise their inalienable right to self-determination. It presupposes a radical redefinition of the Sudanese national identity in favour of the marginalised and the oppressed, the democratic and equitable sharing of natural resources and power. This constitutes a contradiction between the SPLM/A on the one hand, and the other northern opposition political parties, more specifically the sectarian and traditional parties of the Umma and the Democratic Unionist Party, on the other hand, for reasons deeply rooted in the history of the Sudan.

The NIF leaders and thinkers have read this contradiction very correctly. For instance, since on the issue of self-determination for South Sudan, the Nuba and the Ingessina people, the northern opposition political groups do not differ much from the NIF position, the Khartoum regime is likely to exploit the northern fears against the SPLM/A. Indeed, it has already tried to create a political wedge between the different members of the NDA in an effort to weaken the opposition. The NIF has also laboured hard to widen the gap between South Sudanese and that is why it has in an unprecedented haste reactivated the so-called 'Political Charter' it signed with Riek Machar, Kerubino Kuanyin and Arok Thon, among others, in April 1996, and turned it into a political, diplomatic and military weapon to fight the SPLA. The NIF government, after the SPLA - NDA victories in southern Blue Nile, stole the NDA interim arrangements spelt out in Asmara Declaration and incorporated, at least in form if not content, those articles dealing with self-determination and the length of the interim period into its so-called 'peace from within programme'. The regime has signed the so-called 'Khartoum Peace Agreement' with the four southern militia groups allied to it, namely Riek Machar's SSIM, Kerubino Kuanyin's so-called SPLM/A Bahr el Ghazal, Arok Thon's so-called Bor group and Theopillous Ochang Lotti's so-called Equatoria Defence Forces.

The so-called Khartoum Peace Agreement signed by the regime with its own allies on 21 April 1997 is just a sham intended to water down the IGAD peace process. The signing of this agreement in front of the world television cameras and diplomatic representation will not achieve peace and stability in the country. Nor will it resolve the contradiction between the regime and its opponents. These South Sudanese leaders-turned-warlords and militia commanders have reached the height of their capitulation to the regime. Not only that, but Riek Machar has shed all his political pretensions for an independent South Sudan. This so-called 'peace agreement is, in fact, the regime's latest political and military stratagem for southernisation of the war.

This amounts to double treachery and betrayal of the people of South Sudan. In 1991, Riek Machar and his co-traveller, Lam Akol, precipitated the split within the rank and file of the SPLM/A on the grounds that Dr Garang did not articulate well the case of South Sudan for secession. Given their intense hostility to anything Arab or Muslim, the Nuer people massively supported Riek Machar because of this supposed struggle for self-determination for South Sudan. He committed the Nuer people to fight their compatriots, the Dinka, because, according to Riek Machar, the Dinkas are the only obstacle to South Sudan's independence. The result was the bitter fratricidal war that engulfed central Upper Nile, east bank Equatoria, northern Bahr el Ghazal and the Lakes area between 1991 and 1995.

The issue, therefore, is not the leadership of the South, about which he bluntly said 'Garang will get over my dead body'. In my opinion the issue is that Riek Machar and all these pseudo- leaders, who have jumped out of the SPLM/A back into the NIF sinking ship, have not been good converts to the cause of the people of South Sudan and their compatriots in the Nuba Mountains and Ingessina Hills. It is amazing how their conviction about the correctness of the cause, if they ever had any, has been shaken easily by personal considerations of power and leadership.

The only possible explanation is that opportunism had propelled them to use the SPLM/A as a vehicle for self-promotion. Riek Machar rejected the Lafon Declaration, a more honourable agreement between brothers who split and fought against themselves, in favour of an agreement that does not recognise the existence of South Sudan as an entity. By rejecting that declaration, he precipitated another split in the SSIM/A in 1995. The signal Riek Machar seems to be sending out to the people of South Sudan, who have rejected his bid for leadership through capitulation and alliance with common enemy, is that of the Biblical Samson when he got hold of the pillars of the court saying 'on me and my enemies', or put in another way, 'since I can not have it (leadership of the South Sudan), so must it (South Sudan) be destroyed'. This is a contemptible position to be adopted by a man who claims to be the champion of the independence of South Sudan.

In the final analysis, it is a blessing in disguise that these chicken-hearted leaders have opted out earlier. While people like Magar Aciek, Lawrence Lual Lual, Cagai Matet, and others have failed the test of perseverance, their desertion has cleansed the SPLM/A. They have fallen by the wayside when the sun of the NIF regime is setting and the dawn of the oppressed people of the Sudan is breaking. No matter what they do the SPLA is winning the war.

The emergence of small tribal or regional splinter groups, masquerading as liberation movements, which are hostile to each other, but individually maintain strong links with the NIF government, is the latest strategic plan by the regime to break and prevent the unity and solidarity among the people of South Sudan and other oppressed peoples in the country. This is being reinforced by the creation of tribal and sub-tribal districts, provinces, and even states which do not have economic and political viability but serve the purpose of awakening a false awareness and identity in these people, militating against the evolution of a national (South Sudanese) consciousness.

* * * *

What is the SPLM and where is it? With these rather disparaging words a British friend silenced my colleague - a SPLM activist. He had bored our conversation with barrages of SPLM slogans and propaganda, many of them, in fact, completely irrelevant. The place was Kampala and the time was November 1996. My friend could not stomach such batting of the Movement. There was silence, and the friendly atmosphere that had characterised our encounter soured suddenly that we had to depart in order to avoid further embarrassment.

It is four years since that encounter and the Kampala setting but our conversation remains fresh and resonant in my memory. I agreed with my British friend and had tried to convince my SPLM colleague that the question about the SPLM was valid, and that any SPLM cadre must really give serious consideration to the implication of that question. This was at a time I was writing the manuscript which was later published to put the SPLM/A in a bright light by eulogising the fledging process of reforms and liberalisation that had started to vegetate in the New Sudan since 1994. I was to be proved wrong and my enthusiasm misplaced. This is because in a setting other than the Sudan, such important and landmark political conferences like the SPLM First National Convention (1994); the SPLA Senior Officers Conference (1995); the SPLM - UN/OLS Conference on Humanitarian Issues (1995); the Conference on Civil Society and Civil Authority in the New Sudan (1996); and finally the SPLM - Church Dialogue Conference (1997), would have left democratic marks on the SPLM by way of its improved performance.

However, like a process driven by external forces, and, in fact, the SPLM internal dynamics were driven essentially by external forces mediated by the international humanitarian intervention in the conflict and the regional political and military alliances. Those semblance of reforms, democratisation or liberalisation in the Movement were a half-hearted response to the pressure of the international community and a means of relating to it. The institutions and structures of governance created by the First National Convention like the National Liberation Council (NLC) or the National Executive Council (NEC), which gave the SPLM the facade of a conventional government, have yet to become functional and effective. The promised changes remained superficial, unable to penetrate the ossified military core where absolute power was concentrated in the hands of one person as it was before the 1991 crisis.

No doubt, the SPLM leadership methods, unfortunately, have reverted back to the old autocratic and military authoritarianism that characterised it before the Nasir Declaration 1991, which in fact produced it. For how else can we describe the SPLM/A, which after sixteen years of life still does not have a constitution, not even a simple political, economic and social blueprint to guide its activities and the war of liberation. The decisions, including major and strategic decisions, remain the prerogative of the chairman. There is no incident in which a full NEC meeting deliberated on a prepared agenda and its resolutions set for implementation. It is not a secret that the deputy chairman, Cdr Salva Kiir Mayardit, has himself been marginalised and is not consulted on some of these decisions. The SPLM vehicle is on a reverse gear in as far as matters of democracy and governance are concerned. This casts serious doubts on the whole process of liberalisation and reforms that characterised the period following the first national convention 1994.

In 1997, a committee for drafting the SPLM constitution was set up under the chairmanship of its Secretary General, Cdr James Wani Igga, the third officer in the SPLM/A leadership hierarchy. It was the first serious attempt to regularize the SPLM as a political organisation. The committee sat for months looking at the political documents of the National Resistance Movement (NRM) in Kampala. It came out with a draft document which would have formed the basis of a vibrant political discourse at all levels of the SPLM. However, the draft document was handed over to the SPLM chairman who made his changes to produce what was called 'The SPLM Vision 1997', seriously at variance with the original draft. Not only was it tastelessly over-spiced with archaic and tired ideas that rendered absurd the very concept of the New Sudan but the chairman also decreed it as the constitution of the New Sudan, undercutting the democratic process for its formalisation into the Movement's basic document. The National Executive Council and the National Liberation Council, however, later rejected the document.

We are in the last days of 1999. Humanity, including the people of the New Sudan, shall soon enter the third millennium. Considering the political and social environment in the New Sudan, the question of my British friend 'what is the SPLM and where is it?' is an valid today as it was in 1996.

While preparing for the second edition of 'The Politics of Liberation in South Sudan: An Insider's View ', it crossed my mind several times whether or not an analysis of the internal situation in the SPLM should not make the subject of its preface. In doing that, of course, it was necessary to revisit some of the assumptions I made in 1997 and whether or not the political trend proceeded in the manner I had predicted it would. Out of historical necessity and responsibility, I must do that exactly, unperturbed nevertheless, by the criticism generated by the appearance of this book in 1997. Many of my compatriots, both members and non-members of the SPLM/A, rebuked me for '*having revealed SPLM/A secrets which might serve the enemy*'. Some went further to suggest that I should have waited until the liberation war was over to write the book. Yes, a certain David Hole and Sean Gabb of the NIF-funded Sudan Foundation tried to used the book against the SPLM/A in their 1998 booklet: *SPLA fit to govern?*

That notwithstanding, I still argue that I did not reveal any SPLA secrets. What I did was an exposition of mistakes. And mistakes, whether committed by individual SPLM/A leaders or many of its cadres, are no longer secrets, especially when their effects and impact visibly stare the people in the face. Moreover, the initial motivation was to expose candidly and courageously some of these mistakes as a means of collectively working together for their rectification. It was not meant to bring the Movement or its leadership into disrespect for the very simple reason that I myself was a member of that leadership.

Let me briefly run through my own postulates in 1997. I want to reaffirm that the positive aspect of the Nasir Declaration 1991 remains. It has forced internal changes inside the SPLM/A. It was logical to assume that the SPLM/A would not operate on the old methods in a changed political and military environment. It must adjust itself to accommodate the changes that continued to sprout in the political environment, locally, regionally and internationally. That the Movement has reverted to old methods is only unfortunate and the reasons for that must be sought internally.

The most significant political development after the Lafon Declaration was that the *Political Charter* Riek Machar signed with the NIF regime was elevated into the 'Khartoum Agreement' in April 1997 and Dr Riek Machar was absorbed into the NIF system as an Assistant President of the republic, a post unknown in the history of the Sudan, but, of course, resonant with the usual positions occupied by South Sudanese who opt to serve the various Arab-dominated regimes. Dr Lam Akol negotiated his own version of the political charter and signed the 'Pachodo Agreement' which made him a minister in the central government in Khartoum.

It was clear from the start that both the Khartoum and Pachodo agreements represented the NIF regime's long drawn out strategy of defeating the liberation struggle. But they also proved that Riek and Lam have failed to sustain their initial commitment to the aspirations of the people of South Sudan for which they supposedly instigated the split within the SPLM/A in 1991 and unleashing the fratricidal war that followed. Events now suggest that their agenda was more of a power struggle to capture the leadership of the SPLM/A rather than a quest for the secession of South Sudan. And when that failed, they capitulated and joined the institutions of the enemy. Even when opportunity availed itself to delink from the enemy and join his commanders and men engaged in fierce battles in western Upper Nile with the government army, Dr Riek Machar, still harbouring faith in his agreement with the NIF government, condemned his commanders. After a few weeks he made a clumsy turn around by resigning all his positions with the system leaving many of his aides and forces to the enemy.

The National Democratic Alliance (NDA) is still holding together although deep political cleavages have started to rend it. These spring from the inherent dichotomous nature of the alliance. Although the NDA is capable of drawing up a consensus on fundamental Sudanese issues, the individual political parties retain their own political positions on these issues, thus undermining the cohesion and effectiveness of the organisation. While the NDA Asmara Declaration 1996 commits the NDA parties to the exercise of self-determination by the people of South Sudan, the Nuba and the Funj, the Umma Party and the Democratic Unionist Party are individually opposed to this commitment. Their position is reinforced by the hostility shown by Egypt and other Arab countries towards South Sudan's right to self-determination.

The schisms and political cleavages in the NDA are also a product of the flirtation between the Umma Party and the NIF regime. It began with the meeting in Geneva in May 1999 between Sadiq el Mahdi, the Umma leader and his brother-in-law and Dr Hassan Abdalla el Turabi, the National Islamic Front leader and the regime's chief ideologue. This meeting, coming without prior consultation between the Umma and other members of the NDA, created confusion and recrimination in the alliance. This was later followed by another meeting and the signing by Sadiq el Mahdi and President Omer el Beshir of the so-called 'The National Call' in Djibouti in November 1999. That meeting further drove a wedge between the Umma Party and its allies in the NDA.

Although there is nothing in the NDA charter that prevents an individual member party from promoting its own political agenda, and the Umma Party engaged the NIF regime on the basis of that, the minimum programme of the alliance is not strong enough to hold it together. The SPLM engages the regime in peace negotiation through the IGAD process. This has been a matter of concern to the northern opposition and their continued exclusion is responsible for their embrace of the Egyptian-Libyan initiative.

The NIF regime has made significant in-roads into the NDA backyard as a result of this dichotomy. And the NIF manoeuvres came against a backdrop of intense internal power struggle between Turabi on the one hand and Ali Osman Mohammed Tah on the other. In fact, between Turabi and his political faction and the extreme wing of the NIF, which has found it expedient to ally with the military in this power contest, Turabi seems to be losing out. This is borne out by the military intervention of el Beshir, the dissolution of the National Assembly and the declaration of the state of emergency[1]. The

Egyptian-Libyan initiative at reconciling the northern opposition to the NIF regime is another factor in this scenery that may bear fruits if the Umma and the DUP agree to a power sharing formula with the NIF government. This will definitely leave the SPLM/A and other members of the NDA in the cold.

The border war between Eritrea and Ethiopia, which are both members of the IGAD mediating team on the Sudanese conflict, adds to the complexity of the Sudanese political situation. Eritrea hosts the NDA in Asmara and most of the NDA military logistics transit through Eritrea. The border war seemed to push the both Eritrea and Ethiopia closer to the Sudan breaking the NIF regime's regional and international isolation occasioned by its support to Islamic and other rebel groups fighting its neighbours. Viewed against this background, and under the pressure of Arab mediation, the NDA may break up, with the northern parties (Umma and DUP) opting for power sharing with the NIF, forcing a re-alignment of the players along the traditional north-south conflict.

This poses a serious threat to the SPLM strategy, borrowed from the experience of the Eritrean People's Liberation Front (EPLF) and developed since 1995 as well as its effort to assist in building of a broad based Ethiopian People's Revolutionary Democratic Front (EPRDF) that brought about the demise of the Mengistu regime in Ethiopia leading to the independence of Eritrea in 1993. The New Sudan Brigade (NSB) - the SPLA on the eastern front - might have to be withdrawn to the South because it cannot continue to operate as an alien force in the north should the Umma Liberation Army (ULA) and other military groups disband themselves in order to participate in the NIF-dominated system.

There is an apparent stagnation and lack of significant internal developments in the SPLM/A. This has impacted on the development of the war itself. There is a stalemate on all the fronts in South Sudan. Since 1997 SPLA lightening offensive and the skirmishes in Wau in early 1998, there has never been any serious military operations in the South. The fighting concentrated mainly in the Nuba Mountains and southern Blue Nile, allowing the NIF government to shift large forces from the South to defend the Rosseries dam. The other hot spot was in western Upper Nile, where the USDF forces of Riek Machar, with tacit support from the SPLA, rebelled and turned their guns against the NIF army. In hindsight it is perhaps this lack of progress on the war fronts that may have influenced the Umma Party's reconsideration of its position and the attendant flirtation with the NIF regime.

As the year ends, the political environment that characterised the SPLM/A internal situation between 1989 and 1991 seems completely to have set in. The only difference is that dissent could now be expressed openly without fear of repercussions. Nearly everybody in the SPLM/A, except perhaps for a few benefiting from the confusion and the new comers, is agreed that there is something fundamentally wrong in the SPLM. But few are able to speak to point out where things are going wrong. As a result, they have been marginalised and pushed to the periphery to silence them. While the disruption that occurred in 1991 may not replicate itself, the indication is that there is a strong trend to regionalise the Movement. This may be a way of re-energising, re-motivating and re-organising the struggle by bypassing an oppressive centre that has become unresponsive.

There is a parallel in the recent history of the liberation struggle in South Sudan. The Anya-nya, until the centralised leadership was achieved under Joseph Lagu sometime in 1969/70, fought against the Arab-dominated government on tribal and regional basis. The present regional trends inside the SPLM/A, suggestive of a failure at the centre, may replicate the Anya-nya experience until an unquestioned leader that will unite the fighting forces emerges. This failure has sufficiently been manifested in the following: the apparent inertia and the widespread apathy bordering on indifference and discontent simmering in the ranks and file of the SPLM/A; the missed opportunity in Wau; the political crisis precipitated by Kerubino Kuanyin Bol; the crisis of governance that resulted in the military confrontation between the SPLA and the Didinga people in Chukudum and Himan (New Cush); all these and many others point to the existence of an acute malaise suggestive of a political dysfunction in the SPLM/A which may sooner than later have serious political and military ramifications.

Keeping quiet or leaving things to take their course, as some people may want, will not help the situation in the SPLM/A. The structures of the Movement have not been made to function. Those not directly involved with the day to day operations of the Movement have been denied fora for discourse. The resolutions and recommendations arrived at in the SPLM forum remain on paper, because there has not been political will to create the necessary instruments for their implementation. This has made some of us to write freely and openly criticising this pathetic situation. Silence or brooding over mistakes has concealed the rot under this veil of indifferent unanimity reminiscent of the 1991 situation when many people were caught unawares by the Nasir Declaration that there were serious internal contradictions within the SPLM/A leadership.

There has not been a fundamental change in the SPLM/A

The people of South Sudan have been conned into believing that the SPLM has changed its methods. Six years on since its First National Convention, it must be admitted that no fundamental change has occurred in the SPLM/A, but all the pronouncements about change and internal democracy have turned been mere bluffs. The SPLM leader, Dr John Garang de Mabior, still maintains a strong iron grip on the Movement. He makes solitary decisions, the so-called provisional orders, making redundant the structures he himself help create. He shuffles and reshuffles at will the National Executive Council, paralysing its operations.

Dr John Garang has become used to issuing orders that he finds collective responsibility and collegial relations distressing and unnecessary. For instance, in 1997 he formed a structure - the Resource Management Committee of the New Sudan (RMC). It paralysed the functions of the Secretaries of both Finance & Economic Affairs, Industries & Mining, Agriculture and Natural resources, which are concerned with the development and management of the natural, economic and financial resources of the SPLM to curb the collective functioning of the NEC. The operations of the RMC itself were further made difficult by the inclusion of county commissioners and SPLA sector commanders and SRRA officials in that committee, though they were not qualified to be so. To make matters more complicated, the chairman of the RMC got transferred to become the commander of the New Sudan Brigade (NSB), while retaining his portfolio as Secretary for Commerce, Trade and Cooperatives in the NEC. The RMC has now been supplanted by the Coordination Council, made of a few close aides in Nairobi. The NEC, therefore, has been made completely redundant and irrelevant.

The culture of issuing orders works for maintenance of a only small coterie of aides in order to avoid political dialogue in which consensus could be democratically built among the members of the Movement or its leadership. The social and political base of the SPLM decisions, therefore, has narrowed down to a few trusted friends, relatives and new comers who don't know the history of the SPLM/A internal dynamics. Having not been related to the Movement or having been opposed to and fighting it since its inception in 1983, many of these new-comers, after becoming tired of the abuses of the enemy, find the oppressive situation in the SPLM/A even more preferable, acceptable and are ready to endure that situation. Worse still was that many of these newcomers wanted to out do those whom they found in the SPLM/A by exhibiting excessive loyalty, more often bordering on vilifying any dissenting voices in the ranks of the SPLM/A.

In diagnosing the political malaise in the liberation movement, one cannot fail to identify where the rot is in the body of the SPLM. It is unfortunate that one has to agree, again, with those of Riek Machar and Lam Akol that it is Dr. John Garang de Mabior who is the problem and the obstacle to the SPLM transforming itself into a genuine national liberation movement. His leadership methods are averse to democracy and a political culture that puts the people in the centre of the liberation process. A break with him may become inevitable sooner than latter.

It is not a secret any longer that Dr John Garang does not hold in high esteem even his second in command, Cdr Salva Kiir Mayardit. The way things are developing, it may not be long before he jettisons the man who has served him faithfully since 1983 in favour of another favourite. This is because he has been tossing Salva about just like any other junior officer. For instance, he made him a sector commander and does not share with him the strategies of the Movement. Although Salva Kiir Mayardit is theoretically the Chief of the General Staff of the SPLA, he was not privy to the operational plan or the transfer and deployment of SPLA officers. This is not only source of immense worry and danger for the SPLM/A but also for the destiny of the people of South Sudan, their compatriots in the Nuba Mountains and Southern Blue Nile, and the future of the African liberation in the Sudan.

When a guerrilla leader transverses the liberated area in the company of a music band that plays the national anthem of the Sudan at every stop and on every occasion brings people together, there is already a big danger to the liberation struggle. It should not be viewed as a source of inspiration but rather of awe for the people of South Sudan. Dr John Garang *acts* like he is already the President of the Sudan when he salutes the Arab national anthem, and, hence, is not perturbed by the wording of that anthem which denies the African people in the Sudan.

The rigid attitude of ignoring or marginalising others that continues to plague the SPLM/A at its political and strategic level is a recipe for perpetual political and military crisis in the SPLM that may one day spell its disintegration and doom. It paralyses the healthy political discourse that would have promoted healthy development into a genuine national liberation movement. This, without surprise, could lead to the defeat of the SPLM/A at the hands of the NIF regime. Stubbornness is bound to lead to indefinite repetition of own mistakes. It will be the mistake of those who follow blindly, sometimes on account of loyalty and tribal solidarity, if these mistakes lead to the destruction of a grand project like national liberation.

The episode of Wau and the failure to exploit the NIF contradictions

The SPLM and its leadership still operate in the old style and on the assumption that they control the natural development of events. We are not in a hurry to exploit the political and military opportunities that avail themselves, because we attach great importance to the personalities behind these opportunities and how that could disturb the internal power balance in the SPLM.

Thus, while the SPLA High Command was busy infiltrating its officers and men into Wau to help Kerubino Kuanyin Bol against the NIF regime, in what Dr John Garang described on the BBC Focus on Africa as *'the mother of all deceptions'*, the position Kerubino would occupy in the SPLM/A became a matter of concern to some people, even before the Wau operations were launched and the enemy defeated. The impact of this was that the SPLA's support to Kerubino was lukewarm. The operations were denied the armament and artillery pieces it required to liberate Wau. Even the very fact that the capture of Wau by the SPLA with the collaboration of Kerubino was something that would have changed the military situation in the South was not considered at the strategic level. In fact, as it turned out later, there was a conspiracy to murder Kerubino in order to prevent any victory in Wau being attributed to him.

The SPLM/A and the people of South Sudan stood to benefit from the contradiction that emerged between Major General Kerubino and the NIF government. The SPLM High Command needed to formulate a strategy to exploit that contradiction because Kerubino's re-defection to the liberation ranks made insignificant his initial defection to and his Khartoum agreement with the NIF regime. In the realm of political alliances and revolutionary politics, for that matter, the enemy of yesterday is today's friend and vise versa. I don't believe the alliance with the Umma party or DUP in the NDA bear the same mark as that which would have been forged between the SPLM/A and Kerubino Kuanyin Bol as a result of the Wau episode.

Worst still, Kerubino as a person was not fully accepted back into the ranks of the SPLM/A. After pulling out of Wau, a conspiracy was already afoot to separate Kerubino from his forces, leading to the emergence of another contradiction that led in October 1998 to his re-defection back to the enemy eight months after the Wau incident. He finally met his death at the hands of rebelling colleagues in western Upper Nile. This contradiction, provoked by SPLM/A functionaries, which resulted in the death of an SPLA officer in the Kenyan capital could have been avoided.

The decision to send SPLA officers and men to join Kerubino in Wau was not discussed in the NEC nor was it sanctioned by the NLC, the SPLM leadership structures that should have been summoned immediately to discuss the political developments in Wau. That decision was an administrative order by the Chairman and Commander in Chief of the SPLA. The subsequent negative developments relating to Kerubino, therefore, were engineered by Dr John Garang, denying the matter the political and democratic process it merited. The contradiction, therefore, was treated as if it were a personal quarrel between Dr John Garang and Major General Kerubino. Hence, the difficulty for the Movement to draw political lessons from the whole episode.

For historical records, it is absolutely necessary to draw the lines straight. In late 1997, when the situation in Wau emerged, many people in and outside the SPLM/A were interested in the liberation of Wau and turning the tables in the face of the NIF regime. It did not matter to many people whether or not it was Kerubino doing it. But they were ready to forgive Kerubino for the destruction he meted on the people of Aweil, Twic and Gogrial counties in northern Bahr el Ghazal. It was not a major concern whether or not Kerubino would assume the second position in the SPLM/A hierarchy he had held before his detention in 1987. The position Kerubino would assume was a matter of political debate within the SPLM and the forum was the National Liberation Council. As I mentioned above, if the NLC had been summoned to debate the political development in Wau when it emerged, a consensus on where in the Movement's leadership to slot Kerubino would have been reached while the members debated whether or not to assist him against the NIF regime. Avoiding the political institutions of the SPLM is what made the contradiction boil down to personal level, thus losing its political context and significance.

The Torit military fiasco 1998 and the chukudum crisis 1999

Who can reprimand the leader when he commits mistakes or when his error of judgment results in a disaster which has the proportion of a treason? How and who can bring him to justice if he has paralysed the functioning of the institutions which would have held him accountable? This is exactly the situation in the SPLA when in the middle 1998 its operations to recapture Torit from the enemy was planned and commanded by nobody other than its Commander in Chief. It was a lightening attack reinforced with heavy military logistical support from the friends of the SPLA. It did not only end in a failure of immense dimension but was a big embarrassment; people prefer to squint rather than face to discuss.

The failure of the Torit operations, upon which other war contingencies were based, was responsible for the human violations committed by the deserting troops on their way to Bahr el Ghazal and western Equatoria. The break down of law and order in East Bank Equatoria and the situation in Chukudum could be attributed to this military fiasco. The already bad situation in the East Bank was again compounded by the appointment of Cdr Kuol Manyang Juuk as SPLA commander of sector one and as governor of Upper Nile.

It should be recalled that the first elements to desert their positions in the Torit operations were the men from East Bank Equatoria themselves. Angered by the marginalisation of their officers corps, the Equatorians had every reason to desert and leave the battle to the Nilotics. The appointment of Kuol Manyang, against a background of oppressive behaviour of officers from his home area, added insults to the wound that provoked rebellion. The murder of A/cdr Deng Agwang by Captain Peter Lorot in Chukudum, which triggered off the present situation of absolute insecurity in the Kapoeta county, came against this background. This has already claimed the lives of innocent people on both sides, including the Didinga paramount chief Joseph Nakawa and A/cdr Peter Kidi Osman of the SRRA, who were both shot by Dinka SPLA soldiers in Himan on account of vengeance.

Another important dimension to the crisis in Chukudum and other parts of the SPLM administered South Sudan relate to the failure of the governance, instruments. The SPLM has not transformed into reality its rhetoric about the Civil Authority in the New Sudan (CANS). The New Sudan is divided into five regions headed by a governor who is an army commander. The regions are divided into counties and counties into payams. The county commissioners are political appointees of the chairman of the SPLM. There is no link between the governor of the region and the NEC secretaries. Consequently, there is no direct link between the NEC secretary responsible for local government and the county commissioners or for that matter with the local government instruments at the lower levels. In some counties, the SRRA assumes a high profile and runs a parallel system of government besides the office of the commissioner. This is informed by the fact that the humanitarian and relief agencies, which run most of the services in the counties, cannot have direct operational link with the SPLM political and administrative structures. This is a confused situation and explains why CANS has no functional effectiveness.

How can a system operate when there are no linkages between its different organs, laws, guidelines, procedures and rules of conduct of its business? CANS or no CANS, the SPLM has utterly failed to institute a system of governance in all spheres of social life in the New Sudan. As a result, only inertia has set in. East Bank Equatoria, by virtue of the character and traditions of its local population, became a weak link that exposed the SPLM/A administrative inaptitude. This was manifested by its many negative consequences.

First, since the Movement had no programme for social and economic activities, especially for the displaced populations, the area was made dependent on the beneficence of the international community. To make matters worst, the international community discriminated the distribution of relief assistance in favour of the displaced people to the chagrin of the local communities which; due to the arrogance and oppressive treatment by members of the displaced communities, were themselves displaced to the neighbouring countries (Uganda and Kenya); some moved deeper into the hills.

This situation bred instability and the area became pregnant with crime, gun running, cattle rustling etc. These vices extended naturally into northern Kenya and eastern Uganda, where SPLA soldiers were caught gun trafficking, not only breaking the laws of these neighbouring countries, which have hoisted tens of thousands of Sudanese refugees, but fuelling the local rebellion, as in Uganda. Agoro became the gun market which attracted all the rebels in the region. Hundreds of SPLA men and officers are to be found in prisons in Kenyan Turkana district and northern Uganda for crimes ranging from murders and gun trafficking. All these can be attributed to the failure to evolve a system of governance and rule of law commensurate with the liberation agenda. As a result, certain parts of East Bank Equatoria became out of bounds for the SPLA.

The situation in Upper Nile region

While the situation in eastern Equatoria spells disaster for the SPLM/A, a new situation was evolving in Upper Nile region, which could bailout the SPLM/A. It will be recalled that the split within the ranks and file of the SPLM/A in 1991 started in the Upper Nile and was instigated by some of its sons. It neutralised the greater part of the SPLA fighting force while a larger portion joined the ranks of the NIF regime to fight the SPLA.

The whole of Upper Nile was written off as having capitulated to the NIF government and the SPLM/A, unfortunately, had no blue print for reversing the situation. The liberation of South Sudan cannot be realised without the effective participation of the people of Upper Nile, especially if they were to fight on the side of the common enemy. However, because of its lack of commitment to implement its agreement with Riek Machar, the NIF regime's obnoxious intentions showed up immediately precipitating fierce battles over the oil fields. It would have been disastrous for the Nuer population of western Upper Nile, had the Wunlit Nuer - Dinka Peace Covenant not been arrived at in March 1999. The NIF greed has inadvertently united the people in Bahr el Ghazal and Upper Nile in their common struggle against this vicious enemy.

The people to people peace and reconciliation and its dividends in Wunlit and Waat are incentives for uniting the struggle for liberation. This has given rise to the formation of Upper Nile Provisional Military Command Council (UNPMCC), bringing together in a rare unity the different USDF factions in Upper Nile and the SPLA. This is likely to impact positively on the political and military situation in South Sudan, especially the unanimous decision to delink from the NIF regime and any leader still with Khartoum.

One would expect the SPLM/A High Command to support this move, both politically and militarily. Cdr Salva Kiir Mayardit showed magnanimity and statesmanship in dealing with Cdr Peter Gadet and Cdr Tito Biel when they rebelled against the NIF government. Cdr Salva provided logistical support to the two commanders without requesting them to 'join the fold' of the SPLM/A. But this has unfortunately elicited hostility in some quarters of the SPLM/A.

The issue of the people coming into the fold of the SPLM/A is more sensitive to postulate at the moment. First, because of the long period of internecine fighting, the people need a rather long cooling time to enable them overcome some of the hard feelings and animosities that had characterised the relationships since 1991. The people to people peace and reconciliation process and its results must be given time to be absorbed and internalised by the people.

Secondly, there have been no efforts on the part of the SPLM/A to create the impression that internally things are different and to give confidence to any person who has rebelled or disagreed with its leader Dr John Garang that he or she still has a role to play in the Movement. The manner with which Kerubino Kuanyin Bol was received and later forced to re-defect to the enemy is an indication that no one is safe, especially those aspiring to the top leadership position in the SPLM.

Thirdly, since it has been the position of the SPLM/A that unity and reconciliation must be based on fighting the common enemy, then it is too premature to request the combatants to 'return to the fold' immediately without sufficient preparations being put in place for that eventual organic unity of the fighting men.

The situation in Upper Nile, therefore, like the one in East Bank Equatoria, is likely to expose the political and organisational weakness of the SPLM/A and the lack of an agenda for uniting the liberation struggle. Many people in Upper Nile, including some senior members of the SPLM/A, loathe the practice of forcing people into a suffocating political environment in which only few aides have the opportunity to exercise their ignorance and inexperience in running the affairs of the Movement. It is this practice that has unleashed hatred and confusion among the people that has provoked in the past unprincipled alliance with the common enemy in order to protect one's dignity. Unless this trend is reversed, it will prevent the eventual unity among South Sudanese and this could form the basis of our possible defeat by the enemy.

Why not? The defeat of South Sudan and the African people in the Sudan cannot be ruled out in view of the waning support for the SPLM and its inability to adjust to the changing political horizon. If the SPLM/A continues to generate fresh contradictions by committing more mistakes, including murdering chiefs and elders of communities with impunity and without the benefit of learning from these mistakes; if some of these mistakes lead to massive desertions of the SPLA soldiers from the battle field back to their homes paralysing the operational and strategic plans of the SPLA; if the revolutionary zeal for volunteering for the war of liberation has been worn thin by the corrupt practices and lack of concern for the welfare of the combatants, especially those wounded in action; if the leaders themselves have shelved the liberation agenda, and what matters to them is the personal power and welfare of their immediate families, etc. etc., why can't anybody think or contemplate that the NIF regime or a coalition of the Arab parties glued together by the recent Libyan - Egyptian initiative, will reverse all the military gains of the SPLA?

I don't want to play the devil's advocate, but I see the eventual disintegration of the SPLM/A or its regionalisation as a consequent of that, exactly in front of my eyes. It makes no sense behaving like ostriches in times of extreme national danger and when the destiny of the entire people is at stake. We have to face the situation we have nurtured for the last sixteen years. Much would have been served had we listened to each other.

In the NGO's language, it could be called a fatigue - donor fatigue. However, I don't believe there is a war fatigue in South Sudan. The fact that there are desertions in the ranks or if the SPLA, like the NIF government, has to forcefully conscript recruits into its ranks it is simply because the war has lost its liberation agenda. What we see is the projection of power politics and the quest by the leaders to build their power bases which has brought back corruption, nepotism, favouritism and reliance on confidantes and close aides in the affairs of the Movement. This has resulted in the marginalisation of the most able brains in favour of the sycophants, mediocre and the late-comers. This has disillusioned the veterans and desensitised the people to our liberation liturgy that they no longer respond with the zeal they did in their tens of thousands in the early eighties.

The other important factor, which could be counted as responsible for the apathy and indifference among many people in the South Sudan, is that they have not been treated to a social system different from the oppressive and exploitative one they have been used to in the Arab dominated Sudan. The SPLA behaves in exactly the same way as the government army towards the people - its enemies. In some places, what we installed as a semblance of order could have been worse to say the least. We continue to insult the intelligence of our people by projecting false programmes, consequently many combatants prefer to join the enemy or go for resettlement abroad, as a matter of necessity. In fact, some even venture to ask 'what the difference is between stupidity [on our part, suffering the lack of doubt] and treason [their association with the enemy] if the result [the suffering caused to the people] is the same'?

There must be an obsessive fear at the strategic and political level of the Movement for organising the people and their lives; this may explain the apparent reluctance to create a centralised and functional administrative and political system in an area we boast is larger than the territories of Kenya, Uganda and Rwanda combined. Organisation and building of institutions make people conscientious. And if the idea is to perpetuate oppression, then the option is to paralyse any attempts to raise the level of political awareness. The civil society remains cowed and prone to helpless speculation. Thus, what is reigning in that area, what we call the 'New Sudan', is the kind of anarchy and lack of direction that can only be occasioned by lack of government. It is depressingly a very sick joke for a 'revolutionary' to live with after nearly seventeen years pyrrhic military victories.

This situation definitely calls for more thorough reflections, but even after a long time of reflection and soul searching, one comes back to the starting point like in what they usually call a vicious circle.

Whither way SPLM/A?

We are in a gruesomely pathetic reality into which we have cornered ourselves. We refused or rather wanted to subdue the objective laws of national liberation to our own whims. We thought time can wait for us as we engaged in small ticks. We are trying to catch up with the lost time, but, unfortunately, we can't climb onto time at where we should have seventeen years ago because it passed us. We thought we could exploit the cold war rivalries or the regional contradictions. And, in fact, they were there ready for us but we were not there for them. The situation has become more complex and we have not trained ourselves to complex situations.

In view of the unfolding complexities it may not be certain whether the end of the road will be reached. It is even more uncertain now when after sixteen years of relentless sacrifices there is no consensus what that 'end' should be. In retrospect, it would have been better not to embark on such a journey. But the memory of more than two million martyrs and truncated social and economic progress that seem to have pushed the people of South Sudan back into the dark ages are reasons enough to continue the journey. The questions, therefore, are how and who will lead the journey and to where?

Reforms and how deep should they be?

For the SPLM/A to continue the journey and reach a honourable end, it requires some serious soul searching exercise at all levels of its political and military hierarchy. This is necessary and imperative if the situation fed by internal oppression is to be rectified and a nation in the form of the 'New Sudan' is to emerge. This also requires strength and strong will power on the part of the leaders to be able to recognise the fatal mistake they have committed and to be able to organise a go back to where we should have started in 1983.

The SPLM desperately needs not only reforms, but that these reforms must run deep into the core of the Movement occupied by a eccentric personalized power centre in the person of Dr John Garang and his coterie of sycophants and self-seekers. The SPLM should be able to convince the people that their sacrifices was not in vain. This, because the people are more confused now than ever before. Their hopes have been shattered by the lack of clear direction on the part of the Movement.

The people have waited far too long that the inevitable will happen. There is not time for anything short of massive desertions. The last meeting of the National Liberation Council (NLC) should have chartered the way forward. However, the formation of the Leadership Council (LC) and the appointments therein reflect a re-militarisation of the Movement, a return to the old bad days of the Movement which produced the split within the ranks in 1991.

The leadership council, thirteen in number, is made up essentially of the seven surviving former members of the SPLM/A High Command and six new appointees with one absurd promotion dated back to the time the appointee was a leader of the government militia. The appointment is an affront or rather a negation of the democratization process in the SPLM/A. Going by the way things were since 1994, it means that the reconstituted Commissions of the SPLM will just be nominal structures without any meaningful functions. What it means is that the reforms in the SPLM/A have been truncated at a point they have not really taken off. The SPLM/A is on a reverse gear propelling it back into a situation that engenders contradictions and that which jeopardizes its existence.

The appointment of the front commanders is something that may cause serious problems in the army. The fact that all but one front commander hail from Upper Nile region is raising eyebrows in Bahr el Ghazal, Equatoria and Blue Nile. If the bulk of the SPLA human resources hail from Bahr el Ghazal, why it that there is no sensitivity attached to the appointment of the front commanders, especially in view of the fact that the desertion in 1998 that aborted the capture of Torit was attributed to issues of command. This is a case of not learning from one's mistakes which makes a farce of the talk about reforms.

Regionalisation of the liberation struggle

No South Sudanese is interested in a South - South conflict any more, especially when it runs along ethnic lines over the issue of power and leadership. Nobody also would equally remain in a movement that is not growing or in which one is marginalised. In Upper Nile, many people harbour so strong contempt for the leadership of Dr John Garang that they would prefer to remain allied to the Arabs rather than join the rest of South Sudanese groups in the SPLM/A. The reasons for this can be found in the manner in which the split in 1991 had been politicized along ethnic lines. Many Nuer combatants perceive in terms of and equate rejoining the SPLM/A with a surrender to the Dinka, and, hence, prefer to go it alone.

This explains why, instead of reuniting with the SPLA because of the improved relations between the two communities following the Wunlit Nuer Dinka Peace Covenant (1999), the sixteen commanders who met in Waat to deliberate on the political and military situation in Upper Nile, decided to establish a separate military structure. The formation UNPMCC in November

1999 is a precursor of the events to come which may eventually lead to the regionalisation of the liberation struggle in South Sudan.

The reasons for such actions must also be sought in the SPLM/A itself. Since the split within the ranks of the movement in 1991 and, in spite of all the pronouncements about democratisation and democratic institution building, the SPLM/A has failed to create political space for those who broke away from it earlier. Worst still, it has no policy for winning back or creating confidence in those who have differed with it, and that there will be no victimization if they came back into the fold. The experience of Kerubino Kuanyin, following his return to the Movement in 1998, scares people away from the SPLM/A, and in particular the leadership of Dr John Garang, leaving the regionalisation as the only option for anybody who wants to fight for liberation.

Regionalisation, may herald the emergence of separate and independent political and military liberation movements in South Sudan. If that happens, it could be a solution to the present *impasse* that has witness the complete marginalisation of many communities, especially in Equatoria and eastern Upper Nile, and their lack of participation in the liberation struggle. This definitely poses a serious departure from the position we took in 1995 following the Lafon Declaration against parallel existence of separate Movements competing for the leadership of the liberation struggle.

It comes as a natural political development mirroring a failure, of a historical dimension, to organise the people and accrue a liberation process according to its objective laws. Superficially, this looks negative, especially after seventeen years of common struggle and could easily spell doom for the liberation of South Sudan. However, it may prove a better devil than the suffocating political environment that is pushing the combatants as well as the civil population to the enemy garrisons. The challenge will be how to link these regional forces and rally them around a national agenda.

The regionalisation of the struggle may break the present stalemate on the military fronts which has allowed the NIF regime to launch its diplomatic offensive that enabled it to break its regional and international isolation. It brings into the centre stage all the forces that have been neutralised by the splits and factionalisation of the SPLA since 1991. It this vein, it will be a positive action that can invigorate, motivate and effectively involve the people in the war of liberation.

In conclusion, it is disturbing to note that at end of sixteen years of immense sufferings and sacrifices, the people of South Sudan are yet to be convinced about why it was necessary for them to take up arms in the first place and make these sacrifices. This makes it even imperative to consider alternative means if the people of the South are to achieve a just peace and realise their aspiration.

Notes

[1] On December 12th to preempt a national assembly vote to create the position of Prime Minister thus clipping the powers of the president of the state reducing it to ceremonial post as it was before Nimeri's coup in 1969.

Index

Abboud, Ibrahim 18, 64, 73, 194
Abdalla, Peter Sule 103, 131, 132
Abdalla, William Chuol 38, 49
Abuja 66, 75, 99, 100, 127, 155-156, 162
Aciek, Magar 50, 197
Acuil, Dhol 105, 130, 151
Addis Ababa 6, 7, 20, 21-23, 33, 55, 65, 74, 75, 78, 83, 84, 108, 154-155, 158-159, 162, 167, 182
Addis Ababa Agreement 6, 7, 20, 21, 22, 23, 33, 75, 158-159, 162, 167
Addis Ababa Peace Accord 20
administration 15, 16, 20, 40, 47, 52, 53, 56, 61, 88, 105, 132
Adok 96, 107
Adwok 81, 92, 167
Afewerki 193
African National Congress 176
Afrika, Jeremiah 124
Ahmed, Mohammed Mahgoub 158, 186
Ahmed, Ustaz el Radhi Gaaber 156
Ajak, Mungo 156
Akobo 5, 6, 10, 12, 54, 74, 94, 95, 97, 99, 104, 109, 118, 123, 133, 141, 142, 143, 145, 146, 157
Akol, Lam 1, 3, 5, 8-9, 11, 12, 48, 63, 65-66, 69, 71, 72, 75, 82-86, 88, 89, 90-94, 96, 98, 99-100, 102, 103, 104, 105, 106, 108, 109, 117, 118, 120, 122, 126-128, 130-133, 135, 141-142, 147, 150, 151, 152, 153, 154, 155-157, 163, 167-168, 190, 196, 200, 204
Al, Hassan Turabi 99
Ali, Mohammed 14
Ali, Sayed el Mirghani 73, 187
Alier, Abel 22, 32, 33, 73
Americans 61, 122
Anglo-Egyptian Sudan 15
Angola 37, 136, 177
Anya-Nya 7, 11, 21, 26-31, 33-34, 36-38, 40, 43, 46, 48, 49, 50, 51, 67, 71, 74, 80, 92, 97, 98, 124, 136, 138, 141, 165, 178, 186, 203
Anyuak 40, 74, 75, 87, 98
Arab 6, 14, 15, 19
Arabs 14, 19, 73, 108, 165, 213
arap, Daniel Moi 164

Asmara Declaration 160, 161, 183, 195, 196, 201
Assossa 87
Atar 25, 106, 132, 168
Atem, Akuot 37
Atem, Faustino Gualdit 75, 103, 127, 128
Athur, George 116, 117
Awan, Elijah 146
Ayod 24, 28, 97, 99, 136, 138, 145, 157
Ayuen, Dengtiel Kur 118

Babangida, Ibrahim 65, 99, 156
Bahr el Ghazal 23, 26, 29, 38, 40, 48, 49, 58, 60, 72, 77, 97, 99, 101, 105, 108, 130, 133, 142, 145, 164, 185, 196-197, 207, 209, 213
Bailiet 146
Banyping 142
Barcelona Symposium 163
battalions 24, 38, 40, 50, 87
BBC 11, 74, 77, 93-95, 116, 205
BBC Focus on Africa 77, 93, 205
Beja 108, 182, 186, 187
Bentiu 24, 91, 145, 156
Berlin 92
Bilpam 38, 48, 56, 70
Blue Nile 47, 108, 154, 172, 185, 193-196, 202, 205, 213
Bol, Victor Ayual 147
Bonga 38
Bor 4, 24, 26, 28, 29, 30, 31, 39, 46, 51, 54, 58, 71, 74, 75, 97-99, 118, 123, 125, 131, 133, 138, 146, 148, 196
Britain 176
British 15, 19, 20, 65, 95, 120-121, 165, 192, 198-199
British army 120
Butana 167
Cairo 64, 83, 186
capitalism 41
Carter, Jimmy 155
Castro, Fidel 42
CCM 135
Chevron Oil Company 61
Christian education 16
Christian missionaries 15

civil society 159, 169, 172, 175, 191, 192, 198, 211
civil war 17, 73
colonial administration 15, 16, 20
Communist Party 17-18, 33, 41-43, 62-64, 74, 79, 80, 176
Communist Party of South Africa 176
condominium parties 15
conflict resolution 141
Constituent Assembly 78, 80, 187
constitution 19, 44-45, 179, 187, 188, 194, 199
Council for the Unity of South Sudan (CUSS) 23
coup 1-5, 7, 9, 10, 11, 38, 45, 47, 51, 62, 66, 69, 77-78, 83, 88, 90-100, 102-103, 106, 107, 109, 116-119, 124-126, 130, 135-137, 143, 147-149, 151-153, 155, 158-159, 169-173, 178, 180, 181, 184-185, 187-188, 190, 192, 215
Croatia 182
Cubans 37
Czechoslovakia 182

Dak, Kwongo Padiet 156
Damazin 195
Dar Fur 108, 166, 168
de Chand, David 142, 145
Debray, Regis 68, 75, 76, 192
Debri Zeit 83
decentralisation 22, 25
Delos, Romi Santos 135
Democracy 103, 127, 128
democracy 21, 48, 70, 84, 92, 100, 118, 134, 170, 176, 189, 190, 199, 203, 204
Democratic Party 73, 167, 176
democratic pluralism 176, 178-179, 191
democratisation 10, 11, 12, 72, 81, 86, 89, 117, 136, 143, 153, 173, 198, 214
Deng, Daniel Alony 146
Deng, Gatluak 92, 93, 98
Deng, Santino 19, 73
Deng, Taban Gai 75, 96, 99, 127
Deng, Telar 8, 118, 126
Deng, William 19, 73

Department of Humanitarian Affairs 119, 121
Dergue 35, 182
Dimma 55, 56
Dinka 2, 6, 9, 11, 25, 26, 28, 39, 49, 50, 51, 74, 96-97, 106, 119, 124, 126, 131, 137-138, 140, 146, 159, 164, 185, 192, 197, 207, 209, 213
Dinka, Abeyei 26
diplomacy 141
divide and rule 24, 166, 178
Dolieb Hill 97
Duar 99

education 15, 16, 41, 43, 52, 53, 54, 55, 59
Egypt 15, 16, 64, 65, 73, 195, 201
Egyptians 14, 15, 65, 75
el, Ahmed Mahdi 19
el, Ali Hag Mohammed 96, 99
el, Hassan Turabi 35, 154, 188
el, Omer Beshir 35, 62, 89, 142, 153, 161, 164, 166, 167, 201
el, Saddiq Bana 29, 31
el, Sadiq Mahdi 19, 26, 74, 158, 160, 166, 192-195, 201
el, Swar Dahab 26
el Turabi 35, 154, 167, 188, 193, 201
ELF 136
EPLF 87, 136, 176, 202
Equatoria 6, 23, 28, 38, 56, 60, 77, 90, 94, 97-99, 101, 103, 108, 125, 127, 134, 137, 138, 145, 151, 157, 161, 185, 196, 197, 207-210, 213, 214
Equatoria Defence Forces 134, 196
Equatoria Region 28
Eritrea 35, 108, 136, 162, 193, 202
Eritreans 35, 36, 74, 120, 122, 182
Erjok 51
Ethiopia 2, 26-28, 34-38, 48-49, 55, 61, 62, 65, 69, 74, 78, 79, 87, 88-90, 92, 95, 104, 136, 150, 153-155, 162, 167, 169, 182, 202
Ethiopian army 38, 87, 88
Ethiopian regime 35, 36, 37, 38, 74, 75, 79, 87-88, 109

Ethiopians 36, 38, 40, 120, 122, 137, 142, 154, 155
Europe 2, 82, 91, 92, 118

faction 1, 3, 4, 5, 8, 9
Fangak 49, 132, 142, 145, 161, 167
Fashoda 156
federal system 65
federation 17, 34, 160
Focus on Africa 77, 93, 205
Frankfurt Agreement 3, 98-99, 101, 137
FRELIMO 136, 176, 177
French 61, 95
fundamentalist 64, 137, 141
Funj 15, 108, 201
Fur 108, 166, 168, 182, 187

Gai, Samuel Tut 37, 38, 49
Gambella 56, 74, 87, 88, 90, 98, 104, 108, 109, 150, 155
Ganyliel 121, 133
Garang, John de Mabior 1, 8, 9, 11, 12, 30, 36, 38, 43-48, 52, 58, 63, 66, 69, 72, 73, 75, 77, 79, 82, 83, 86, 87, 88, 89, 90, 95, 96, 99, 100, 102, 105, 106, 107, 118, 120, 124, 126, 129, 133, 136, 137, 140, 143, 147, 148, 168, 170, 171, 180, 190, 194, 195, 203-206, 210, 212, 213, 214
Gassessa, Abu 156
Gatwich, Simon 109, 123, 168
Gawaar 87, 97, 98, 131
Germany 92, 93
Gezira 167
GPLM 74, 75, 87, 98
guerrilla army 1, 107, 116

Hani, Chris 176
Haroun, Mohammed Kafi 163
High Command 1, 9, 36, 44-47, 50, 55, 57, 69, 71, 72, 75, 78, 82, 88, 90, 91, 93, 103, 108, 117, 118, 128, 144, 153, 170, 205, 206, 209, 213
High Executive Council 21, 22, 33
Hindi 188

Horn of Africa 61-62, 78, 88, 105, 182
House of Commons 176
human rights 1, 11, 39, 47, 81, 84, 94-96, 100, 117, 118, 136, 190
humanitarian aid 54
humanitarian assistance 54, 89, 121, 134, 154, 155
humanitarian worker 8

ideological awareness 68
ideological education 55
ideological issues 57
ideological orientation 30, 54
ideological position 37
ideological strategy 141
ideological struggle 9, 37, 170, 174, 175
IGAD 12, 105, 160, 162-163, 165-166, 196, 201, 202
IGAD Peace Initiative 12, 105, 162, 163
IGADD 156, 159, 160, 168, 184
IGADD Declaration of Principles 160
Imatong Liberation Front 103, 126
imperialism 79, 192, 194
INEC 104-106, 109, 118-120, 122, 125-126, 128-130, 132-133, 137, 143-144, 150-151
institutionalisation 136
Interim National Executive Committee 96, 118
internal conflict 163
Internal Settlement 166
international community 72, 95, 98, 105, 120, 129, 138, 141, 143, 149, 151, 154, 172, 173, 198, 208
international humanitarian intervention 95, 138, 198
Intifadha 38, 63, 194
Intisar 38
Islam 15, 34, 137, 180, 188, 194
Islamic Charter Front 18, 187
Islamic constitution 187, 188
Islamic sharia laws 23, 26, 27, 31, 39, 187
Israelis 122
Italian 135
Itang refugee camp 69, 81, 87, 108

Jarad division 51
jihad 164

Jikany 49, 98-99, 104, 107, 109, 123, 133, 141-144, 148, 150
Jonglei Canal 22, 24-25, 61, 74, 75
Jonglei province 25
Juba 6, 20, 21, 23, 24, 28, 29, 30, 31, 38, 40, 43, 44, 46, 61, 74, 77, 79, 80, 101, 104, 108, 212, 124, 145, 148, 159, 166, 171, 184, 186, 195
Juba Airport 31, 61
Juba University Sudanese Staff Association 79

Kampala 103, 119, 128, 131, 198, 199
Kaya 54, 195
Kazuk 38
Kenana Sugar Company 66
Kenya 38, 62, 75, 95, 101, 128, 134-135, 139, 161, 208, 211
Kenyi 150, 151, 163
Ketbek 98, 99
Khartoum 3, 6, 12, 14, 18-20, 23-27, 29, 35, 36, 40, 49, 50, 51, 62, 64-66, 78-80, 96, 99, 104, 107, 108, 120, 124, 132, 136, 139, 141, 142, 150, 151, 153, 154, 157, 159, 160, 163, 165, 166, 167, 177, 182, 183, 185, 188, 193, 194, 195, 196, 200, 206, 209
Khartoum regime 40, 51, 196
Kiir, Salva Mayardit 8, 44, 47, 143, 149, 199, 205, 209
Kiplagat, Bathuel 95
Koang, Gordon Chol 118, 126
Koat, Daniel Mathews 140
Kodok 85, 135, 146
Koka Dam 158, 167, 192
Koka Dam agreement 158
Koka Dam conference 158
Koka Dam Declaration 158, 192
Kongor 4, 26, 46, 97, 98, 103, 117, 118, 128, 132, 133, 138, 144, 146, 151, 168
Kony, Joseph 134
Kowa, Yousif 157
Kuanyin, Kerubino Bol 28, 29, 31, 47, 67, 70, 75, 102, 103, 127, 141, 145, 159, 203, 205, 206, 210
Kulang, John 46, 50, 132, 142
Kunda, Yusif 124

Kur, Ayang 23, 85
Kurmuk 33, 74, 87, 195

Lado, Lakurnyang 51
Lado-Gore, Alfred 66, 103, 128, 129, 131
Lafon 5, 8, 11, 12, 106, 139, 142, 148-150, 173, 197, 200, 214
Lafon Declaration 5, 8, 11, 106, 139, 148-150, 173, 197, 200, 214
Lagu, Joseph 20, 22, 134, 203
Latjor State 149
Leer 82, 96, 99, 122, 157
Liberal Party 17, 18
Liberation movement 1, 2, 8-10, 20, 28, 44, 47-48, 52-54, 56, 60-61, 67, 70-71, 79, 86, 107, 108, 116, 120, 129, 135, 140, 142, 149, 152, 156, 158, 162, 163, 166, 170, 175, 176, 178-179, 191, 204, 205
Libya 73, 127, 201, 202, 210
Lokichoggio 120, 121, 135
Lonrho 66, 103, 128
Lou 8, 12, 14, 22, 40, 49-50, 57, 71-72, 82, 87, 91, 94, 97, 98, 104, 107, 109, 117, 123, 129, 133, 136, 142-144, 148, 150, 169, 176, 187-188, 196, 209
Lual, Lawrence Lual 197
Luc, Jean Siblot 121, 122
Luk, John 8, 9, 11, 12, 75, 125-127, 132, 136, 140, 142, 147, 149, 151, 155, 161

Maban 83, 94, 146
Mabor, Jiech 97, 98, 104
Machar, Riek 1, 5, 6, 8, 9-12, 35, 50, 65, 69, 72, 75, 77, 82, 83, 85, 86-93, 94-109, 116-126, 128, 131-134, 136-168, 188, 190, 196-197, 200, 201, 202, 204, 209
Magar, Nikanora Acie 50
Maguek, Simon 121, 122
Mahdiyia uprising 14
Maiwut 145
Majier, Martin Gai 45, 133
Maker, George 140, 147, 149
Makuei, Kawach 147

Malakal 44, 74, 92, 97-100, 102, 103-104, 109, 121, 123, 126, 137, 146, 151, 153, 159, 168, 186
Manajang 132
Mandari 2, 39, 40, 74
Mankein 133
Manyiel, Martin 40, 86, 93, 94
marginalisation 17, 37, 48, 51, 54, 81, 129, 170, 207, 211, 214
Mario, Michael 25
Marxism 175
Marxist ideology 27
Marxist philosophy 54
Marxist phraseology 28
Marxist theories 55
Matip, Paulino Nhial 141, 156, 167
Mayom 150
Mayong, Akwoc 94
MedAir (Swiss) 135
Medani 79, 108, 195
Melut 83, 146
Middle East 16, 20
militarism 1, 53, 55
military authoritarianism 55, 199
military coup 1, 2, 3, 9, 62, 91, 116, 155, 158, 180, 184, 187
military hierarchies 55
military training 41, 59, 72, 83
Ministry of Finance 31
Ministry of Foreign Affairs and International Coop 95
missionaries 15
Mohammed, Gaafar Nimeri 20, 61, 194
monarchy 44
Morobo 195
Mour Mour division 38
Movement 6, 8, 28, 46, 57, 131, 145, 178, 199
movement 142
Mozambique 136, 177
MPLA 5, 37, 45, 65, 68, 83, 85, 95, 136, 176, 183-184, 210
Mubarak, Hosni 65, 154
mujahideen 157, 164, 183
Mulla, Richard 134
Murahalieen 26, 97
Murle 2, 26, 40, 138
mutiny 17, 28-29, 31, 46, 71, 74, 192

Nairobi 3, 4, 10, 11, 12, 66, 75, 93, 95-96, 99, 100, 102, 103, 105, 109, 119, 121, 122, 126, 127, 128, 131, 133-136, 143, 146, 150-151, 153-155, 157, 162, 165, 182, 192, 204

Nasir 1-11, 38, 47, 51, 54, 65-66, 69, 74-75, 77-78, 82, 83, 89-109, 116, 117, 118, 119, 120, 121, 122, 124-128, 130, 134, 135-140, 142-143, 145, 147, 148-153, 155-157, 161-162, 169-173, 178, 185, 189, 190, 192, 199-200, 203

Nasir coup 3, 5, 47, 83, 94-96, 102, 106-107, 117, 118, 124, 130, 136, 137, 147, 148, 169, 170, 171, 172, 173, 178, 190

Nasir Declaration 1, 3, 4-11, 51, 77, 78, 82, 89, 91-92, 94, 102, 124-125, 140, 152, 161, 190, 199, 200, 203

Nasir faction 1, 3-5, 8-10, 65-66, 75, 78, 90, 93, 96-103, 105, 109, 117-119, 122, 124, 125, 126, 127-128, 134, 135, 137, 138, 139, 142, 150-151, 153, 156, 162, 171

Nasir leaders 3, 5, 8, 75, 77, 92, 100-102, 106, 117, 126, 136-137, 153, 169, 190

National Alliance for National Salvation 63, 79, 158, 180

National Convention 4, 52, 55, 119, 143-144, 146, 148, 169, 170, 171, 192, 198-199, 203

National Council of Churches of Kenya 95

National Democratic Alliance (NDA) 177, 201

National Islamic Front 18, 26, 63, 154, 158, 177, 180, 192, 201

National Liberation Council 118, 143, 144, 146, 170-171, 198-199, 207, 212

national liberation movement 1, 9, 10, 28, 44, 47, 52-54, 61, 66, 70, 86, 116, 120, 135, 152, 170, 176, 178-179, 204, 205

National Resistance Movement 178, 199

National Unionist Party 17, 73, 167

nationalism 4, 7, 80, 93, 124, 152

New Sudan Council of Churches 95, 127

New Sudan Islamic Council 35

NGO 138

Index 221

Ngor, Francis 45, 50
NIF government 3, 5, 8, 10, 35, 62, 65-67, 95-96, 98, 99, 100-103, 105-107, 120, 123, 126, 128, 129, 131-135, 137, 139-142, 148, 153, 154-157, 160, 162, 163-165, 169, 171, 183, 184, 190, 194, 196, 197, 201-202, 206, 209, 211
NIF leaders 4, 157, 194, 196
NIF regime 3-5, 62-63, 65-66, 78, 93, 98, 100-102, 120, 124, 126, 129, 130, 141, 144, 153-163, 170, 177, 182, 183, 187-188, 191, 193-195, 197, 200, 201, 202, 205-207, 209, 210, 214
Nigeria 65-66, 75, 99, 127, 156, 162
Nigerian 66, 75, 99, 156, 162
Nimeri regime 21, 23, 24, 28, 35, 39, 42, 61, 73, 74, 79, 80, 158, 180, 188
Nimule 162, 171, 172
Northern Sudan 17, 19, 64, 86, 143, 185
Nuba 8, 15, 27, 56, 139, 143, 154, 160, 163, 166, 174, 181-183, 185-187, 191, 196-197, 201-202, 205
Nuba Mountains 8, 15, 139, 143, 154, 160, 163, 166, 174, 181, 183, 185, 191, 196, 197, 202, 205
Nuer 6, 11, 13, 23, 26, 40, 49, 50, 51, 53, 67, 85-88, 90, 94, 97, 98, 102, 106, 107, 108-109, 120-121, 123-126, 131-133, 136-138, 140-141, 143, 145-147, 150, 155, 159, 161, 164, 185, 197, 209, 213
Nyok, Joseph Abiel 142, 145

Obay 25
Obur, Ben 124
Ochang, Theopolus Lotti 151
Oduho, Joseph 45, 84, 103, 128, 147
Okuch, Marconi Aba 94
OLF 44, 75, 87
oligarchy 44
Operation Lifeline Sudan 120, 135
Operation Moses 61
Organisation for African Unity 34

Orinyo 135, 142
Owikyel 85

Pachodo 200
Padiet 50, 156
Pageri 127
Pal, Thowath 87
Palestinian Liberation Organisation 176
Pan-Arabists 64
Panyagor 138
Papwojo 50
Pariang 94
Patriotic Resistance Movement 66, 103, 128, 131
PDP 18
Peace Accord 20
Peace Agreement 196
peace from within 135, 157, 196
People for Peace in Africa 95, 127
Phow State 106
Pibor 24, 40, 54, 138, 146
Piny-udo refugee camp 87
Pochalla 28, 31, 54, 74-75, 78, 95, 146, 151, 172, 193
political 9, 35, 45, 51, 53, 69, 75, 102, 106, 120, 133, 134, 141-152, 154-155, 157, 159, 160-161, 163-168, 176, 189, 191, 196, 200
Political Cadres Group 69
political charter 35, 102, 106, 120, 133, 134, 141, 142, 152, 154, 155, 157, 159, 160, 161, 163, 164-167, 196, 200
Presidential Decree 22

Radio Omdurman 89, 167
Radio SPLA 27, 53, 68
Rasas, Gasimalla 22
reconciliation talks 49, 75, 95
referendum 33, 160, 183, 188, 189, 191
regional government 6-7, 20-21, 23, 25, 29, 31, 33, 43, 46, 80, 171, 186
relief workers 120, 121, 122, 135
RENAMO 136, 177
reunification 5, 8, 9-13, 106, 124-125 128, 130, 139, 140-141, 144-

145, 148, 149, 155-156, 163-164, 167, 173
revolution 7, 36, 37, 51, 52, 55, 75, 80, 96, 147, 192
revolutionary nationalism 152
revolutionary politics 152, 206
Rokon 38
Round Table Conference on the Southern Problem 33, 166
Rowlands 127, 128
Rumbek 49, 151, 195
Rwanda 7, 49, 211

Sahel belt 14
Salauddin, Ghazi el Atabani 165
Secretary for Information and Culture 120
sectarian parties 79, 80, 180-183, 187-188
sectarianism 160, 181
Serbs 182
Shilluk 6, 10, 11, 23, 25, 50, 71, 73-74, 85-86, 90, 94, 97, 101-102, 106, 109, 126, 131-132, 135, 142, 146, 154-156, 167, 185
Shukary, Ahmed 177
Slovak 181, 182
Sobat river 25, 38, 95, 123, 153
social and economic development 15, 22, 171
socialism 36, 41, 42, 61, 79
South Africa 37, 136, 176, 177
Southern Front 18, 21, 28, 33, 73, 167, 186
Southern patriotism 136
Soviet Union 2, 42, 168
SPLM Manifesto 7, 29, 33, 42, 44, 73, 74
SPLM/A 2, 3, 4, 5, 7
SPLM/A training camps 27
SSIM National Executive Council 140

State Security Organisation (SSO) 2
Sudan African National Union 18, 21, 73
Sudan Socialist Union 2, 21
Sudan Unity Party 19
Torit 31, 47, 54, 78, 97, 102, 161, 184, 192, 207, 213
training camps 27, 38, 39, 49, 51, 52, 59
tribalism 43, 80, 108, 120, 131, 150, 170, 179, 189, 191
Uganda 38, 62, 101, 102, 127, 128, 137, 139, 161, 162, 178, 208, 211
Umma Party 17, 19, 36, 62, 64, 80, 108, 161, 167, 181, 183, 187, 192-194, 201, 206
Upper Nile 23-25, 29, 48, 49, 58, 60, 61, 64, 71, 75, 77, 82, 83, 85, 90, 91 94, 96, 97, 98-99, 101-102, 106-109, 116, 121, 125, 138, 145, 146, 149, 150-151, 156, 164, 185, 193, 197, 201, 202, 206, 207, 209, 210, 213, 214

White Nile provinces 24
Wilson, Simon 122
with the regime 27, 40
World Food Programme 135, 121

Yabus, Khor 172, 193
Yahyah 51
Yambio 53, 54
Yei 26, 28, 33, 38, 77, 145, 151, 195
Yuai 138, 151

Zalzal 38
Zande 6, 53
Zenawi, Meles 193
Zeraf valley 132
Zindiya battalion 39

www.ingramcontent.com/pod-product-compliance
Lightning Source LLC
Chambersburg PA
CBHW071352290426
44108CB00014B/1520